# Contents at a Glance

by Anna Kennedy

**Business Development For Dummies®**

Published by: **John Wiley & Sons, Ltd.,** The Atrium, Southern Gate, Chichester, www.wiley.com

This edition first published 2015

© 2015 John Wiley & Sons, Ltd, Chichester, West Sussex.

*Registered office*

John Wiley & Sons Ltd, The Atrium, Southern Gate, Chichester, West Sussex, PO19 8SQ, United Kingdom

For details of our global editorial offices, for customer services and for information about how to apply for permission to reuse the copyright material in this book please see our website at www.wiley.com.

Wiley publishes in a variety of print and electronic formats and by print-on-demand. Some material included with standard print versions of this book may not be included in e-books or in print-on-demand. If this book refers to media such as a CD or DVD that is not included in the version you purchased, you may download this material at www.dummies.com. For more information about Wiley products, visit www.wiley.com.

Designations used by companies to distinguish their products are often claimed as trademarks. All brand names and product names used in this book are trade names, service marks, trademarks or registered trademarks of their respective owners. The publisher is not associated with any product or vendor mentioned in this book.

For general information on our other products and services, please contact our Customer Care Department within the U.S. at 877-762-2974, outside the U.S. at (001) 317-572-3993, or fax 317-572-4002. For technical support, please visit www.wiley.com/techsupport.

For technical support, please visit www.wiley.com/techsupport.

A catalogue record for this book is available from the British Library.

ISBN 978-1-118-96271-8 (paperback); ISBN 978-1-118-96269-5 (ebk);

ISBN 978-1-118-96270-1 (ebk)

10  9  8  7  6  5  4  3  2  1

# Table of Contents

# Introduction

*W*hatever role you play in your company, finding out more about business development gives you a broader perspective on how to make the firm grow. The purpose of business development is to drive growth, or whatever form of expansion is important to you right now.

Absolutely everybody in the company can make a contribution to growth, and this book not only gives you a grounding in business development – it also shows how people in different areas of the business can do their bit. As the saying goes, the sum of the parts is greater than the whole.

People commonly move into business development from other parts of the company, and leaders often have to manage business development and all its component parts. This book helps you do that.

The book is intended for small to medium-sized companies that offer services to other businesses – so-called business-to-business (B2B). Such firms are as diverse as lawyers and architects, corporate event planners or video specialists, technology implementers, branding and marketing companies. I keep the content general enough to be applicable to a wide range of people and organizations. Product companies will also find this book useful, along with anyone who wants to be expert in business development.

## About This Book

After 20 years working in business development, you'd expect that I've learned a thing or two. One fact I discovered is that people are confused about what business development is. In this book I set out to dispel that confusion and provide a model for business development that anyone can use.

Another thing I found out is that companies go through spurts of growth, interspersed with periods of flat revenue, or even backsliding. For smaller companies, say those with less than $10 million in revenue, this variation can result in periods of severe peril. Therefore, I want to provide ideas as to how you can mitigate that danger through robust business development.

Also, when company growth stalls, what you did yesterday to get new business probably isn't going to work for your next phase of expansion. That pattern keeps recurring and you'll find that some things from the book are a no-brainer to do today, whereas others may be more relevant in two to three years' time. Yes, here is the book that keeps on giving.

I include lots of good advice for executives who need to plan for growth, but aren't sure what to prioritize or how to manage people with different capabilities to their own. In the early years, you can't afford top leaders for every part of your organization – you have to wear a lot of hats until you have the money to start handing those areas over to others, who may often be new employees.

When I started my career in the US, I was in charge of delivery and also tasked with getting more business. I learned from my then CEO how to be effective in selling, contract negotiation and customer management. I later began to dig into and understand marketing and how to make partnerships pay off. In other words, it all had to be 'painted on' – it didn't come naturally.

Even today, I know the areas that I'm really good at and the ones best left to someone else. I've come to realize that nothing's wrong with me – the best leaders know their weaknesses and get help. So if you're used to going it alone, this book provides you with a pathway to surrounding yourself with the right people to take you where you want to be.

I wouldn't be able to share my experience authentically unless I 'fess up that I've experienced failure as well as success. Every great business leader I've ever known has done the same and has the capacity to handle failure and learn from it. I'm really excited that you want to join their ranks.

I attended a seminar recently. The leader said, 'This isn't television. I'm actually talking to you and I require you to respond.' Similarly, I don't see this book as a leisurely bedtime read – it's an interactive experience. Study, think, write. Keep a pad and pen handy throughout. You're about to reinvent how you do business.

## Foolish Assumptions

I assume that you're an ambitious business owner or leader who wants to grow your company, but for whom business development holds some mystery. Whether you're directly involved in strategy, marketing, selling, customer management or working with partners, you need to understand the strategies and tactics for making your business grow. Marketing folks, salespeople and customer managers will find this book useful as well, if they want an overview of business development to improve their own practices or better understand other disciplines.

Perhaps you've been dissatisfied with your company's expansion, or your revenue growth has slowed down or even halted. If so, this book gives you a fresh look at how to push forward to the next stage in your company's history.

I assume that you don't want a sit-back-and-relax book but are willing to commit to active reading, participate in 'try this' experiments, use tools to help you make plans and develop ways to measure your results. I give you strategic direction and on-the-ground tactical tools and advice and assume that you're going to take what's useful and apply it in your own organization. I wrote this book to contribute to your success, and that can happen if you use it and share it.

# *Icons Used in This Book*

This icon highlights techniques or approaches that you can use to improve your business development.

I use this icon to point out important information you may want to keep in mind as you apply the techniques and approaches.

I use this icon to point out concepts that are a little more involved.

This icon stresses potential pitfalls and danger spots.

I use this icon to provide you with a task – perhaps something to do in your armchair or take to the office and work on with others. Think of it as an experiment and see what comes out of it.

This icon provides real-life examples of business development that worked and, in some cases, didn't.

# Beyond the Book

This book is chock-a-block with business-development guidance, tools, tips and tactics to make you successful. You can find additional tools at www.dummies.com/go/businessdevelopment and some free bonus articles at www.dummies.com/extras/businessdevelopment. You can also access the cheat sheet at www.dummies.com/cheatsheet/businessdevelopment.

# Where to Go from Here

If you're new to business development, I suggest that you read this book cover to cover from Chapter 1. If you ever thought that business development was just sales, you'll change your mind by the time you're done.

Even experienced business developers probably want to read Chapter 1, which defines what business development is and ensures that the rest of the book makes sense. One of the most common issues with business development is that company leaders are overly centered on their own services and how great they are, but not necessarily on what the customer cares about. Part I turns that on its head, and so is an important foundation for the rest of the book.

For Parts II through VII, you can focus on what's most important to you. If you want to get to grips with something specific quickly, take a look at the contents pages and dive right in. I provide plenty of cross-references to help you find what you need to supplement any chapter.

I encourage you to share the book with your co-workers. Business development takes teamwork, and so if you decide to adopt any of the practices in this book, pass it on to others who need to be involved. I make clear where that involvement is important and how everyone can contribute.

As you read this book and work with some of its ideas, I hope that you recreate your view of business development. Above all, being in business is a game that you play to win; how you do business development determines whether you win the game.

Digest this book in your own time and I wish you well with your business growth.

# Part I

# Getting Started with Business Development

*For Dummies* can help to get you started with lots of subjects. Visit www.dummies.com to discover more and do more with *For Dummies* books.

# In this part . . .

- ✔ Gain a clear understanding of what business development encompasses.

- ✔ Realize why business development can be problematic for small, growing companies.

- ✔ Look at business development from the customer's point of view.

- ✔ Align your business development with the customer lifecycle.

- ✔ Use business development tools to secure your business growth.

# Chapter 1

# Introducing Business Development for Services Firms

. . . . . . . . . . . . . . . . . . . . . . . . . . . . . . . . . . . . . . . . . . . . .

*In This Chapter*

▶ Defining business development

▶ Looking through your customer's eyes

▶ Making time for business development

. . . . . . . . . . . . . . . . . . . . . . . . . . . . . . . . . . . . . . . . . . . . .

*I*f you ask ten people what they think business development is, you probably get ten different answers. Chances are that even your own view of business development isn't completely aligned with others in your organization, unless you've taken special and unusual steps to make it so.

Whether you're a business owner, involved in business development or just interested in discovering more, you probably inherited your view of business development from your business experiences, gleaned it from Google, created it yourself or perhaps used a mix of all these influences.

In this chapter, I set the scene for the whole book, providing a clear definition of business development, which involves strategy (see the chapters in Part II), marketing (Part III), sales (Part IV), customer management (Part V) and partnerships (Part VI) – and I set out why business development matters. I also describe the central role of your customers and tackle the problem of becoming overwhelmed, discussing how and why you need to find time for business development in your company.

# Answering the Question: So What Is Business Development Anyway?

Here's the $64,000 question: What is business development? Is it something to do with sales? For sure. Is it related to business growth? It had better be! Does is have anything to do with your business strategy? Probably.

When you set out to create something, say, a new company, a growth plan or a new service, nothing says how it ought to be: in other words, your 'something' is what you *create* it to be. You may have noticed, however, that in business what gets created soon becomes the norm, the accepted way, the way it *has* to be. So that when you try to change something, someone always says, 'but we've always done it this way'. Boy, don't some people take themselves seriously!

When this happens, you can find yourself forgetting that you created it, whatever it is, and that therefore you can *recreate* it. Successful businesses take *re*creation seriously – recreation is built into their DNA. Recreating is how they keep their *offer* (the service they bring to the marketplace and something I discuss in detail in Chapter 5) fresh, how they assimilate new ways to market themselves, how they reduce their sales cycles and how they find great partners to help them grow their businesses.

Check out Chapter 2 for lots more on the importance of business development.

## *Recognizing that business is a serious business*

If you're thinking that business is a serious matter, I agree with you. Professional football is a serious game (and a big money business). It has a purpose (get that ball over the touchline – or in the goal if you're thinking soccer), it has rules and it's clear what winning looks like (and the winners receive prizes!). Think about business like that and it becomes fun; well, some of the time.

Given the different ideas people hold about business development, having a definition is useful. Here's mine:

*Business development is the discipline required to achieve growth through the acquisition of profitable net new customers and expansion of existing customers.*

Clearly business development is concerned with growth and most companies achieve growth by getting new customers. Even if you grow by acquisition, you're still, at the root of it, acquiring new customers (though note that, unless they're profitable to you, you really don't want them). You also have existing customers and many firms neglect the opportunity for growth that lies within those existing (or historical) customers.

Discipline is required to acquire, keep and grow customers. Discipline has two meanings here:

✔ **Discipline is the serious study of business development as a business competence.** I'm frequently amazed how many people think that they can do business development when they've never studied it for a moment. If you think about your offer and the knowledge and experience it takes to do what you do for your customers, you probably don't take that lightly. So start thinking of business development the same way. You have to study it, become an expert and use the discipline.

✔ **Discipline is the rigor of doing business development every day.** When small firms have plenty of business, they neglect business development, and when they're running out of business they panic and start scurrying around for new opportunities. This approach is disastrous. Getting new business takes time. If you're not looking ahead to where your revenue is going to come from in three or six months' time, you're facing the spectre of horrible revenue swings, which stress your company, your cash flow and your co-workers/employees.

Business development gives you a disciplined approach to creating your offer, taking it to the market, acquiring customers, developing them to enhance your success and partnering with others to grow still further.

The discipline helps you smooth out the bumps in the road. You know – the bumps that caused you to pick up this book, whatever they were.

## Understanding how business development differs from selling

I need to dispel a myth: a lot of people equate business development with selling, but in fact selling is just one of its functions, not the whole thing.

### Selling is only part of business development

*Sales* is the art and science of presenting a solution to a prospective customer's need and getting to a transaction, where the customer 'buys' your solution.

By contrast, *business development* is much broader. To develop a business, you have to create solutions to the problems or pains that are sufficiently common in the marketplace for you to build a viable business. Then you have to figure out how to take that offer to the marketplace and generate results.

Business development encompasses:

✔ **Your offer:** Creating the solution you have or the reason your business exists. Move on over to Chapter 5 for more on your offer.

✔ **Marketing:** Making the market aware of your offer. Chapters 8 to 12 contain all you need to know about marketing in the context of business development.

✔ **Selling:** Acquiring new customers. Chapters 13, 14 and 15 are your guides here.

✔ **Customer management:** Delivering your solution so that you retain, expand and leverage your customer base. Check out Chapters 16, 17 and 18 for more on customer relationships.

✔ **Partnerships:** Joining with other firms to expand your opportunities. Chapters 19 and 20 are your friends here.

✔ **Feedback:** Using opinions to improve your offer (in other words, quality assurance). Chapters 3, 7 and 17 cover feedback from customers, from your staff and from the delivery department, respectively.

You can see that business development is cyclical – a feedback loop, with the potential to improve, recreate and enhance your performance. The power of business development lies within that cyclical nature (more on that in Chapters 3 and 4).

People always buy because they have a need. Even a 'want' such as 'I want a diamond ring for my 25th anniversary' is a need. I need to show myself, and everyone else, that my husband still loves me. I need to look good to the neighbors ('did you see that ring he bought her!'). Businesses experience needs as problems or pains that need to be solved. So the purpose of selling is the same whatever the context – fulfilling customer needs.

Businesses that think of business development as only sales often have big gaps in their business development cycle that lose them money. Closing those gaps is one way you can boost your results – often dramatically.

Getting those spectacular results takes more than one person. It takes a village or, in a small company, a few key people pretending to be a village (also known as wearing multiple hats). Growth is dependent on creating the vision for business development and then dealing with the reality (something I tackle in the later section 'Taking stock of where you are').

### Problems that result from getting things wrong

When companies confuse sales with the wider practice of business development, they often end up taking the wrong approach to growth.

Imagine that your firm has reached a certain size and as the owner you're totally stressed trying to keep up with everything you have to do. You've exhausted your own network for getting customers, and sales are slowing down.

What do you do? Hire a salesperson, of course! Customer acquisition becomes the salesperson's responsibility and you can get on with all the other stuff. The problem is that salespeople are born to sell and selling is a specific discipline related to taking prospective customers from a twinkle in the eye to signing a contract.

Nonetheless, you hire a salesperson, give her a title like 'Director of Business Development' and sit back and wait for the sales to roll in.

On her first day, your salesperson shows up for work. At 10:00 a.m. you meet with her to get her started. You talk about what the company does, you talk about your customers and you ask about who she's planning to sign up first. She interrupts you with three questions:

> 'What's in *my bag* (what offers am I taking to the market)? Where's my *collateral* (where's my marketing stuff)? Where are my leads?'

You look a bit uncomfortable:

> 'Umm. Aren't you supposed to do all that, Ms Director of Business Development?'

> 'No, I'm a salesperson. I sell. Period.'

Ooops!

I'm painting an extreme picture here, but it happens; I see it all the time. The salesperson is left on her own. She sighs, pulls out her metaphorical rolodex, makes calls and tries to close business. Six months later, she's let go, not because she's no good (although that's often the conclusion) but because the company didn't understand that selling is just one part of business development. The firm sent the salesperson up the creek without a paddle.

The sad thing is that some business owners repeat this sorry cycle three or even four times before coming to the (wrong) conclusion that salespeople are worthless and that the firm better go back to how it was doing things before. Like a popped balloon, bang goes any chance of business growth.

Business development is a wide-ranging game – if you only focus on the next sale, you're missing the point.

## *Breaking business development into bite-sized chunks*

If, as I define it in the earlier 'Recognizing that business is a serious business' section, business development is all about achieving growth, acquiring net new customers and expanding existing customers, how do you go about that? What do you have to do in practical terms?

One place to look for answers is at companies like yours that have grown to $10 million ($6.3 million), $20 million ($12.6 million) in revenue or beyond. What do they do to get there? Well, they focus on key things that ensure growth and success:

- ✔ They keep an eye on the marketplace, what's happening in it and what services the market is demanding.

- ✔ They watch the competition, assess their strengths and weaknesses, and try to out-maneuver them.

- ✔ They define their target customers clearly.

- ✔ They get their name out there and proactively pursue the customers they want.

- ✔ They understand the customer journey clearly, with special attention to the buyer's journey.

- ✔ They know where the buyer is at every stage and interact appropriately.

- ✔ They're willing to walk away if a deal isn't a fit, or they refer it to someone else.

- ✔ They pitch, sell and close business with efficient speed.

- ✔ They choose partners who can make them more successful than they can be alone.

- ✔ They deliver well (of course) *and* they use their customer base to get new customers and to provide valuable feedback.

- ✔ They're in a state of continuous improvement.

Long list, huh? To get to where these firms are includes you strategizing, marketing, selling, managing your customers, partnering, evaluating how you're doing and reinventing. Then around you go again (sorry to make you dizzy!).

If you're feeling a little overwhelmed right now, don't worry. I deal with that in the later, appropriately named section 'Dealing with overwhelm'.

# *Placing the Customer Experience Center Stage*

If you don't have customers, you don't have a business – so obviously your customers matter to you a whole lot. You need to be interested in what they need right now, not in what you want to sell them. If you're just trying to sell, your ears are closed to any opportunities that may lead to a large breakthrough in your business – a referral to a new customer, a testimonial, an opportunity for a business partner.

Before you worry too much about how to do business development, step back, put customers first and look at things from their points of view (you get the chance to do this in depth in Chapters 3 and 4). What happens is that you start to see things you haven't spotted before and you start to do things differently.

## *Deconstructing the customer lifecycle*

One way to dig into the customer experience is to understand what an interaction feels like for a customer.

As a taster, what do customers say they like and not like about services firms? Table 1-1 gives you a few things to chew over. Do any of them seem familiar?

| Table 1-1 | What Customers Say They Dislike and Like |
|---|---|
| *Customers Dislike Vendors Who . . .* | *Customers Like Vendors Who . . .* |
| Don't listen | Are clear about what they'll do and how their actions are going to help |
| Talk about themselves all the time | Understand my business and how it works |
| Don't ask questions | Ask lots of questions (so that I get to talk) |
| Try to 'sell' me something I don't need | Are interested in my goals and needs |
| Don't seem interested in my business | Give me exactly the right information at the right time |
| Don't finish the work | Help me understand how to fix my problem – if they're not the solution, they say so |
| Over-promise and under-deliver – namely, they don't give value for money | Charge fees that are fair and I get what I expected (or more) |

Good business development gives customers what they need at every stage of the relationship.

Customers often have a fractured experience: they don't receive calls back from the service firm, they have to answer the same questions over and over, they don't hear enough about project progress, they just see a lot of invoices. You can use the chapters in Part I to help avoid these sorts of issues.

Understanding the customer experience is the key to great business development. You want to talk to your customers, and your prospective customers, as much as you can.

## Mapping business development to the customer lifecycle

The closer you get to your customers, who after all represent your marketplace, the more clearly you see how to develop your business. Just like you, they're trying to stay ahead of the rest of the market. They know, if they're any good, what their competition is up to. They know the trends in their industry. They can give you insights that rock your world, hopefully in a good way, but not always. Either way, you need to know.

At best, your customers help you develop your business. How cool is that!

# Making Business Development Manageable in a Small Business

If your response to business development is 'I hear what you're saying, but what you're saying is not my reality. I'm just surviving from day to day. I don't have the time to worry about what my customer thinks', this book is *definitely* for you.

If you're living in survival, that's a sure sign of overwhelm, namely being too busy to take on yet one more thing. You're working *in* the business, not *on* it. That needs to change.

## Dealing with overwhelm

You're in a high-stress mode right now or you will be – it's inevitable. In the end, you have to move away from the 12-hour (or more) workdays, total exhaustion and feeling like a hamster on a wheel. Larger, successful companies have a business development engine, cranking away, supporting the growth of the company. Do leaders in larger firms work hard and experience stress? Of course they do. The difference is that those larger companies have worked out the strategies for dealing with challenges and have the resources to tackle what the market throws at them, most of the time.

To start moving in this direction, you need to take two steps:

1. **Break the cycle of overwhelm by stepping back and creating a plan of action.** If you can't see the wood for the trees, how can you know where you are?

2. **Implement the most important, pressing aspects of the plan.** In this way, you start making a difference right away.

I describe creating and implementing your business development plan in Chapters 6 and 7, respectively. But to get to the plan, you have to do some self-assessment. I'm sure that you're doing certain things efficiently, but certain things you may not be doing well, or at all. You can unearth gold when you uncover your shortcomings. The section 'Looking for the obvious and not so obvious problems' in Chapter 2 helps you with this task.

No silver bullet exists. Luck does, like a new customer calling you out of the blue, but you can't build a business on luck. The sooner you start taking control of your business growth, instead of just hoping this growth is going to happen, the sooner you see results. If it was easy, companies would never fail.

## *Anticipating growth and its impact on your business*

Companies often say, 'We just need more work.' Maybe that's true – but I have to quarrel with the 'just', as if having more work solves every business problem. Growth is exciting, but also dangerous.

In a sense, where you are right now is comfortable. I'm not saying that you have it easy, just that you probably have a fixed way of working and when problems arise, you know what to do and what your co-workers need to do too.

But if you're at $1 million ($630,000) in revenue today, do you know what your $5 million ($3.15 million) company is going to look like? For sure it won't look the same, act the same or do things that same way. You'll have more people and cash flow challenges, be awarded bigger projects of higher complexity; maybe quality slips, and process and formality become important. Your role changes and the nature of the pressure is different. You'll need to become expert in things you don't have that much experience with today. You'll need to plan for those changes too. They're a-coming and maybe faster than you think. Get ready for some discomfort. It's heady stuff.

## Taking stock of where you are

You probably want to see growth. If you don't, that's okay – you can still find ideas in this book to make life easier on the business development front. Unless you're involved in a start-up, you're dealing with an existing situation, whether you're new to the company or you founded it.

### Knowing the services-firm growth patterns

Doing more of what you're already doing can work, but, and this 'but' is a big one, the patterns of growth in services companies are pretty predictable and surprisingly revealing. They look something like Figure 1-1.

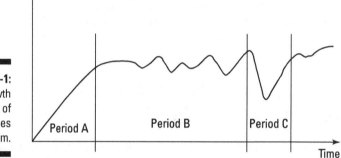

**Figure 1-1:**
Growth pattern of services firm.

Here are the phases in the growth pattern:

- ✔ **Period A:** Spell of initial growth fuelled by your network, or a growth spurt after a 'flat' spell.

- ✔ **Period B:** A plateau, sometimes flat but also sometimes a gentle but worrying seesawing of revenue. Enough to keep the owners awake at night.

- ✔ **Period C:** Loss of a major customer or some other catastrophic event. Now no one is sleeping.

After periods of growth, services firms typically settle around an average revenue level where they seem to get stuck. Why is that? Well, imagine that you acquired 12 new customers last year and your revenue was $2 million (£1.26 million). You'd like to double that next year to $4 million (£2.52 million). So you need at least one of the following three things to happen:

- ✔ Find 24 new customers this year of the same size as last year.

- ✔ Obtain fewer, but larger, new customers.

> ✔ Fill the gap between the revenue from customers that will carry over to this year, even if they give you more business.

Whatever the stage of your company's development, you're probably facing one of these scenarios. I guess that you were busy last year, just getting the 12 customers. You're going to need to do more or different things than you did last year to be successful in doubling your revenue.

### Reacting to the signs that your firm needs to change

You may succeed by doing what you did before, but you'll have to do more of it. That strategy can certainly work when you're in a growth phase and you haven't fully tapped the potential of your current approach.

If that thought makes you nervous, however, perhaps you know that your current tactics won't work or you can see a Period-B plateau looming. Those signs indicate that you need to change your strategy.

The other sign that things may need a shake-up is when you start losing your biggest customers. Sorry to be so full of warnings, but that's the reality of small businesses. You're at high risk until you have a broad portfolio of customers where the loss of one is a nuisance and causes a wrinkle, but doesn't result in terminations or shutting the company down. Time to burn the midnight oil reading this book and selecting tactics that you can initiate immediately. You're in danger of going down.

When experiencing a risky situation, or even just when stuck, business owners say things like:

> ✔ I worry about making payroll.

> ✔ I don't know what my projected revenue will be in three months.

> ✔ We keep losing on price.

> ✔ I guess this is as big as we're going to get.

> ✔ I think I'll go and do something else.

Ask yourself what you're worrying about the most? Before you can move on, you need to be clear about where you are and realize the implications of not doing anything about it beyond your usual approach. Don't resist the facts of your current situation. Write down the specific business issues you're stressing about.

When you've done that quick exercise, starting to look for solutions becomes much easier. In a way, you're going through the same journey your customers do when they're faced with business challenges that threaten their situation. Relish what's happening – first, because you're ready to take a long, hard look and, secondly, because you can find solutions – and quickly.

# Chapter 2

# Finding Damaging Gaps in Your Business Development

**In This Chapter**

▶ Staying strong by addressing weaknesses

▶ Discussing dilemmas for services firms

▶ Assessing where your business is now

*G*aps can be a real pain and usually indicate a weakness of some sort, whether they're gaps in business knowledge, like not feeling comfortable with marketing, or things you haven't attended to, like gaps in clothes that need repairing! Identifying and fixing weaknesses takes money and effort, but the cost of not addressing them is higher. You can't do things you don't understand and you may lose a sale when a hole appears in your worn suit during a meeting, turning you instantly from successful entrepreneur to hobo!

I assume that you're reading this book to discover how to do better in business development, whether your firm's revenue has plateaued or is seesawing (check out Chapter 1 for more details). Perhaps you're wondering why getting business is so difficult when your firm is good at what it does and provides value to its customers. You're busy, you want more business, so maybe you just need to do more of what's been working. Unfortunately, simply working harder can overwhelm you and lead you to feel that life is nothing but work. As a result, you experience a knock-on effect on your health and wellbeing – and on your family and leisure time.

Doing more of what you did yesterday just isn't enough. You may have been fine up to now, but growth needs robust business development – it's the engine of your business. This chapter helps by uncovering some of the gaps in your business development practices. This chapter is about taking stock – don't skip or short-change it. Take a real, long look as I describe the signs of inadequate business development and the particular challenges that services firms face.

If your first thought on hearing the phrase 'business development' is 'sales', read Chapter 1, where I break down business development into its component parts.

# Spotting Patchy Business Development

You're not a leader for nothing. You're where you are now because of your ambition, strengths, capabilities and, like everyone else, weaknesses.

Your strengths originate in your innate capabilities and preferences: in other words, you're doing what comes naturally to you. Your weaknesses stem from trying to do what's not natural for you. Any chance these weaknesses may be connected to the gaps in your business development? Bingo!

In this section I give you a heads-up on the dead giveaways of poor business development, discuss some of the obvious and less obvious problems, and help you think like one of your customers.

## Recognizing the tell-tale signs of weak business development

If your business development is patchy, you're likely to see signs such as the ones I list in Table 2-1. Which ones have you experienced?

| Table 2-1 | Tell-Tale Signs of Weak Business Development |
|---|---|
| **Signs** | **Consequences** |
| Your revenue plateaus. | You feel stuck. You spend time trying to maintain your revenue level/retain your staff. |
| Your revenue fluctuates. | You're caught in a seesaw of uncertainty. Do you need to lay off people? Do you need to get a line of credit? How do you survive the next 'low' and make it to the next 'high'? |
| You can't predict what your business will look like in three months. | Stress and uncertainty. You can't make hiring or firing decisions. You can't make commitment to any investment. Can you even survive? |

| Signs | Consequences |
|---|---|
| You do business development only when you seem to be running out of work. | Extreme panic. You take whatever you can get. You approach opportunities in a desperate frame of mind. You don't really have a sales 'pipeline' or if you do, the pipeline is way too small to meet your revenue goals. |
| You have limited market reach. | Your database of contacts, both prospects and other business contacts, is limited and your market recognition is low. |
| Your employees' morale is low. | Staff don't feel as if they're working for a dynamic and thriving organization. |
| The competition is killing you. | You're losing ground to new players who are more credible and who have a better market presence and a better offer. |

The signs in Table 2-1 mean that you have an on-again-off-again approach to business development *or* you have gaps in your business development that limit the opportunities to engage with your customers. These gaps can result in serious problems:

✔ You and your people doing activities that don't generate results

✔ An offer that's getting out of date

✔ A lack of overall goals and plans to achieve them

✔ Unpredictability in the business

Ouch!

## *Looking for the obvious and the not-so-obvious problems*

Why is business development problematic for smaller firms? I hear the following misconceptions regularly:

✔ Something else is always more urgent.

✔ I'm fine when I get in front of a prospect – I just need more leads.

✔ I have plenty of business right now – I don't need any more.

✔ The firm hasn't needed it up to now.

✔ There are only so many hours in the day.

Everyone has well-worn paths in the brain that make change hard. For example, consider the pattern of how you go about your work each day. Do you do the same things and have the same habits? What's your first thought when you get out of bed? Is it:

✔ How on earth am I going to get everything done today?

✔ How can I make sure that my largest customer doesn't cancel its contract?

✔ How can I find time to write that proposal for prospect Oddball Documentaries Inc. ('Weirdness is our speciality!')?

✔ How can I pay for the supplies that the business needs?

If your day-to-day life looks like the above, you're in survival mode, doing only whatever seems most urgent. Maybe you're juggling a lot of urgent issues and you only give your customers and your business development attention when you're about to run out of business. That's like giving your life partner the time of day only when they throw a tantrum or threaten to leave you.

You can discover a lot by tracking your time for a week. Yes, I know you don't have time to do that, but do it anyway. You need to know, because it reveals where you're focusing your time and where you're not:

1. **Take a piece of paper and divide it into four boxes.** Label them along the lines of 'Administration', 'Business development', 'Leading/Working on a customer project' and 'Working with staff' (or whatever four divisions are appropriate for your situation).

2. **Take a stab (in the meantime so that you can get on with this chapter), at predicting what you'll find in the timekeeping exercise.** Where do you spend your time in each of the four areas? (Look at the bullets below for ideas.)

3. **Compare where you're actually spending time to where you think that you're spending it.** This exercise can be really illuminating.

Here's a little more detail on the four areas:

✔ **Administration:** Finance, general email, rearranging your desk and engaging with admin staff or professionals such as accountants, legal or HR.

✔ **Business development:** Planning, reviewing progress against goals, researching and studying the market, spending time with prospects/customers, writing proposals and contracts, creating/developing business ideas, doing marketing and going to networking events.

> ✔ **Leading/Working on a customer project:** Being the project manager or subject matter expert (that is, *leading the team*) or doing actual work on a customer engagement (namely, *being on the team*). Clearly, the more time you spend being on the team, the more swamped you get as your business grows.
>
> ✔ **Working with staff:** Hiring, developing, planning, delegating and inspecting the work of your staff.

Don't make the mistake of saying that business development is getting little time because you're busy with customers, you love administration or you're always facing a higher priority. Business development *is* your highest priority!

## Thinking like your customers

Business development can be weak because you're inwardly focused – in other words, running the company and doing 'the work'. Nothing's wrong with that, but you need to look outside too – at the market, at your competition, and at your prospective and actual customers and their needs.

I suggest that you adopt a new take on business development. Shifting to the point of view of the customer provides that new perspective and has you balance your efforts across key activities that you and your customer both need. Take your shoes off, move to another chair and imagine that you're in the head of one of your customers. Ask questions such as:

> ✔ What are my customers concerned about? What are they trying to accomplish?
>
> ✔ What keeps my customers awake at night?

Whenever you work on your business development, make that mental leap into a customer's head. I talk a lot more about developing a deep understanding of your customers in Chapter 3.

Your customers don't care about your business development practices – not one jot. They care about their own survival and the problem that's staring them in the face. That's why the best meetings are usually ones where the customer does 80 percent of the talking.

From your point of view, the customer relationship is cyclical. It repeats over and over, sometimes with the same customer, definitely with others. Figure 2-1 illustrates the business development cycle from a prospect/customer viewpoint.

Take a tour round the circle to absorb its general drift. Start at the top with CREATE and go right around the circle, making sure that you're in the customer's head as you do so.

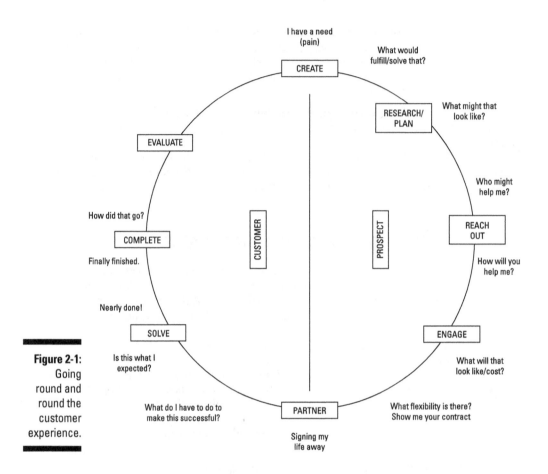

**Figure 2-1:** Going round and round the customer experience.

Here are a couple of things to grasp about how your business development is relevant to the customer:

✔ Customers want to be the one and only and to know that they have your attention from the first conversation to the point when you complete their work, get their feedback and move on. They want you to be obsessive about them. That's their point of view – and there's no shifting it.

✔ A couple of critical aspects of the customer experience in Figure 2-1 don't involve customers – one is when you EVALUATE their feedback and the other is when you do your own 'Create' (aka invent/reinvent your offer). I cover inventing your offer in depth in Chapter 5.

The customer's perspective is so important because you can all too easily fall into the trap of thinking that the customer is interested in you because you're the greatest thing since sliced bread.

In reality, customers are interested in you *only* if they identify a need/ problem/pain (call it what you will) *and* you can solve it. Imagine that Oddball Documentaries Inc. needs a film crew and your company supplies videographers at short notice. If you can connect when the need arises, you're going to get a shot at doing business with that customer.

I use the word 'need' to identify why customers buy. It connects to Maslow's Hierarchy of Needs (a 1943 theory by Abraham Maslow about human motivation), those fundamental human needs, such as eating, being safe and being appreciated, that everyone walks around with and that drive everyone's actions.

The whole purpose of business development is to identify needs in the marketplace and create and deliver solutions that solve them. You have to understand the customer need deeply – not only the overt need (like my partner's suing me – I need a lawyer!), but also any hidden ones (the ones people have but don't usually admit to, like being respected or being a hero). In Chapter 3, I help you uncover those hidden needs. They're big drivers for why people buy – or do anything else for that matter.

# Understanding Business Development Challenges for Services Firms

Business development presents particular issues for services firms, not least because the value of services is hard to articulate. When buying a product, businesses know what to expect, but the market doesn't really want to pay for *services* unless it perceives a clear and tangible value. For that reason, searching for gaps that are damaging to business development, and hence to growth, for a services firm requires special consideration.

In this section I discuss the idea of value for services firms, just how important you are as leader and the vital need to be proactive.

## Identifying value in a services firm

Services firms enable customers to do business more efficiently, more effectively. They help them answer tough business questions, resolve problems they have, do things they can't do today, grow and thrive. As a services firm, you're the source of these types of benefits for your customers. The tangible value lies in the fulfillment of need/removal of pain (see the earlier customer experience diagram in Figure 2-1). The journey for the customer starts with, 'I can't . . . ', 'I want to be able to . . . ' or 'I'm threatened by . . . '.

Your customers and prospects want their pain fixed.

When you sell services, you're selling people – their expertise, their track records, their credentials. The value lies in the people and what they can deliver. For example, if you're a patent lawyer, a branding or marketing agency, or any kind of consulting company, you produce a work product. You need to demonstrate that your work product provides *value*. For example, if you solve a huge customer pain, that has value. Flip to Chapter 5 for how to get at the value that your services provide.

The customer is also buying *from* people. Research from Google and CEB (titled *The Digital Evolution in B2B Marketing*) shows that 57 percent of any business-to-business (B2B) sales process now happens online, before the customer ever talks to you – you can read what to do about that in Part III. Fortunately for you, business happens between people and you have to talk in person – you and your prospect, your team and their team. If a prospect is going to let you into its business to solve knotty problems, it wants to be comfortable with you and your people.

Therefore, the leaders of those people need to get their act together. And who leads your team of people? You do.

## 'You're the top!' The owner-led sale

Cole Porter's song says it well: in the end, the customer wants to talk to the top – the big cheese, owner, partner or long-standing leader in your firm. This section is for owners, or others who've been leaders in the firm, maybe since it started. No one, I repeat, no one can sell your business like you do. If you don't have living proof of that in your own business, I'll eat my hat (and I must be confident because my hat is pretty large, with all the trimmings – fruit, foliage, feathers, the works).

The problem is, if you're the last port of call to a sale and everything that leads up to it (and even more so if you're also involved in delivery), you can all too easily be the bottleneck to your business growth.

If you just want to maintain your services firm's current level of success, that's all fine and dandy, this book helps you do that. If you want expansion, however, the time comes (and you may already be there) where you just don't have enough hours in the day to do more. You can't solve the problem by working harder. You need to address the fact that, despite all your efforts for the firm, you may be strangling the growth because of how you approach business development.

### 'Everybody wants to talk to you'

(Sing the heading to the tune by Tears for Fears!) As an owner, partner or long-standing leader in your services firm:

- ✔ **You have natural authority.** It comes with your title.

- ✔ **You know the whole history of your company.** You have intriguing stories of how you achieved X for company Y, in fascinating detail.

- ✔ **You position your business better than anyone else in the organization.** You create confidence in the mind of prospects that your company can make a difference to them, so you're on the hook for making sure that your firm does.

If you really are the only person in your company that can close a deal, manage a customer and bring the effort to a conclusion, you can't be surprised when absolutely everyone wants to talk to you.

After they meet you, customers won't let you go. Much as you love your company, your capacity (that is, your involvement in so many aspects of your business) is the problem.

### 'Don't bottle things up!'

When you can't squeeze any more productivity out of yourself, you're involved in every sale, every delivery and sometimes every decision: you *are* your business and without you, it simply doesn't exist. This position is unhealthy, untenable and can't scale.

Business development gets you to your goal – whatever that is. If your business can't function without you, you're unlikely to be able to reach that ultimate goal. Growing your business, your revenue and your profits, means that you need to get help. Expansion requires hiring people, outsourcing, bartering for support, whatever it takes.

If your firm is over-reliant on you, you have to transition your role from the 'I'm it, I'm doing everything, I have to jump in here' to a leadership role. It won't happen overnight – you have to plan for that shift. Part II of this book shows you how to create your plan and how your role as a business development leader will emerge.

# Being proactive rather than reactive

Do you react to threats to your revenue stream, to the phone ringing, to a customer complaint, to an upstart competitor? Of course you do. But that's what needs to shift about your role within your services firm – from reactive to proactive. When everything you do is reactive, you basically get what the world throws at you. When you start to be proactive, you create your destiny. Being proactive about your future business is what business development is all about.

### Applying consistent effort

Business development produces results when the *discipline* and *practice* of business development become as important as other activities such as administration, working with customers and working with staff.

For example, tomorrow you may decide that business development is less important than some administrative tasks you have to get done. That would be ridiculous, right? But that's what thousands of business owners and managers do every day. They set aside business development because they're too busy – they may characterize it as handling priorities. I suggest that they have their priorities wrong.

Strive to make business development a consistent part of your day-to-day activity.

If you haven't already completed the time analysis exercise I mention in the earlier section 'Looking for the obvious and the not-so-obvious problems', do so now. (By the way, reading this book comes under the Business Development heading, in case you weren't sure!) Consider where your time goes. What percentage of time do you spend on the following:

- ✔ Creating or refining your market offer
- ✔ Educating your prospects
- ✔ Presenting to your prospects, based on a real opportunity
- ✔ Proposing work with pricing
- ✔ Contracting, including negotiation and legal paperwork
- ✔ Delivering services
- ✔ Completing on services
- ✔ Evaluating your offer

Small services businesses give attention to talking to 'real' prospects, writing proposals and contracts, and delivering: in other words, being reactive to opportunities. But they're often less strong in broader tactics, such as proactively reaching out to the market, educating prospects, asking customers how the work's going, or in critical introspection, analysis and creation. Make sure that you don't make this mistake.

### Realizing that the world's your oyster: The power of proactivity

Taking on yet more work than you already have can be daunting, but here's the upside: you start to work on what matters, not so much on what comes up on a daily basis.

Initially, small firms grow more by accident than by design. They take on whichever customers show up at the door, people they're referred to or those they meet at a networking event. They don't necessarily select the customers they want to work with, create proactive approaches to those customers, control the sales process or fire unprofitable clients.

Your services firm benefits when you visualize a world in which you create your destiny in the marketplace and approach it proactively. To help, Table 2-2 describes a few symptoms of reactive versus proactive business development.

### Table 2-2    Reactive versus Proactive Business Development

| *Reactive Business Development* | *Proactive Business Development* |
|---|---|
| Time spent talking to ugly duckling prospects in the hope that they'll somehow turn into swans. | Little time spent on ugly ducklings. They're not the customers for you and you gracefully back off. |
| Lots of hard work chasing prospects, getting them to return calls or take the next step. | Prospects collaborate with you in the process. If they don't, you back away. |
| High levels of deal loss. | Prospects that aren't a good fit are eliminated early (they never get to a 'deal'). |
| You discount a lot. | You talk about price early and you negotiate when and if you're selected, not earlier. |
| You lose on price. | You win on value. |
| You fear the competition. | The competition fears you. You win the deals you want and you let them win the ones you don't want. |
| Your reputation in the marketplace is scattered (you take on anything). | Your reputation in the marketplace is clear – you work with customers that fit your requirements, not with those who don't. |
| You try to do whatever the customer requests. | You do what you do and you regularly review that in case it needs updating, extending or replacing. |

Assess now whether your firm is mostly reactive or whether you're garnering some of the benefits of proactive business development. When you have a good handle on where you're being proactive and where reactive, you can plan for a more proactive approach (something I help you tackle in Part II).

# Taking Stock of Where You Are

At any point in your business growth, stopping and taking stock is well worthwhile – and I'm not talking about products in a warehouse (I hope that activity's a given!). I mean asking yourself questions such as: are things going well; are you enjoying your job; are you worried to death?

In this section I help you orientate yourself in relation to business development, which involves analyzing the state of your firm, what you're doing and what you're not doing. The damaging gaps are to be found in what you're not doing.

Business development is about mastery – you never get to the top of the mountain, because another peak is always on the horizon. At any time, some areas in your business need work – glory in that fact.

## What you're not doing – and being okay with it

Unless you were entrepreneurial at 7 years old and you've carried on creating new ideas and new companies, you likely worked for someone else before you decided to start you own business.

A useful exercise is to ask yourself why you set up your own firm (what was in your mind at that time?) and then contrast it by thinking about what you're saying to yourself today. To help, compare the columns in Table 2-3.

| Table 2-3 | When You Started Your Firm Compared to Today |
|---|---|
| *Then You Said* | *Today You Say* |
| I can serve customers better. | It was much more fun when I started. |
| I do all the work; but I get no share of the profits. | I guess this is as big as the firm is going to get. |
| I'm tired of 9 to 5 – I want some flexibility. | I worry about making payroll. |
| I have a great idea. | I don't know what my projected revenue is in nine months' time. |
| I have historical customers I did work for who'll give me their business. | The firm keeps losing on price. |
| I want to work for myself (any version of 'my boss sucks', 'I don't want to report to anyone', 'I'm better than so and so'). | I think I'm going to do something else. |

TRUE STORY

## You scratch my back . . .

I'm part of a CEO group, founded by Jeff Cohen, called 'C-Level Group: No Business Left Behind'. We're self-help, so people bring their problems to the group for objective advice. Someone around the table is likely to have tackled what I'm dealing with, tried solutions, failed and succeeded. Growing a business is a team game, so if your internal team is light on experience, go outside.

Each member creates a goal for three years out for their business and then works backwards for where they need to be in two years, one year and so on. Finally, they look at the next three months in detail, specifically what they need to do for the next month to keep moving forward. Sometimes they identify areas where they know that they have a weakness – in recruitment, in doing the books or in how to grow.

Rod, Owner of West Coast Gaskets, a manufacturer and installer of a specific refrigerator parts needed by shops and restaurants, couldn't see how to expand his business without hiring lots more installers. We brainstormed two ideas: (a) putting an eCommerce site together to sell to other installers and (b) partnering with installers all over the country and supplying them with parts. Both actions would expand his business by increasing his manufacturing – he's actively working on them.

If you want to set up a group like this, connect with Jeff Cohen (www.linkedin.com/in/jeffcohen) and tell him you want to get started with your own support group – he'll be delighted to help.

You took the leap and created that small business. You were excited. You knew who your first customers were going to be to give you that initial revenue stream, and you relied on referrals and your broader network for your initial growth. You worked really hard to get to where you are.

If you're not the owner, your motivation for joining a small business may be similar or something entirely different. Think back to what encouraged you to make the leap.

In that early period of your business, you ran on string and sticky tape. Not everything was buttoned down, not everything was perfect, but it was exciting and you survived. At times you weren't doing things and you were okay with that. You did everything you could until you fell into bed exhausted at the end of every long day, including weekends.

When your revenue starts to plateau and you have to work just as hard to stand still as you previously did to grow, you're saying some of the things in Table 2-3's second column. The 'beating-yourself-up' that business owners go through, the determination to work more, faster, harder, is the sign of true commitment, but it doesn't get the desired result.

To create what's next, you need to rekindle the excitement you had when you started. One way to do that is to pretend that you just acquired the very company you already own or work for. You're the new owner or leader. Ask yourself what the firm does well and what not so well. Ask how you're going to grow it from $2 million to $10 million and beyond. Stop blaming yourself that things aren't perfect today. They never will be.

Forgive yourself for where you are and get to work on creating a new future. A much respected CEO friend of mine said: 'Be the company that's $10 million and you'll get there.'

Plugging the gaps in your business development may take more objectivity than you alone can provide. Check out the sidebar 'You scratch my back . . .' for an example solution.

## It's a numbers game: How's your firm really doing?

Do you know how you're doing? If you don't, disaster can strike suddenly and take you down quickly.

See whether you can answer the following questions:

- ✔ What was your revenue last month, last year?
- ✔ What's your gross margin percentage?
- ✔ What's your goal for this year? How are you measuring your progress?
- ✔ How many prospects are you talking to right now? Is the number increasing, decreasing or staying about the same?
- ✔ What's your highest revenue customer? And the next? And the next?
- ✔ Which customers are you losing money on?

Don't beat yourself up if you don't know all the answers. You're a great company and you're in good company. But if you're not tracking key metrics, making good decisions is that much harder. Turn to Chapters 12 and 13 for some good business development metrics.

When you combine metrics with a goal and plan for how to reach it, you have powerful tools for seeing whether you're on track or for changing course if you're not.

# Chapter 3

# Diving Inside Your Customer's Head

*In This Chapter*

▶ Understanding your customer's requirements

▶ Building your business development lifecycle

*I* know that this chapter's title sounds a bit like one of those Hollywood movies where a scientist is shrunk and injected into another person's body, but you can relax. I'm talking metaphorically here and simply mean that understanding your customers is essential.

In fact, if such a thing as a magic key to business development exists, you find it in a deep understanding of your prospective, current and past customers. They represent the marketplace and they can provide the clues as to what the marketplace wants.

In Chapter 2, I focus on you and your business development health, but here I ask you to step into your customer's world more fully. After all, love 'em or hate 'em, customers are the reason you're doing business, and shifting your focus to the customer's viewpoint helps you to see new possibilities.

In this chapter I drill down into the early stages of the customer relationship, which are typically where vendors most commonly make the wrong moves. You take a deep breath and dive into thinking about your customers, seeking to interact seriously with their concerns and desires. I describe a business development concept that focuses on them and not on you, which allows you to see where and why you may need to change your approach.

# Uncovering Your Customers' Real Needs

All kinds of customers exist: one-time, repeat and those who spend a lot upfront and then need ongoing support or maintenance of some sort. Acquiring and serving customers is part of the practice of business development and your efforts need to depend on understanding not only who your customers are, but also on what they're thinking at every stage in your relationship with them.

Write or print out a list of your current and past customers (and prospective ones too, if you have that info) and think about what sorts of organizations or individuals they are.

Ask yourself the following questions:

- **Size of your customers:** Are they big business, mid-sized, small? Do they belong to specific *verticals* (industries)? Are they for-profit or non-profit?

- **Within your customers:** Which roles do you interact with in your dealings with your customers? Who specifically signs your contracts, who has a say in the purchase, who consumes your services? A number of people with different job titles may well be involved.

- **Nature of your customers:** Which customers are 'great' and which are 'not so great'? What defines a nightmare customer for you?

Yup, those nightmare customers sure do keep you awake at night. Take a look at the following list to see whether anything sounds familiar. Do you have any customers who:

- Don't co-operate with you

- Are late with their part of the work – unprepared for you, not providing the information you need and so on

- Pay late

- Are judgmental, even abusive when things don't go well

- Are disrespectful

- Don't appreciate or value your services

- Refuse to provide references when asked

- Never provide referrals to prospective customers

- Show no interest in your business (and after all you've done for them!)

Surely, a good customer is the exact opposite of this description.

Perhaps you're thinking (like Kylie) 'I should be so lucky' to have perfect customers, but luck isn't the only factor involved in what customers you get. You can start by being clear about what sorts of customers you're looking for and turning away others.

Yep, that's right: I said it! Turning away customers. And I mean it. You'll never have the sort of business you want, the sort of working existence you want, unless you have the right customers. For more on getting such customers, flip to Chapter 5.

Unlike your prospects, your past customers have one thing in common – they wanted what you have to *offer* (that is, what you say your customers get when they work with you) and were ready to buy it. You need to be clear what it was that they were willing to buy.

---

# A tale of social media

Imagine that you're the customer and you're asking yourself whether you should use social media in your business. If you were to seek help from a social media agency (a company that manages your presence and content on social media), what would you be buying and what would they be selling? Jot your thoughts down and then take a look at this table.

### What I'm Buying versus What They're Selling

| *What You're Buying* | *What They're Selling* |
| --- | --- |
| Help in using social media to promote your business | |
| Getting your Facebook page, LinkedIn profiles and Twitter account set up and then managing them | Strategy and execution for social media *reputation management* |
| Writing content to post on social media | |

The key phrase is reputation management. The social media agencies exist to manipulate the social media (in a good way) on your behalf. They're building your reputation and, just as importantly, protecting it from harm by taking corrective action when someone says something nasty about you. What you thought you wanted may not be what you actually need – 'nuff said.

## *Understanding what customers need today and whether they know it*

Sometimes, what you're selling and what your customers are buying are aligned, sometimes they're not. Customers think that they know what they need, but their perspective is different from yours. You may well say, entirely without arrogance, that you know better. You want to say to them, 'You think you want this but you actually need this.'

Ask yourself this question: is your offer aligned with what customers say they need, or is it a struggle to have them understand why they should buy what you're offering? If your answer is the latter, don't worry – you're in good company. After all, if customers knew exactly what they needed, they'd have to know what you know and they wouldn't need you anymore. That's the beauty of services – you bring your special knowledge to solve a customer's pain.

Another reason that prospects are sometimes slow to buy is that they have *hidden needs* (the ones that don't get talked about). These hidden needs are at least as important as the overt need or problem they're trying to fix. If you can take care of customers' fears, hopes and dreams, their experience of working with you is elevated to a whole new level.

While asking yourself what your customers clearly need (items directly related to their pain), don't forget those hidden (deeper) needs. At the very minimum, they're thinking (subconsciously), how they can:

- ✔ Hire the right vendor
- ✔ Avoid getting fired
- ✔ Look good (to boss, board, partner)
- ✔ Be a hero by solving a business issue that's driving people crazy

Believe me, no one buys anything unless it fulfills a need – whether that need is hunger ('I gotta eat right now') or to look good ('my next car needs to be a Jaguar'). Purchases are a response to a need, whether you know you have that need or the ad industry created it for you.

Consider the following: when you bought this book, what was your overt need? What are your subconscious needs? Now repeat the experiment for your customers. What's their overt need and what are their hidden needs?

The ways in which humans take action to fulfill their needs is a complex matter, so stay on the lookout for unspoken needs. Use Chapter 5 to tweak your offer to account for those hidden needs. At the very least, you'll refresh it; and if you can fulfill known needs and deal with hidden ones, your customers will keep coming back for more and talk about you to everyone they know.

## Staying current with your customers' needs

I don't have to tell you that the world is changing – fast. The great offer that you have today may work just fine tomorrow, or it may not. You have to keep an eye on the marketplace – your antennae need to be up all the time, feeling for what's in the wind.

If you use social networks at all, you know how quickly the latest YouTube video, diet tip, travel destination (or whatever topic you're interested in) gets shared, goes viral and then just as quickly dies down. My friends at Influence Ecology call this *the current*. As with the current in a river, you can get swept up in the hype of the marketplace.

The business world has a current too, except that the trends aren't quite as volatile (unless you're a daily trader). Moving the mountain of a large corporation, or even the hill of a middle-sized one, takes a little longer than persuading an individual to book a massage. The business-to-business (B2B) market moves more slowly, shifting in weeks or months, rather than days. Even so, a current (an opinion as to what matters and what doesn't, what the latest 'thing' is and whether it's any good or not) exists and if you try to swim against it, you're certainly going to struggle. Swim with it and life gets much easier.

---

### Not changing; drowning

Sanjiv has a lifetime of experience in a specific software solution used to power manufacturing. Over many years, despite all the software manufacturer's efforts to refresh its product, the marketplace started to replace the system with newer, more up-to-date software. Sanjiv was convinced that companies still needed support for the original system, especially as programmers started to move into new technologies. His argument was that people had been buying what he offered for 20 years. He expected business to stay the way it had always been.

You won't be surprised to hear that Sanjiv no longer has a business.

---

If you're losing business to competitors and you suspect that they're more up-to-date than you with their solutions and services, you may need to update. No point sitting around with no work, fingers crossed that the market wants your offer. That only happens if your offer's current.

Table 3-1 shows ideas on where to look to see whether your offer is relevant to today's marketplace and the questions to ask yourself.

| Table 3-1 | Placing Yourself in the Market |
| --- | --- |
| **Where You Look** | **What You Ask** |
| Google (or your preferred search engine). | Do we need to account for any new trends? |
| Blogs, Twitter, industry analysts and market influencers. (Follow a few leaders in your space and see what they're talking about.) | Should we improve or change our offer (streamline, apply better methodology, automate, create a product)? |
| Competitors (websites, social presence, blogs, news). | What are they communicating to the marketplace and where/how are they doing that? |
| Professional trends (professional associations and their events, online groups, for example, LinkedIn). | Do we need to acquire new skills? Should we extend our capabilities? |
| Prospects (who they are, what they're asking about, who they're working with). Often found on competitor sites and on social sites. Also use information from prospect interviews (after the sales process is done). | What are they interested in? What are they asking questions about? What are your prospects giving as the reason for not awarding you the business? |

Set aside three or four hours a month to spend time researching the marketplace to see what people are talking about. Try to do this research somewhere other than your office – a library or coffee shop is a good idea. Personal life permitting, a couple of quiet hours on a Sunday morning also works well.

Re-examine your offer on a regular basis to keep it current. Take feedback from your customers, staff and market intelligence seriously and then use Chapter 5 to reinvent/reinvigorate your offer. It may need a small twist or a major revision. Either way, get it done, get it communicated to your team and get it out to the marketplace; and get used to reinvention. You'll be doing it again and again.

# Powering Growth Using Your Customer's Viewpoint

The secret to growing your business is to get a handle on where your business is right now as regards understanding your customers' priorities and proceeding from that point effectively and purposefully. To help you achieve that aim, in this section I describe conducting customer interviews, investigating your customer's journey, orientating your business to your customers (not expecting things to work the other way around!) and exerting your influence.

## Focusing on your customer: Why you should care

Telling people how good your business is at what it does misses the point. They may believe you, but frankly they don't give two hoots.

Instead, when you pay attention to what your customer is saying you obtain the intelligence you need for creating and recreating your own business.

At two specific points in your relationship with your customers, you can interview them in a structured way:

- ✔ **When you win or lose a deal:** I cover a sample interview process in Chapter 14 and at www.dummies.com/go/businessdevelopment.
- ✔ **When you complete a project, or midway through a longer project:** Flip to Chapter 16 for a method at this stage.

Interviews with customers provide valuable information for you to use in designing your offer, adding to your marketing or leveraging for references and referrals. The interview is one of the most powerful yet underused tools in a services firm's toolbox.

Check out Table 3-2, which contains an informal approach to these interviews.

| Table 3-2 | Questions to Discover What Your Customers Think about Your Services |
|---|---|
| **Who to talk to** | **What to ask customers** |
| Customers (getting them to talk to you is usually fairly easy). | 'When did you decide to get help with [the specific need or problem that your firm solves]?' |
| | 'Where did you look for information on how to solve the problem? What was most useful to you during that process?' |
| | 'How did you find out about us?' |
| | 'Who else did you consider?' |
| | 'Before we signed our contract, what worked best for you about our interactions?' |
| | 'What was least valuable?' |
| | 'What did our competitors do well?' |
| | 'What caused you to choose us/not choose us?' |
| | 'When we started working together, what was effective for you?' |
| | 'What didn't work so well?' |
| | 'Did we fulfill your need/solve your problem?' |
| | 'What feedback would you have wanted to provide when we completed the work?' |
| | 'Is there anything you would specially have valued that we didn't do or didn't do enough of?' |
| Prospects (usually best to interview them when they've given you, or not given you, the business). | Same as questions for customers down to:'What caused you to choose us/not choose us?' |

| Who to talk to | What to ask customers |
|---|---|
| Your staff (who'll be delighted to spill the beans). You get fuller answers to different questions, depending on who you talk to. | 'How well do you think potential new customers understand what we do?' |
| | 'Do they understand how we'll do things?' |
| | 'Do we tell them the right things before they make their decision to work with us (or not)?' |
| | 'Do you think we're well aligned with our customers when we start the work?' |
| | 'Are there any surprises as we kick off the work/project?' |
| | 'What goes well for the customer and for us when we're working together?' |
| | 'What doesn't go so well?' |
| | 'Do we get enough feedback from the customer?' |
| | 'Do we use feedback as fully as we could?' |
| | 'Do you think what we offer customers is what they need?' |

Prospects and customers can (and do) say things that take you by surprise. Often, these observations are really positive about your perceived or actual value to them, how well you understand them, their business and their industry, what they'd like you to do next so that they can give you more business. Sometimes, they tell you what they think you should fix in your business. From these interviews, you get an insight into how your customer sees you. How cool is that!

Don't be tempted to set up online surveys as a substitute for talking to your customers. If you have a lot of customers you can gather information online, but still select the most valuable customers and interview them live, preferably in person; telephone is second best. You don't get the detailed feedback you need from an online survey and your prospects/customers don't get the sense that you really care to listen to what they want to say. There's gold in them there hills. Go mine it.

## *Mapping your customer's journey*

The period from the time that a prospect identifies a need, to the point at which that need is fulfilled, is the *customer journey.* To get fully into the customer's head, you need to understand that journey and use it to your advantage.

As I mention in the earlier section 'Understanding what customers need today and whether they know it', remember that a business relationship has two sides:

- ✔ **Your firm:** With your view on how the relationship should go, what should happen in what order, how the services should be delivered and what works for you.

- ✔ **Your customer:** With its needs, its search for solutions and services, what it does and in what order, its engagement in the solution and the delivery, and what works for it.

Clearly you see the relationship one way and the customer sees it in quite another.

Figure 2-1 in Chapter 2 shows the cycle from the customer's point of view. Figure 3-1 switches to your viewpoint. This is the *business development life-cycle.* Certain steps in the lifecycle don't involve the customer, specifically EVALUATE and INVENT, so this version covers stages that you and your company need to pay attention to but that don't involve your customers directly.

Review this version of the lifecycle, download it from www.dummies.com/go/businessdevelopment, print it out and slide it into this book – and pin a copy to your wall alongside Figure 2-1. You're going to get to know these figures as well as you know your face.

As you upgrade your business development, which by the way never stops, use Figure 3-1 to help you plan your business development approach and then implement your plan. Chapter 2 helps you see the areas that aren't working so make these areas your priority: you can't implement everything at once. You build your high-level plan and then fill in the detail and tackle it a bit at a time.

Turning your business-development engine on requires that you:

1. **Understand what your customers are looking for at each stage in their experience.**

2. **Understand the stages and how to interact with them at each stage.**

3. Map your business development to the customer experience – which includes planning your business development to fit your company.

4. Implement the plan that you create.

5. See the engine working (and not working), then rinse and repeat.

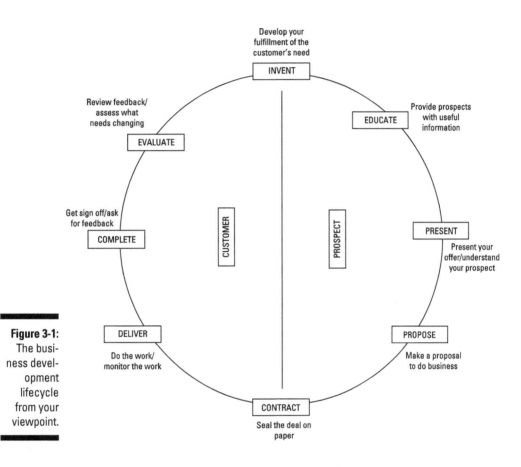

**Figure 3-1:**
The business development lifecycle from your viewpoint.

After the initial go round, which can take weeks or maybe even months to complete, you use it again and again to refine and improve your business-development practices and expand your results.

Breaking down the stages in Figure 3-1 clarifies any questions you have about the lifecycle. See Table 3-3 as its instruction manual.

| Table 3-3 | Stages in the Business Development Lifecycle |
|---|---|
| *Stage* | *What Happens* |
| INVENT | You're creating or reinventing your *offer* to the marketplace. Your offer articulates the essence of how you help to fulfill a customer's needs and solve its pains. This process is rigorous, requiring a deep dive into what customers want, what the marketplace is saying and what your staff can do. |
| EDUCATE | You have valuable information to share with the marketplace and you distribute that information to educate your customers and influence their (later) decision to talk with you and do business with you, when that specific need arises. Don't expect everyone to be interested in your information – they're only interested if the information is timely for them (that is, if they're in the RESEARCH phase of the cycle). |
| PRESENT | You introduce your offer and gather information from the prospect about its business and its need. You're assessing each other (like a first date, though hopefully less awkward!). |
| PROPOSE | You have enough information to propose a specific service that fulfills on the customer need. You only give a proposal if the customer fits your profile of what a customer should be, co-operates with you in gathering information and has the time and budget to commit. |
| CONTRACT | You specify what you'll provide/deliver, what the customer will provide/deliver and what the terms are under which you're willing to engage. |
| DELIVER | You kick-off the work with the customer – you set the ground rules, the communication plan, the tools and the escalation process if things go off the rails. You also establish the contacts you need to operate effectively together.<br><br>You do the work in collaboration with the customer. You monitor the work to make sure that everything is going as planned, you adjust accordingly if not and you receive ongoing feedback from the customer's team and from yours. |
| COMPLETE | You follow a formal completion process that has the customer sign off that you're done with the work to its satisfaction, you make sure that you get final payment and you ask for specific feedback, references and referrals. |
| EVALUATE | You take your experience with this customer (and all your others), feedback from all interested parties and intelligence from your research of the marketplace, and you review whether your offer is still current and whether how you're delivering it is working for customers, for your team and for your business. You start the cycle over again, working the feedback in periodically to refresh your offer. |

TRUE STORY

## Joe's early customer journey

As an example of what customers do and think in the early stages of the lifecycle, read about Joe's journey.

Joe owns a tool-manufacturing company with revenues over $100 million (£63 million). His firm sells B2B all over the country with some overseas orders too. His current website is informational: it has a catalog, but it's available as a pdf file, so you can't easily search for a specific product, nor buy a product online. The company that created the website five years ago has gone out of business, so Joe knows he has to start over with a new vendor.

Joe's business spends a lot of time (and hence money) serving smaller customers that represent about 15 per cent of his business. They mostly fax orders in, sometimes using an old catalog with inaccurate orders, which causes Joe's firm a lot of trouble. Customer Service has to make phone calls to straighten things out. Joe wants to provide online ordering for his smaller customers, including taking payment upfront (saving his accounting department time chasing payables).

His IT department has never implemented a website, never mind an eCommerce system. His marketing team is two people, who spend all their time doing the catalog and placing trade adverts.

Joe realises that he needs to go through a number of progressive steps before he can consider doing a website/eCommerce project. He consults his IT application manager Sheetal, who knows how to make minor changes to the website, and his catalog compositor Phil, who posts the updated catalog to the website in pdf format regularly, but doesn't touch any other pages in case he 'breaks something'.

Despite the team's lack of knowledge, Joe's motivation is high as he launches into the process:

*Education*: Sheetal researches a number of available eCommerce solutions, while Phil looks at competitor websites and how catalogs are handled. He also analyzes the firm's own site, to map what's there. He calls a couple of smaller customers to ask what they think of the site. They reveal that they look at the catalog sometimes if the paper catalog has gone missing. They've even printed out all 200 pages, just to find the few specialized items they actually need to buy. Both customers would like to do online ordering – they're used to that with other suppliers – and think that paying with credit cards would be fine. Joe gets the number of faxed orders and average order value from an ERP report. The firm takes around 5,000 orders per year that are $3,000 (£1,890) each on average.

*Research/Planning*: Sheetal finds a great whitepaper on the web about B2B eCommerce, which Joe devours. He discovers that it can be hugely complex and expensive, but that if he keeps it simple he can probably get a website up and running within a few months. The team define the specific problem they're trying to solve – providing an easy-to-use catalog and customer-ordering system on the web for smaller customers. Phil mentions a few other areas that they need on the website and gives Joe a list of the required pages.

They discuss hiring a person to lead the eCommerce efforts, but Joe feels they need more advice before trying that. He decides to talk to a few eCommerce companies. If you were an eCommerce software or services company, this point is when you'd hear from him (providing he'd ever heard of you, that is).

You can see how similar Figures 2-1 and 3-1 are. They represent the two viewpoints: the customer's and yours. The prospects go through a number of buyer or 'customer experience' stages (education, awareness, consideration, evaluation, justification, commitment and purchase) and then become customers. Yaay! The better you understand the buyer's journey, the better your business development lifecycle and plan is. Ask yourself, all the time, what would the customer think of this (what I'm saying, emailing, advertising, promoting, presenting, promising).

The two diagrams are necessarily generic. The skill is to take your customer's viewpoint into account and map your actions, resources, communication, analysis and responsiveness to its needs at any given moment. To do so, you use your business development lifecycle to design your approach and then follow through in practice – and you start to have happy customers.

Now, I know that customers aren't right all the time. I'm guessing you've experienced that yourself. Sometimes they're downright jerks (but as I say in the earlier 'Uncovering Your Customers' Real Needs' section, you're not going to continue working with them going forward, are you?). But if your organization has a culture of dissing the customer ('They're such a pain', 'They want everything perfect first time', 'They never say thank you, or well done'), you want to put a stop to that.

Using your customers' viewpoints as the core of your thinking means that treating them as enemies or spoiled children doesn't make sense. They're your source of revenue, reputation, profit and, ultimately, wealth. Treat them with respect – they have hopes, dreams, challenges and fears, just like you. Listen out for these viewpoints and 'be' service. It pays.

Grasping the customer's journey isn't easy. Ask yourself the following questions. (If you want, also read the sidebar 'Joe's early customer journey' and draw parallels with your own business.) What sort of thinking do your customers go through before they ever talk to you? How many decisions have already been made? What can you influence and what's already decided? How can you start to bring influence into the earlier stages? Is that even possible? I address these types of questions in Chapter 4, as you shift to becoming fully customer-centric.

## *Tailoring your solution to your customer's need (not vice versa)*

Most services firms live in a delusion that they're so good at what they do, any customer would want to work with them. Selling to a friend, acquaintance or referral is easy – you already have an 'in' – but in the tough world of the open marketplace you're dealing with people who don't know you or your work. You have to show that you understand their needs and that what you're saying is relevant to them and adds real value to their business.

If you misunderstand the customer experience and its different stages, you can make the mistake of trying to sell customers something when they're not yet ready to buy. From their point of view that appears pushy (customers complain about that a lot and you've probably experienced it yourself, as a customer).

To engage early on in your customer's journey, you have to abandon 'selling' and be willing to contribute to customers' research and planning. This approach means being eager to educate them and can even include suggesting that they look at solutions that aren't yours. Ouch, that hurts! But if you aren't willing to walk away when you see that the customer isn't looking for exactly what you have to offer, you'll end up chasing customers who don't really want to buy what you're offering and wasting time trying to convince them that they do. Mostly, they simply won't return your calls.

When customers gather information, they sometimes do so accurately and sometimes not. (Check out the earlier sidebar 'Joe's early customer journey'. Joe formed a bunch of opinions before ever talking to an expert.) They start to shape their judgments on what help they need and what they can do themselves, what's valuable, what's not, how long it should take, how much it will or should cost. You're faced with pre-conceived ideas and judgments that you may have to upset before you can sell your services. Of course, you should only sell your services if the customer needs them and they really are a fit. That doesn't mean that, initially, the customer has to agree with you that the purchase is a great idea, but the customer does need to be open and listening and you need to be demonstrating your value, so that they come around.

Table 3-2 in 'Focusing on your customer: Why you should care' earlier in this chapter gives you some questions to think about when mapping your customer journey. If you find these questions hard to answer, you may need to interview customers, prospects and staff to ask for their thoughts.

You can extend the interviews to partners and others in your business circle. If you go to the trouble of asking people for their help, thoughts and feedback, you'll hear things that surprise you. That's why the exercise is so valuable.

Review your research alongside the business development lifecycle in the earlier Figure 3-1. Does it help you see where you need to do some work? Where are your gaps? Flip through this book's contents or index and pick the chapters that help you dig more deeply into those areas.

And don't feel bad – every business has gaps and plugging them makes a big difference: conversations with prospects become easier and you can see more clearly what to do next. You feel powerful about how you're driving your business.

## Using influence to get the outcome you want

Power is a highly enabling experience. I'm not talking about the sort of power that people use to bully others into doing what they want. I'm referring to the kind of power where you present yourself and your company in the most compelling, authentic, honest, nothing-hidden way. This form of power is where you don't need to smear the competition to win, or cut your price to a point where the business is hardly worth having: with this power the customer is your ally, not your adversary. If something goes wrong, you're attentive and respectful and you can powerfully compromise without giving the farm away.

You want every available tool to support you in getting the result you desire. As I discuss in the earlier section 'Understanding what customers need today and whether they know it', some of the most powerful motivations (including your own) are hidden needs. You should be using every type of ethical *influence* (factors that sway things in your favor) to push customers' hot buttons.

Imagine that your customers are working in big business, in the C-Suite (that is, they reside on the top floor, maybe in those coveted corner offices). Unless you're visiting a social-media company populated by 20-somethings, you probably wear a business suit, ensure that your shoes are clean and your hair neat. If you turn up in a grubby T-shirt and jeans, would they respect you?

The fact is that you're not Warren Buffet and neither am I: you don't win business looking a mess. Give some thought to why that is.

In his seminal book *Influence,* Robert Cialdini highlights certain types of influence that make people do what they do. This wide-ranging book is highly relevant to business development. I want to draw your attention to four specific influencers on a sale:

✔ **Liking:** People buy from people they like. Prospects who think that you're a jerk don't buy from you unless they have no other option. More than that, people tend to buy from people who are like them: people who shares common values, have common aspirations, pursue the same goals. If your prospect likes football and is trying to get her kids through college, she relates to you if you're doing the same sorts of things in your life.

Be as like your prospect as possible. If you hate football, that's okay – you can create liking in all sorts of dimensions, down to what you wear, the car you drive or the music you like.

✔ **Authority:** If you carry authority in your field, that's a big influencer. You have automatic authority if you're a CEO, an expert or a person who can do things others can't – or if you're asked to speak at events, have an authoritative blog or are associated with others of high authority.

Look for ways to build authority. Certifications work well, high profile business associates are good, hiring top performers who are known for their expertise is great.

✔ **Social proof:** People want to do what others do – it gives them comfort that they're making the right decision. You need proof that you've created results for others and that good, respected companies buy your services (they can then say, 'See, ABC Company hired them, we should too').

For this reason, recognizable logos and case studies are hugely influential – these great companies must know what they're doing, so customers can be safe doing the same.

✔ **Scarcity:** If you think that something may be running out, or not be freely available, you value it more. Scarcity is an influence that has customers acting faster, paying more money and valuing what they're getting. Don't be too available. Keep yourself and your services a little scarce – it makes you more valuable.

Say things such as 'We only work with companies that . . . ', 'We take on three new customers a year; that's it' and 'We can start your work the month after next'.

You may want the world to be different, but in the big, bad marketplace, companies are using influence all the time. Influence drives people to act, make the choices they make and feel good about those choices. Use influences ethically – they're really powerful.

# Chapter 4

# Using the Lifecycle to Your Advantage

*In This Chapter*

▶ Knowing what you're selling

▶ Getting pre-sales right

▶ Working on after-sales

*I*f I say to you 'the customer is king', what's your reaction? You think worrying about the customer is all very well, but you want your moment in the spotlight? Well, here's your chance, because whereas Chapter 3 talks about the customer's perspective, in this one I look at the customer experience from your point of view.

I want you to look in detail at your business and ask whether you think that your experience of working with customers is enriching or sometimes a disaster. I cover how to align your business development with that customer experience, helping you to grasp the stages of business development as they relate to the customer's mindset, concerns and goals at every stage. Examining your business in this way allows you to develop a customer-centric approach to its full potential.

I have complete faith that, after you and the customer shake hands on the deal and the contract is in negotiation or about to be signed, you know what you're getting into and the work's going to go well.

 Check out Figure 2-1, which represents the customer experience: notice its stages, that it has a cyclical nature and that customer experience is a complex beast. Dealing with customers at multiple stages in their experience can feel like juggling plates – once in a while a plate falls to the ground. Just getting a handle on their experience is a major achievement. All the way through, you're balancing the customer's needs with your own. Start spinning those plates!

# Clarifying Precisely What You're Selling — and How

Your business needs to have its act together to get a sale *closed* (to sign a contract). You've already been doing a version of business development in your business – I just point out a few useful things to know or try to expand your 'good' stages and tackle your weaker ones.

If you're inclined to change or collapse the stages in the lifecycle, hold off for now. I recommend that you read through Chapters 2 to 6 before rewriting it! If you think that a part of the lifecycle is unnecessary and shouldn't be included, the chances are that the part you're resisting is a weakness in your business – worth checking.

Plenty of customers are out there; most of them you've never met and most you never will. From time to time a prospect appears on your horizon, and you start interacting with this potential customer (or indeed with others who take an interest in what you do and may direct you to new prospects). When you start this interaction, be clear about how you want that interaction to go. That includes knowing what you're selling: it includes your specific services of course, but you're also delivering safety, confidence and peace of mind (see the later section 'Creating the customer experience'). In this sense, you come to appreciate that you're selling more than you think you are.

## Being in control

When you're clear about what you're selling, you want to think about who you're selling to and how. Controlling the customer experience builds a strong, resilient business for you. Take a look at the sidebar 'Are you in control?' Establishing and maintaining control is a recurring topic throughout this book.

Here's the scoop. One of the hidden needs of customers is that they want to experience a confident, organized service provider that looks like it knows what it's doing.

You may be asking 'How can I be in control? Surely the customer chooses to whether to work with me?', but you're probably not saying 'Be in control? I don't want that!'

## Are you in control?

Business is only fun when you're doing the right things for the right customers at the right time. The challenge is how you get to that position. If your approach is to grab every piece of business that walks through the door, chances are you'll never get to that level of fun.

If you want to love your business life, you need to design your interaction with prospects and customers and not let it be accidental. Flying by the seat of your pants causes all sorts of problems:

✔ You look unprepared/unprofessional.

✔ You lose some of your authority.

✔ You struggle to establish trust.

✔ You definitely lose the upper hand.

✔ You're not in control.

Being committed to serving your customers doesn't mean that you have to be a punching bag. In fact, it means quite the opposite. You establish control of the business development lifecycle by being clear about what needs to happen at every step. Establishing control is especially important in the first interaction, because you're setting the tone for the whole relationship.

The lion is a powerful animal, but a lion tamer, although physically weaker, is a master of how to be in control. If you don't want to get eaten for lunch, take control of the customer's experience.

The ultimate goal is to guide the customer around the lifecycle (because you know that it works). To be that kind of guide, you need to train the customer. Have you ever wondered why a customer pays some vendors on time and not others? It does so because the vendor that gets its money on time has trained the customer to pay on time. That training starts on day one.

It's your business. Make sure that you say how things should go.

You're definitely selling your firm's expertise, your authority as one of the leaders in your firm, your track record, your references, your results. That all makes sense, right? Thing is, you don't want to wait for customers to dictate the next step: to enquire as to your references, review your case studies or ask you for a proposal. You want them to buy immediately into the fact that you're in control of the process. For them, control that's powerful and authoritative doesn't show up as arrogant – it makes them feel safe. They can relax and be fully engaged in telling you about their business and their problems, instead of trying to figure out whether you're any good at what you do.

When you display competence on day one, it accomplishes three important objectives:

✔ Customers see that you know what you're doing.

✔ Customers heave a sigh of relief (believe me, they've seen plenty of incompetence in their time).

✔ Customers start to trust you.

If you can achieve this level of authority and control in your first interaction, subsequent meetings and discussions go well (as long as you can keep it up – that takes planning and lots of practice). People buy from people who seem competent and they can trust, and you set yourself up for success.

These interactions are commonly handled amazingly badly. Compare the two versions of the same meeting in Table 4-1.

| Table 4-1 | The First Customer Interaction (the Good, the Bad and the Ugly) |
|---|---|
| **The Customer's in Control** | **You're in Control** |
| You come to the meeting knowing next to nothing about the customer's company or the specific contact. | You've done your research and you have a good overview of the customer's business, size and how long it's been around. You also know something about the contact. You have a sense of whether it's a target customer. |
| The customer drives the agenda and controls how the meeting goes. | You have an agenda. You outline it to the customer and get agreement. You're clear about where you expect to be at the end of the meeting. |
| The customer tells you what it thinks you need to know about its situation/need. | You introduce your company very briefly, so that the customer immediately gets the value. |
| The customer's hard to interrupt. You can't get a word in. | You ask questions that you need the answers to in order to determine whether this prospect is one you want to work with. |
| The meeting runs short of time or runs long. | You keep an eye on the clock. You leave time to cover the vital three items below. |
| Budget is never mentioned. | You talk price. You tell the customer what you typically charge. If the representatives are still on their chairs, go to the next step. |
| You're not sure what the customer's buying process is, who to makes the decision, who else is involved, who signs the contract. | You ask the representatives to outline their roadmap to making a decision (assuming that you're in a competitive situation). Get the decision-makers' names and roles and understand the timeframe. |

| The Customer's in Control | You're in Control |
|---|---|
| The meeting ends with no action items set, or commitments to next steps. | If you think you're on to a winner, ask whether the representatives are willing to entertain the next step (whatever that is). If they say yes, let them know what you need to happen to move forward. Don't ever give anything without getting something back. ('Before we send you a proposal, let's set a date to review it together – we expect [the decision-maker] to be at that meeting.') |

I'm sure that you can see from the table that the customer feels way more confident with the approach in column 2 (Chapter 14 has loads more about selling under control).

If things don't smell right at the end of that first meeting, *walk away* (the chapters in Part IV tell you why). Take the same strategy with future meetings.

If you didn't immediately rush to Part IV (and I wouldn't have blamed you if you had), let me just add one thing. One of my favorite treats as a child was those little netted bags with gold chocolate coins. Think of those coins as representing you, your customer and the relationship. On one side of the chocolate coin is what you're selling. In big gold letters, it says 'authority in every move you make'. On the other side of the coin is what the customer is buying: it says 'peace of mind'. The chocolate in the middle is 'mutual confidence and trust'. Oh, I love analogies featuring chocolate!

## *Keeping your offer fresh*

You're not stuck with your current offer as it is. Your offer has to be relevant and flexible, open to small shifts and changes without high risk:

- ✔ Your offer has to serve customer needs as they are today (check out Chapter 3 for all about assessing your customers' real needs).

- ✔ Your offer needs to be current (in the sense of up-to-date) and *technically appropriate:* 'technically' in the broad sense of your specialized knowledge, your methodology, the tools you use and how your service gets delivered.

# Technology and its impact on services firms

Did you have a car 10 or 20 years ago? When you went to have it serviced, way back when, it was a different experience. These days car service is all computerized, pinpoint diagnosis – never mind that cars are just way more reliable than they used to be.

I asked a group of CEOs of small businesses how technology had changed their businesses in the past ten years – changed how they *get* the business and how they *deliver* on it:

## How Technology has Changed Some Businesses in the Past Decade

| Type of Company | Biggest Technology Impact |
|---|---|
| Executive search firm | LinkedIn for Candidate searches |
| | Specialized recruitment software |
| Event planning and design | Social media |
| | Easy availability of design ideas online |
| | Remote working (Skype, WebEx) |
| | Design software |
| Software as a Service (SaaS) | SaaS-based Customer Relationship Management (CRM) |
| | Project management and issues tracking systems |
| | Search Engine Optimization (SEO) to get traffic to the website |
| | Remote meetings |
| Custom art manufacturer | Website has increased traffic ten-fold |
| | YouTube 'show and tell' of art pieces |
| Design and construction | Email, blogging and social media for extended communications |
| | Design software/much less printing and paper |
| Law firm, investment group | Email, social media |
| | Remote meetings |
| | Website and SEO to attract customers |
| | Template libraries for proposals |
| | Online legal research |
| | E-filing for legal cases |

| Type of Company | Biggest Technology Impact |
| --- | --- |
| Business coaching | LinkedIn for networking |
| | e-Newsletter |
| | Online calendaring |
| | Online communication with clients |
| Consumer goods marketing | LinkedIn for contacts |
| | Being able to work anywhere (mobility) |
| | Texting |
| | YouTube, Instagram and Twitter for sharing work |
| | Adobe products for design |
| | Better presentations |

How has technology changed your business? Were you doing things the same way ten years ago? How has what you're selling changed? Has that happened in the past two or three years? Should it?

For an example, read the sidebar 'Technology and its impact on services firms', which examines how technology (in the narrower sense) has changed the offers of a sample of companies over time. The questionnaire for this mini-survey is available at www.dummies.com/go/businessdevelopment if you want to use it on your own company.

In essence, you need to ask how certain forces in the marketplace, including the escalating rate of technological change, are impacting your offer, how you take it to market and how you deliver it.

When you make the decision to change your offer to keep it fresh, extending from what you're already doing makes the most sense. Keep to the path, don't go wandering out into the woods. You're in a dangerous neighborhood. Moving too far away from your core competence starts to confuse the marketplace. I discuss creating or modifying your offer in Chapter 5.

Some people have particularly clear offers (yes, people have offers too – it's not just companies), whereas other people's offers are rather confusing. Take a look on LinkedIn for a few minutes to see what I mean. Perhaps you see a person going from studying the History of Art, to becoming a hairdresser, to going into marketing and now he's in a sales role. If you saw that background, would you hire that person into sales? No focus, no logic to his career, probably light on expertise and experience in a number of areas.

Serial entrepreneurs and leaders in society can get away with a richly varied profile, but I recommend that you stick to what you do best. I also happen to write novels, but I don't talk about that in my business life – I don't want to dilute my offer. Apply that thought to your business offer and you start creating a strong reputation.

## Investing to stay up-to-date

As your offer changes (as I cover in the preceding section), so does how you deliver it. I look at deciding whether your business and its offer is up-to-date or not in Chapter 3, but here I describe allocating your resources to take the necessary actions to decide what your offer should be today, such as being aware of the latest thinking, practices, trends and technologies.

Maintaining your staff's skills in this context often involves professional development, and you need to invest in this area. Table 4-2 shows examples of where to place your bets and how to make your investment pay off.

| Table 4-2 | Staying Current: Where Your Investment Needs to Go |
|---|---|
| *Your Investment* | *Accountability of Staff* |
| Create a staff development plan for key individuals in collaboration with them and aligned with their goals/ responsibilities. | Follow the plan. |
| Arrange for training, courses, conferences. | Attend and be focused. Share what you've learned (update and feedback sessions for other staff). Apply new knowledge. |
| Study time – set policy to give staff weekly study/research time. | Locate appropriate courses (certified if possible). Choose study that's relevant to the company/strategic direction. |
| Review processes/methodology. | Suggest improvements. Implement agreed changes. |
| Gather feedback from staff development. | Contribute to the thinking. |
| Gather feedback from prospects and customers; keep an eye on the competition. | Ensure timely feedback into the pool of ideas. |

| Your Investment | Accountability of Staff |
|---|---|
| Keep abreast of current market trends and developments. | Share new findings/ideas (typically this task is a leadership responsibility, but research can also be delegated). |
| Incorporate all the above into how you do business (offer, methods, deliverables). | Incorporate any new direction into daily business processes. |

Don't forget to keep looking for new staff, too. Interviews are a great way to find out what's new in technology, alternative approaches and so on.

If your staff members are out in the wider world keeping up-to-date and sharing what they're seeing, you have a source of new ideas for your business. You want them to be enthusiastic about making a contribution to the business, but you also need to be realistic about how much change you can initiate and follow through on at any one time.

## *Creating the customer experience*

Beyond just a sale, the customer is buying much more than the services you deliver, as I discuss in the earlier section 'Being in control'. Ultimately, the customer is buying the whole experience – every aspect of the interactions between you and your customer is part of the deliverable. In the services arena, customers depend on your expertise, judgment, objectivity, communication and warnings. You have the opportunity to be a trusted advisor. You also have the potential to let customers down.

Attention to the customer experience journey is critical to ensure that you're lockstep with the customer's expectations.

Compare the two halves of the business development lifecycle in Figure 3-1 (the part before the contract and the part after) and see what you notice.

All kinds of thoughts may pop up, perhaps things you never noticed before. Here is a selection of my ideas:

✔ **The mood of customers doesn't stay the same throughout their journey in looking for and implementing a solution to their need.** They can go from optimistic, even elated, to depressed, almost despairing (especially if their needs have a serious impact on their business or are complex to solve).

- **A big swing exists from the subjective to the objective in the first part of the cycle.** In the early stages, anything is possible. The customer's research can be quite wide-ranging, looking at a lot of options, not all of which are apples-to-apples comparisons. As they progress round the cycle, they start to eliminate possibilities and hone in on what they think may work for them, for their situation, for their budget. The move is from a subjective enquiry into an objective one, from 'What might I do?' to 'What will I do?'.

- **Choosing is decisive.** Literally. When they choose you (or anyone), do they heave a sigh of relief? Absolutely. They've moved from a world of uncertainty to one of certainty. Now they know who they're going to be working with. The engagement ring has changed hands.

- **The contract is the pivotal point.** This point is where objectivity really matters. Customers have to be clear what they're getting. Any looseness at this stage can bite both parties later on.

- **Delivery is an uncertain time.** Customers can be unsure what to do when the contract is signed. Should they stand back and let you get on with it, or do they need to be active and participatory? Should they minutely inspect everything, or should they trust you? Are they confused about what's going on, or clear?

- **What does 'done' really mean?** You may think you're done, but does the customer? Is this part of the process sometimes a point of disagreement and why is that?

- **What now?** Does the customer expect something beyond the delivery, such as a post-project review, a thank-you note, a dinner?

One person can't do everything around the customer experience cycle and be really good at it all. I'm not just talking about the fact that you'd need to be Super(wo)man, but that the stages in the lifecycle require different skill sets from your team. Someone who's good at pitching your services in a live presentation to a group of C-level people and fielding their questions isn't necessarily the person to write your contracts or deliver the work. Try getting a project manager to expand his relationships in a key account to see whether you can get more business, and you'll see what I'm talking about.

Key personality traits fit the various stages of the business development lifecycle, as shown in Table 4-3.

When you're a small company, people who carry multiple roles have strengths and weaknesses. No point blaming them for that – it's how they are. You can ameliorate weaknesses, but you can never make, say, a great salesperson out of a great bookkeeper.

### Table 4-3          Lifecycle Stages and People's Personalities

| Stage of the Business Development Lifecycle | Personality of Your Team Member |
|---|---|
| EDUCATE: Served by marketing | Typically creative, detail-oriented (every word matters). Not always great with numbers (although detail orientation can help overcome this). |
| PRESENT: Served by sales | Self-confident, loves to mingle, relate to people, perform. Prefers talking to writing. Willing to take risks. |
| PROPOSE: Served by subject-matter experts | Authoritative. Can be arrogant, but takes great pride in expert knowledge. Cautious about commitment. |
| CONTRACT: Served by proposal writers, contract people | Fanatical about detail. Leaves nothing up in the air or uncertain. Accounts for every possibility (of what may go wrong). |
| DELIVER and COMPLETE: Served by subject-matter experts, project and account managers | Lives in a task-driven world. Loves lists. Can push back quite hard if the customer asks for flexibility. Gets the job done, no matter what. |
| EVALUATE and INVENT: Served by executives/strategists/visionaries and also by quality control, finance people | Interested in the big picture, the broad sweep of things, but can also lock onto detail. Inspires the customer, but sometimes thinks things can be done more easily or quickly than they can. Looks for new possibilities and aims to find what's positive. Loves to create new business ideas. By contrast, the quality/finance folks are judgmental and number-oriented, and are looking for problems and what not to do next time and why the CEO's next idea won't work! |

By the way, your customer has a personality too. Check out Chapter 14 for how to sell to different job roles and personalities.

# Considering the Pre-Sales Stage

From first contact to contract signing, you're in the phase of the customer lifecycle and relationship referred to as *pre-sales*. Pre-sales is a period of getting to know: dating, courting and making the offer. You want to look your best, say the right things at the right time and not mess up.

## Selling without looking like you're selling

Here's a loaded question: when are you selling and when are you not? Clearly you can only close a deal when the customer's need exists, the time is now and the prospect is ready to buy, but the prospect being ready to buy doesn't mean you have to get all 'salesy'. You may take the viewpoint that you should never be selling or the viewpoint that you're selling all around the lifecycle, or something in between. Take whichever viewpoint you want – what's important is that you're responsible for the customer relationship with your company throughout the whole lifecycle and for how that 'feels' for the customer at each stage.

In the end, every relationship is emotional. Customers have sensations around their business pains – if these sensations don't get solved, they're a threat to a person's view of himself, his career advancement and whether he keeps his job. In Chapter 5, you get to turn those threats into value statements for your solution.

Imagine that you're about to buy something. You know that you need it and you're considering what the next steps are. Someone who tries to 'sell' aggressively is going to fail, because some of the key questions you have (such as 'Do I like the person?') really matter in services sales. Pushy people aren't likeable. The question that trumps all the others is 'Do I trust the person?'. If the answer is yes, it's because you've proved yourself trustworthy throughout.

## Dating the customer: EDUCATE stage

During the EDUCATE stage (see Figure 3-1), obviously the earlier you can get in on the conversation, the more influence you have over early judgments and decisions that the prospect is making. This stage is the domain of marketing – to ensure that you're well represented in the marketplace to your target customers and to bring some influence into their early decisions.

You can get this influence in two ways:

✔ **Analyze where the customer has been looking and see how you can insert yourself.** The advantage of this method is that the customer is already in the lifecycle – just at an early stage. You need to create the connection points between your business (and business-development activities) and the customer's lifecycle. This approach takes effort and is better suited to companies with some marketing and sales resources.

✔ **Create an offer where the value is immediately evident to anyone you talk to.** The advantage is that the prospect doesn't have to be in the customer journey or even a target customer at all, but if its reaction is 'Really? You do that?', you're in a strong position to determine early on whether you can create a need or not. If not, the customer may be intrigued enough to refer you to other business contacts, or consider you later on. I work on this aspect in Chapter 5.

Take a look at Table 4-4 for where you can have some early influence, for where you may already be engaged and for a few additional things to try.

| Table 4-4 | Exerting Early Influence | |
|---|---|---|
| *What Can You Use?* | *When to Use it* | *When Not to Use it* |
| Cold calling | Your offer is distinctive and offers particularly high value at a senior level in your customer base.<br><br>A good-sized segment of the market needs what you offer.<br><br>Your target customers need your services on a cyclical or ongoing basis (that is, they buy with frequency, for example if you're a product marketing company and your target releases a distinctive product on a reasonably regular basis). | Your target contacts are bombarded by cold calls from companies just like yours.<br><br>You're operating in a local market (such as a town or small city).<br><br>The market only uses your services in specific and/or rare circumstances. |

*(continued)*

**Table 4-4 *(continued)***

| What Can You Use? | When to Use it | When Not to Use it |
|---|---|---|
| Offline event participation, networking, speaker engagements | You can identify events where your customers may hang out.<br><br>You're willing to consider sponsoring or exhibiting at such an event, which gives you the right to say hello to everyone there.<br><br>You have someone who's really good at working a room (relating well to people quickly, forming a connection that can be followed up on).<br><br>You're a great presenter and people come up to you afterwards wanting more. | The time provided for networking is limited.<br><br>The events are attended more by vendors than customers.<br><br>The cost of getting more deeply involved is prohibitive.<br><br>You hate talking to strangers, you don't care why they're there and you don't really want to be there either.<br><br>You dislike doing presentations to more than five people. |
| Online events | When you can sponsor or have some say in the content and audience.<br><br>When you get an opportunity to present, however briefly, your value proposition. Even better if you can present some content of value to the audience (see next item). | You're participating, but without a specific role (such as a presentation opportunity) or any influence on the topics and audiences. |
| Authoritative content | The heart of early engagement, great content, means that you have something to say that people want to read or listen to (or share with others or blog about).<br><br>You can provide simple tools that help customers who are confused during the customer journey.<br><br>You can demonstrate exceptional results from your work with your customers (preferably quantitative, but qualitative is good too).<br><br>You, or someone in your organization, is great at writing content for a specific audience.<br><br>See also social media below. | Your offer is pretty general (for example, you're an accounting firm, but you don't have any specialized services).<br><br>Your customer journey is simple (as in something's broken and the customer has to fix it right now). |

| What Can You Use? | When to Use it | When Not to Use it |
|---|---|---|
| Social media | Your customers can be found online, on Twitter, in LinkedIn Groups, even on Facebook, or on specialized social networks.<br><br>They follow specific leaders in your area of work or customers who'd buy your services.<br><br>They follow/read bloggers who are expert in your area of work and provide objective content to the marketplace. | Your customers aren't found on social networks such as LinkedIn (especially the specific people you want to connect with).<br><br>The cost of buying into their network (e.g., becoming a Vistage member or joining a virtual executive roundtable group) is prohibitive. |
| Social events/ non-profits/ community efforts | Unless the gig is incredibly noisy, social and community events are a great place to practice your pitch and get others interested in what you do. Most people work for one company or another – you never know. | The people around you aren't in the right networks to provide the referrals you need. Keeping the conversation social is fine – just keep looking for a suitable opportunity. Some organizations also prohibit promoting your business, in which case, respect that. |
| Email marketing | You have compelling content that the prospect can sign up to receive, or good content for a regular informational newsletter. | Blasting out to large numbers of people who haven't asked for your communication (which is illegal). |

Don't waste time seeking out quick fixes to broaden your customer base (believe me, none exist!). Chapters 10 and 11 in Part III provide thoughts on developing and executing on your marketing tactics – to ensure that you're picking the right things to do that are appropriate to your stage of development as a company and to what's going to attract the prospects.

## Courting and proposing: PRESENT and PROPOSE stages

You're in the PRESENT and PROPOSE stages of Figure 3-1 here. Deep into the sales process, you're building the customer relationship – extending it from the person you initially spoke with towards other important players on the customer team and your own. Mostly, customers want to know that you're not the only person in the company who knows what he's doing, unless you're a one-person shop (in which case, tag, you're it).

Customers want to be able to trust everyone and to use you as an escalation point. You don't want to show up as a bottleneck. You also want to know the players on their side – who's going to make the decision, how will others influence that decision, who will you be working with day-to-day if you move ahead with this deal and who needs to be in a relationship with whom?

At a minimum, you want three roles in your company represented, even if these roles are combined into one or two people. Here's who to bring to the party from your side:

- ✔ The lead for the sale (sales person/account manager)
- ✔ The lead for the work (project manager or other senior expert)
- ✔ The lead for the customer relationship (account manager/account manager)

If you're the business owner, don't dominate the conversations. Allow your team members to show their strengths and speak for themselves. Prepare for customer meetings in advance, especially if your team hasn't worked in this way before. Start to plan out who's going to take care of what. Teamwork at this stage helps the transition to the actual work go smoothly, something customers like.

Maintain control of the sales process using the same approach I discuss earlier in the 'Being in Control' section (see Chapter 14 for the deep dive).

Your aim as you work on the relationship during the sales process is to give the customer *peace of mind* and to instill *trust*. Even if you never do business with this particular prospect, your reputation in the marketplace is built piece-by-piece from every encounter you ever have with people outside your company (and inside it, come to that). My favorite comment from a prospect is, 'I hope one day I'll be big enough to afford you.' Don't you just love it when they say things like that?

## Confronting reality: CONTRACT stage

You've got to the CONTRACT stage of Figure 3-1, the halfway point. Well done!

The first half of the customer lifecycle goes from 'everything is possible' to 'this is what we're actually going to do' – a move from the subjective, happy-clappy, aren't we such good friends, to a serious, contractual business relationship. Rather like negotiating a pre-nuptial agreement, moving from proposal to starting work is a tough transition. I tell customers that this stage is the low point in the relationship, but that it gets better when we start to work together. Just know that you have to deal with it – you can't shy away or compromise to your own disadvantage. I provide more tips on this stage in Chapter 14.

Contracts are an important part of the customer's experience of you. Don't do business without one. At the very least, you need something in writing and signed by the customer that captures what you're going to do, what they're going to do, what they get and what you're going to be paid and when. This contract is one of your most important control mechanisms. If you start work without that agreement, you lose your leverage and regaining it is difficult.

# Handling the After-the-Sale Process

You're in, you're trusted. Just as in the pre-sales phase in the preceding section, you want to set the tone for the relationship and continue to manage the customer relationship with care and attention.

I don't mean diving in and doing all the work for the customer (unless you're a one-person business). I mean that someone needs to be responsible for the relationship and for taking the temperature of the customer from time to time – call them the account manager (which could, of course, be you). If possible, this person should be separate from the person managing the work – the project manager. The attention of the account manager is different from a project manager. Salespeople often take on the account manager role, but review Chapter 13 while considering whether that's a good idea.

Ongoing customer relationship management has all kinds of benefits and I cover how to garner those in Part V.

## Moving from 'Yes' to 'Done': DELIVER stage

You're at the DELIVER stage. Only you know the detail of what happens when your business is delivering its services, but customers often get a feeling of abandonment by the people they've met from your company (and have come to trust), into the hands of a stranger (no doubt competent, but not yet trusted). Transitioning from the first part of the customer experience to the second part is a delicate maneuver. Someone needs to be responsible for that transition, and time spent on finessing this move saves you oodles of grief later on.

Here are some general guidelines that are the responsibility of the account manager in the second half of the customer lifecycle:

- ✔ **Understand the scope of the work/do a handover.** Make sure that your team has a firm grip on the contract, its terms, the scope of the work, what the customer is supposed to be providing, contributing or doing, what the deliverables are, what the process is for engaging with the customer and who's going to be involved on the customer side. Prepare for a kick-off meeting with the customer.

- ✔ **Lead or attend the kick-off meeting.** The purpose is to go through, with the customer, what you just went through in the handover meeting. Getting the scope clear, how the work will proceed, what the timeframe is, who does what and when. In simple projects, this doesn't take long, but it helps get everyone aligned. On longer projects you encounter clear phases to the work, points of sign-off by the customer that it's satisfied. Involve the account manager at these points, and make sure that the sign-off is obtained and that the kick-off for the next phase is just as effective as the initial one. Above all, check in with the customer on how things are going.

- ✔ **Make the project manager your friend.** Project managers are incredibly focused – they're totally committed to getting the job done on time and within budget. Good for them – where would you be without them? At times, the project manager is going to have problems. Make yourself his trusted advisor. If issues exist, you want to know about them so that you can support the project manager and/or take corrective action with the customer or your own management. Set up a regular meeting with the project manager, or attend internal project management meetings.

- ✔ **Continue the courtship throughout.** Send customers useful information from time to time, make an occasional call to see how things are proceeding and take them to lunch. Express interest in their perceptions of how things are going on the project. Do they want to say anything? Give them the space to do so.

Customer management is the most underused method for expanding your business. That's why I dedicate the whole of Part V to the topic.

## *Wrapping up delivery: COMPLETE and EVALUATE stages*

You've arrived at COMPLETE. You need to tie up all loose ends – and get the customer to sign off that you're done and to pay you that final invoice.

Here's where companies leave gold on the table: they don't follow through to get customer feedback. Eager though you may be to get to the next job, spend time with the customer in a structured interview process. Make this review meeting separate from the final meeting with the delivery team.

You're bound to uncover opportunities for new business with this customer: get permission to use it as a reference or to build a case study, testimonial or press release; get introduced to another part of the organization or to contacts it has and can refer you to. You also get feedback on the project and how it went – what the customer liked about working with you, what it didn't like or would've appreciated more of, how to improve your relationship with it – and with other customers. See Chapter 17 for details on maximizing your customer's feedback and value to you.

If you're wondering what happened to INVENT, I cover that in Chapter 5.

# Part II
# Planning for Business Development

| A | B | | E | F | G | H | I | J | K | L | M | N | O | P | Q |
|---|---|---|---|---|---|---|---|---|---|---|---|---|---|---|---|
| **1** | **TOTALS** | | White cells are booked/firm. Gray cells are projections | | | | | | | | | | | | |
| **2** | | | | | | | | | | | | | | | |
| **3** | **Current month : APRIL** | | GOAL FOR THE YEAR IS $950k | | | | | | | | | | | | |
| **4** | | | Month 1 | Month 2 | Month 3 | Month 4 | Month 5 | Month 6 | Month 7 | Month 8 | Month 9 | Month 10 | Month 11 | Month 12 | TOTAL |
| **5** | **2014 Goal and Milestones** | | $32,500 | $32,500 | $47,500 | $47,500 | $47,500 | $50,000 | $75,000 | $110,000 | $120,000 | $120,000 | $120,000 | $120,000 | **$922,500** |

Visit www.dummies.com/extras/businessdevelopment for a free bonus article on keeping your business in touch with the market via feedback loops.

## In this part . . .

- ✔ Craft a perfect business offer for what you provide.
- ✔ Align your offer with what the market is looking for.
- ✔ Build a business-development plan that's right for your firm.
- ✔ Put your plan into action and ensure that everyone's behind it.

# Chapter 5

# Getting Ready for Business Development

- - - - - - - - - - - - - - - - - - - - - - - - - - - - - - - - - - - - - - - - - - -

## In This Chapter

▶ Building an offer that succeeds

▶ Preparing your offer properly before the sale

▶ Moving confidently beyond the sale

- - - - - - - - - - - - - - - - - - - - - - - - - - - - - - - - - - - - - - - - - - -

*I*'d like you to take a moment to picture business-development heaven (clouds and harps optional). Imagine that every one of your customers is as good as your best customer – that your work delights them. It also inspires you and your team to leap out of bed every day, impatient to get on with the work. Wouldn't that be gre at? Does it have to remain a dream?

Not at all! The key to living this sort of life is ensuring that you align your offer with what the market wants. Don't worry about customers who want something that your company doesn't provide. That's not your problem.

To run a successful and profitable business, all you need are enough customers who want what you do and are willing to pay a fair price for it.

The process I describe in this chapter helps you to create your market offer and to design how to take it to the market and deliver it. I offer valuable insights into the high-level dos and don'ts. Please make the effort to answer all the questions in this chapter and perhaps consider doing some role-playing or working with a trusted advisor. Believe me, the efforts you put in here pay off when you're planning in Chapter 6 and actioning in Chapter 7.

## Developing an Offer that Sells

The business development lifecycle gives you a tool for managing the growth of your business, making you think clearly about what your customers want and how to give it to them. As a result you can fend off the challenges of the marketplace, which are sure to assail you whether you like it or not.

You can only grow your business if you wrap your services into an engine that can deliver new customers and new projects. In this section I ask you to look deeply at, focus on and effectively convey your offer. I also discuss making your chosen specialty really special, to trump the competition.

You're in the INVENT (or, if you prefer, 'reinvent') stage of the business development lifecycle (Figure 3-1). How do you invent an offer? In this section, I cover a few important considerations and give you tools for inventing your offer.

I want to start with a quick exercise that takes you back to the early days of your company.

Why did you start your business or become involved in it?

Do you have:

- ✔ Specialized skills that you wanted to bring to the marketplace (you're a subject matter expert)?
- ✔ Business skills that can support the growth and development of a business (you have business development skills)?
- ✔ Entrepreneurial skills (you know how to build a business)?

Any one of these skills can be the genesis of a fine business leader. All skills are valuable, but the most valuable to the market, and hence to your prospects and customers, is the application of deep domain knowledge (what you know that the customer doesn't) to the solution of business problems (the needs of the customers).

Everything else your business needs to do is centered on your offer and how you:

- ✔ Make the market aware of the needs you fulfill
- ✔ Conduct powerful interactions with prospects to have them buy from you, instead of from the other guy
- ✔ Do the work
- ✔ Leverage your happy customers, that is, use successful projects as the basis for business expansion

If you're a business owner, you have a different perspective from a leader of business development. That's okay. Sharing what you're uncovering from those different perspectives doesn't hurt at all.

## *Ensuring that you're giving the market what it needs*

If your offer doesn't take care of a customer need, it's not going to sell. People buy because they need or want something.

### *Specializing*

Imagine this scenario: It's morning, I need a coffee. Coffee has low value – technically, you can make it yourself. You can also visit an abundance of places to get coffee. The market's hugely competitive and has heavy price pressure. But people are willing to pay a ridiculous amount for an individually crafted coffee. I can buy a cup for coffee in the garage for $1 (63p), but I wait in line at Starbucks for 20 minutes to pay $3 ($1.89). Tuck that thought in your back pocket.

I'm not suggesting that you open a coffee shop, but rather that you need to uncover what's high value to the market so that you can charge more. Coffee isn't always coffee – sometimes it's an experience.

Here's another example. Say that I just invented a device that can help people keep their cholesterol low. I'm going to be rich! I need a patent lawyer, because I know 'I can't do this, I don't know anything about patenting.' Plus, lots of patent lawyers are around, patent law is complex and so are the products that get patented. The lawyers don't just know how to create and file a patent with the patents and trademarks office. They also have to understand their clients' area of business – they specialize. They may represent healthcare inventions, or software, or manufacturing equipment or any other area of business you can name. The deeper their specialization, the more value they are to me, their customer.

Specialization is valuable, so you need to consider it carefully for your business. Four results arise from firms' increased specialization:

- ✔ Their knowledge becomes deeper.
- ✔ They're more valuable to their customers.
- ✔ They're scarcer (less competition and limited availability).
- ✔ They can charge more.

Although the market you have if you're highly specialized is smaller than if you offer something more general (more widely applicable), a more focused offer is easier to position and harder for the customer to resist. Why would a customer go to a lawyer who knows nothing about their space and risk something going wrong? Specialists can point to those risks, have probably seen them happen and can justify why the customer should work with them and pay more.

### Breakdowns

Time to take a deeper dive into what starts the buying process for customers – breakdowns. My thanks go to Influence Ecology, an education company, for teaching me everything I know about breakdowns. Its definition of *breakdowns* is as follows:

> A breakdown is the collapse of function and/or continuance in taking care of an immediate or future concern. A breakdown means that life, as we know it, is or is about to be out of balance.

Simply put, a breakdown is something not working. It causes a need that creates an opportunity for a solution, aka your offer.

You can sell an offer to a customer in two situations:

- ✔ The customer has a *current* breakdown in its business and knows that the breakdown exists and that it has to act. In you go.

- ✔ You can also point to a *potential* breakdown that the customer (a) doesn't even know it has today (it's hidden), or (b) one that's coming tomorrow (the customer doesn't see it coming). With the right offer, you can create a need in the customer's mind.

Luckily(!), the world contains plenty of breakdowns, though not all are opportunities for profitable businesses. I have at least five business plans that solve real and common breakdowns but clearly wouldn't work for any one of a number of reasons (for example, the offer isn't specialized enough, the market isn't big enough, the market price is too low or needs too much capital to start).

For all kinds of reasons, many people are picky about what they eat. The breakdown is that, wherever you are, you're presented with things you shouldn't eat. I had an idea some years ago for a restaurant where you profile your needs and dietary restrictions and the menu is customized for you with only the things you can eat. Great idea, but I have no specialized knowledge in running restaurants.

Based on the True Story, think about your own company and note down what your customer's breakdown is, how you'd describe your customer's need and what offer you can make to solve that breakdown/fulfill that need. Don't over-think this situation right now. Write no more than three short sentences.

Now, if you're the customer with that need, do you buy your company? Are you, the customer, convinced that your firm's offer solves the need? Do you feel the urgency to act right away, or are you willing to 'think about it', 'talk to my business partner about it', 'look around' – in other words procrastinate like Hamlet on an indecisive day. How confident are you that, faced with a customer that has the right breakdown and need, she would buy your services, and quickly. If your prospects don't seem that bothered, you want to examine why.

One of the things services firms complain about is that customers are slow to act. Here are a few reasons for their reluctance:

- ✔ The need is one of many problems they have to solve (and the problem you solve isn't top of the stack today).
- ✔ They worry about different things today than they did yesterday, and so even if they start a promising conversation with you, their priorities are constantly shifting.
- ✔ They're totally overwhelmed (short on staff, trying to do everything at once).
- ✔ They know that they're going to have to put effort into the project and they're worried that they may not have the time – engaging with you actually produces more work for them for a while. Doing nothing and living with the problem can look like a viable option.
- ✔ Your offer just isn't compelling (imperative) enough for the prospect to take action, right now (that's the donkey kick).

Yuck, I know, but look anyway. Some suggestions for how to deal with this list are below. If you're having problems closing new customers, you need to reconsider your offer, or at least how you position it and to whom.

As you write down your customers' needs, look for the imperative. If you can't feel it, or it's a bit wishy-washy, spice it up (see the next section). The market hungers for solutions that solve imperative needs: keeping up with the latest fashion trend, getting your water tank fixed or looking for consulting advice on fending off new, aggressive competitors.

---

# Is it a bird? Is it a plane? No, it's an imperative!

If the water tank in your attic starts leaking a ton of water into the bedroom ceiling, which is bulging and threatening to collapse, you don't procrastinate. The need is imperative and propels you into immediate action (faster than Superman can find a phone box). You *can* hang about (checking that your superhero underpants are neatly on outside your fetching tights) and wait until the ceiling collapses, but common sense tells you that this problem is just going to get worse if you wait. That's what an imperative looks like.

To sell quickly and successfully, customers have to understand the consequences of inaction and experience how serious that would be. When they get the full impact, they're primed to buy.

## *Making your specialty really valuable*

You know that old expression, 'It's not what you do, it's the way that you do it'? My version is, 'It's not what you do, it's how you position it.' But don't worry. I'm not about to go all fluffy marketing speak on you. Quite the opposite.

Services firms struggle to articulate their unique value. Maybe you're thinking, 'My offer isn't unique', and you're right, it probably isn't. But when you can draw out the value to the customer and express it in the most compelling way, your offer can look unique, even if it isn't.

If you create your offer to look unique, you start to deliver it as if it is.

Don't fall into the trap that some firms make, when they say that they do something 'miraculous' but in the hurly burly of doing the work forget to check that they've fulfilled on 'miraculous'. A common example is when firms talk about developing 'strategy' and continuing to keep an eye out for the customer but quickly devolve into delivering on tactics and so lose their strategic hold on the customer. The result is disappointed customers, because they're not getting what they expected. They say things like 'you do really great work, but . . .'.

You need to create a *value proposition,* expressed as an *inspiring positioning* (a description of your services that declares the extra-special value). Two things can happen when you do that (one great, one bad): your organization is right behind the positioning and lives out that promise every day – or you do something like the example above (strategy declining into tactics) and the promise isn't fulfilled in practice.

If you're going to get big with your promises, you better align the rest of your organization to follow through. Your task is to take a need, known or *hidden* (one the prospect doesn't know it has), make it an *imperative need* (often called a 'pain' or 'business pain') and state the value of the solution as a business concept that you can present to a prospect, in other words, as an offer.

When buying solutions, much of the purchase is emotional, driven by survival. This exercise digs into that emotion. Follow these steps and answer these questions about your customer's needs and your value:

1. **Write down your offer (as you expressed it earlier in the Try This exercise in the earlier 'Breakdowns' section).**

2. **Ask yourself: which individual do you sell to in the customer organization?** Whose pain is the greatest? What's this person's role? Who really needs what you've got?

If you have more than one answer (for example, head of HR may say one thing, chief operations officer another, general counsel something else), pick the role of your most common customer contact, the one who most often consumes your services and keep just that person in mind as you answer the rest of the questions.

3. **How would that person describe her pain/need?** Start your answer with 'I can't . . .', 'I don't trust . . .', 'I'm afraid that . . .', 'I panic when . . .' and the like.

4. **What's the consequence of the answer in Step 3 for the customer's business?** For example, 'We might not . . .', 'It could result in . . .', 'We won't be able to . . .', 'We might lose . . .'.

5. **What are the emotions associated with the things you write down in Step 3?** Is it fear, panic, feeling incompetent, helpless? The customer would say, 'I feel . . .'.

6. **What are the opposite emotions?** What would the person be feeling if the problem was solved: for example, fear becomes confidence. The customer would say 'Now I feel . . .'.

7. **How does your service address the pain and the emotion?** 'We do . . .', 'The results are . . .', 'You'll feel . . .'.

8. **What's the benefit of your solution to the business of the customer and to this individual's emotional state?** 'You'll be able to . . .', 'You'll stop . . .'.

9. **What would your contact say about her situation if she had the solution already in place.** 'I'm really . . .'.

10. **Restate your offer.**

Big task, right? What shifted for you in your view of your offer? Are your people capable of delivering on that restated offer?

Jack had a thriving product design company. Firms came to him to work their ideas up into market-ready offerings. The problem was that over time, he did less work on envisioning the products and more on designing the marketing of the products. When he rethought his offer, he was able to craft a new positioning for his value – to help people practically with ideas to create a better product, not just a better-positioned one.

Can you see your own value more clearly, more strongly, after answering the questions? If you can, great, keep refining it. Do the same exercise on a different role in the customer organization. Each time you repeat the process, you may find new value you didn't know you had. These aspects are key things to know when you're selling.

If you find this exercise hard, try doing it with someone else – a trusted business friend or a key person in your organization. Think about the hidden needs of the customer representative – the things that are going on in her head but she doesn't articulate. Dig deep into what the customer is thinking and experiencing.

## Assessing your competition

If you don't know who you're competing with, you better find out pretty darned quick (I touch on competition in Chapter 4).

Try to uncover what competing firms think their value is, but you won't find doing so easy. Most companies articulate their positioning (the needs they fulfill on, the offer they have) badly, with even their websites often giving little clue as to what they actually do! Seeing just how badly some companies present to the marketplace is a salutary lesson. Don't make the same mistake.

The good news is that you can do it better; the bad news is that you don't really know what competitors are saying to prospects, what they're promising and what they're saying about you or companies like you, unless your prospects tell you.

At a minimum, profile your competition and start a dossier on each one you've recently lost business to. If the timing is good, ask some recent losses what caused them to choose another firm. Tell them that you're reworking your positioning and that their input can really help. They'll take the call. People love to be helpful, especially when they can tell you what's wrong with you!

If the loss was just that the other firm did something better than you in the sales process, take note and use that in planning your sales process in Chapter 13. However, if the loss was *price, better fit* or (heaven be praised) *higher value,* great, you're onto something.

You shouldn't be losing on price. If you do, you probably didn't do one of two things:

- ✔ **Walk away early enough:** In other words, the customer wanted cheapest, not best. If your positioning is 'we're the cheapest', that's fine, but then you wouldn't have lost on price.

- ✔ **Get your unique value across:** Doesn't necessarily mean the value doesn't exist, just that the competitor did a better job of creating a value proposition ('if you hire us, you get this specific value').

Consider carefully how to beat the competition. You need a value proposition that steps to the outer edges where competitors can't go and to position a compelling value story that speaks to the customer's emotional needs.

In the earlier section 'Ensuring that you're giving the market what it needs', I say that customers are sometimes slow to act, even with a high imperative, because they can't see how they'd dedicate the time or resources to work with you. If you, hypothetically, can take a lot of that burden off their shoulders and minimize the commitment they have to make, that can have value for them – as long as they are involved in key information transfer and key decisions along the way. If you're talking to the right prospects, they quite possibly would pay for it.

How much would you pay for a new website: $5,000 (£3,150), $50,000 (£31,500), $500,000 (£315,000) or even more? These prices represent different value propositions, in terms of what gets delivered and whether it's effective *and* in how the work gets done. The value has to match the price unless you're in the enviable position of being able to charge whatever you want.

## *Accepting that the grass isn't always greener*

When business is great, when lots of prospects are a good fit for your offer and when you're running at 100 miles an hour to keep up with the growth, you probably don't spend much time gazing over the fence at the next field.

If business is tight, if you're losing a lot and if you're beginning to doubt whether you have the right offer, even an innocent question from a customer or prospect along the lines of 'Do you do so-and-so?' can make you wonder whether, even though you don't do so-and-so, easy money is out there.

The correct answer is, 'No, we don't do that.' Better still, '. . . but we can refer you to someone we trust completely'. If you're tempted to say 'yes', thinking that you must get money in the door somehow, *stop,* at least long enough to read this section.

Considering adding services to your offer can be tempting. From your position, that company in the next field seems to have lots of business in that so-and-so service area. Apparently, a lot of demand exists for that service out in the marketplace.

When you eye a new service offer to consider whether you should be doing that too, doing so is called *diversification,* namely offering something different than you do today. The thinking is that offering different types of services is a hedge against one area not doing so well.

If you're General Electric, with billions in the bank (I'm just guessing here, I know nothing), you can afford to diversify. If you make a bad move, you can just back off while the rest of your empire is humming along. But you're probably not GE, and so behaving like you are is a bad idea.

If you're tempted to grow by expanding your services, the following is a list of reasons why that may not be a good idea. If expanding still looks like a good idea after considering these items, by all means go for it. Just don't jump in naively thinking you're going to find any kind of quick fix:

- **You're in a panic.** One or two customers asked you for 'so-and-so' and you start to wonder whether offering that would maybe be a fix to your near-term revenue problem, maybe even bring you lots of new business.

- **You think that more business is 'over there'.** That other field may look greener, but it's not. Walk over and see. The field is full of mud and stones – more brown than green! Talk to someone in that business who offers those services and ask whether it's really so easy. If the area is highly lucrative, you can bet on a lot of competition – you're the newbie and you're likely to lose a lot before you win, maybe even your shirt (and it's chilly out there!).

- **You think you can do that service.** You probably know something about what it would take to become a so-and-so company. The problem is that what you don't know probably outweighs what you do.

- **You think you can slide into it quite easily.** Likely not. You have to retool a lot of stuff: train or hire staff, create a new methodology, invest in new tools, create a whole new offer (market positioning, presentations, proposals, contract formats, and on and on). Starting a new service area can be a major distraction, a real money sink, and can even take your business down.

- **You think you can create a product.** This one's a real gem for services firms. If your service (or a part of it) lends itself to *productization* (such as a book, a training course, a do-it-yourself process, a software solution), unless you've done productization before, take it from me, you know next to nothing about what it takes. Services business is extremely flexible, you can shift and change it, compensate for any shortcoming or minor customer dissatisfaction. Products are nothing like that – they stand or fall on providing enough value 'out of the box' to compensate for any deficiency in the product. Before you consider it, talk to people in services who've tried to productize an aspect of their businesses. Ask them how it went.

The bottom line is that fixing what you have is the fastest route to growth. When your business is performing and you have capital to invest in a new offer and time to dedicate to shepherding it through, go for it. Don't try it when your business is struggling, cash flow is tight and you're already working 12-hour days. Tread warily.

# Developing focus – or it's all over

Al Ries has written a great book called *Focus* (Harper Business): when you've read this book, read that one. It's excellent. You'll discover that customers really appreciate narrow and deep expertise. In fact, over time, even your deep domain knowledge becomes more like general knowledge and you have to adapt.

Take the example of www.legalzoom.com. Once upon a time people had to go to lawyers for contract documents, now they can just use the Internet. But that presents a problem for lawyers: what do they do to survive? They have to go deeper into areas of legal complexity that the general public have no chance of understanding from a casual review of an article on www.about.com.

When you can say, 'We do this and nothing else, but we're the best' (and I mean the absolute best), you're in a powerful position. Single-minded focus is the key to small-business success (check out the sidebar 'Just call me Adair, Red Adair').

# 'Really? You do that?' Articulating your offer

Imagine meeting famous fire-fighter Red Adair at a cocktail party (now that dates me!) – read the sidebar 'Just call me Adair, Red Adair'. What would his offer have been like? Perhaps it was, 'I put out oil well fires, guaranteed.' Your reaction may be, 'Really? You do *that*? Tell me more.'

That phrase comes from my friend, Kirkland Tibbels, President of Influence Ecology, and it's a great test for your positioning statement. When you tell people what you do, you're after that 'tell me more' reaction.

So if I say to you 'I'm the CEO of HRFixIt and we're an HR consulting company', you can be forgiven for changing the subject or going to talk to someone more interesting. But if I say 'I'm the CEO of HRFixIt. We help you *not* get sued when you terminate staff', you may say, especially if you have employees, 'Really? How? Tell me more.'

Kirkland calls it *agitation*. People don't act unless you agitate them with an impending threat – in the case of the HR company, 'Yes, you could get sued. Want to insure against that?'

Take a look at your offer and value proposition and see whether you can rewrite it to get the response, 'Really? You do that? Tell me more.'

## Just call me Adair, Red Adair

Oil well fires are the devil's own job to put out. It can take weeks or months and is dangerous – plus the fire is polluting and millions of dollars are lost. Red Adair was the Ninja Master of oil well fires. In fact his name became synonymous with the task of putting oil well fires out.

Naturally, Red was able to charge huge bucks, because his fee was relatively trivial compared with the impact of the fire continuing. If companies decided not to hire him (because someone else was cheaper), they sometimes regretted it later. They had to come back, tail between their legs, and ask him to help them. He got out in the field (himself) and nailed that sucker. It was awesome to behold. He worked well into old age. Check out the website (just search for 'Red Adair') or documentary programs about him.

Of course, having something pithy to say at a cocktail party is one thing, but taking that principle and driving a sale with it is quite another. Read the next section to discover how.

# Presenting Your Offer

After your firm has built a great offer statement (see the earlier section 'Developing an Offer that Sells'), you need to know who to take it to. In this section, I discuss finding out who and where your customers are, as well as engaging successfully with them as you approach a sale.

Defining your *target market* (types, sizes, location and profile of customers) saves you masses of time. It allows you to disengage quickly when the prospect doesn't fit the profile. As the saying goes, 'just say no'. Doing so may be really hard, especially when you're short of business, but is key to building the business you want. Don't work with customers your offer isn't built for.

Working with the right customers – those that your offer is specifically designed for – is the pathway to growth and success.

## Finding your customer

To discover whether you have a definition of your target customers, answer any of the following questions that are relevant to your business:

✔ Are they local, regional, national or international?

✔ What size are they in revenue and number of employees?

✔ What types of companies are they (for profit, non-profit, public sector)?

✔ What industries are they in?

✔ What roles do you work with in these target companies?

✔ What specific need do they have?

✔ What budget do they have?

✔ What would have them need you now where they haven't up to this point?

At this point, you should be able to fill in the sentence 'We work with . . .'. You can append this sentence to your offer statement – the one that starts 'We do . . .' or 'We help companies . . .'. For example, 'I'm the CEO of HRFixIt. We help you not get sued when you terminate staff. We work with companies smaller than 100 employees where legal action could ruin their business.' Da, da!

With data about companies that fit your profile to hand, you can find out a lot more about these organizations and their business people.

Pick 100 companies that you want to do business with and create a company initiative to do the research. Using data sources such as Bloomberg, Inside View, Data.com, LinkedIn and a myriad of others, you can find out what's important to them right now, who just joined the company, who's left and how you may be able to network to get to the right contact.

Undertaking this kind of project moves you from reactive to proactive business development. Proactivity is a source for getting the business you want. Check out Chapter 2 for why proactivity is so important.

Although you can buy lists of companies of the right profile and contacts with the right roles for relatively little money, please don't do that and then start blasting them with emails. Doing so is illegal. You need to become somewhat familiar with anti-spam legislation (check out Chapter 11).

## *'Tell me what you want, what you really, really want'*

As well as a clear statement of how your services help customers, be ready with a barrage of answers to questions from your prospects. As with exam preparation, study upfront to succeed on the day. No surprise that you're in the PRESENT stage of the lifecycle (see Figure 3-1).

Build your own story that stands out from your competition. Study your competitors, but don't mimic them. Prospects buy the solution that resonates best with them, whether that solution is articulated by a competitor, by you or by the customer's internal team (as in, 'We can do that ourselves'). Closely align your offer with the customer need and you win more often.

The prospect's head is full of questions such as the following:

- What's my need?
- Can it be solved and, if so, how?
- What are my options?
- How much can I expect to pay?
- Who can I talk to for good advice?
- Do they seem to understand my issue?
- Are they interested in me and what I want?
- Am I learning things I didn't know? Do I need to account for those?
- Do they seem to know what they're doing?
- Can they articulate the solution? Do I understand what they're saying to me?
- Do I have questions? Can they answer my questions to my satisfaction?
- Can the budget and timeframe work?
- What do their customers have to say about them?
- Do I want to work with them?
- Do I feel safe?
- Do I trust them?
- Are they my best, my safest, my right choice?

Think about each of these questions ready for when they come up in the buying cycle – they're not always overt. When they do arise, make sure that you have an answer.

Great salespeople are worth the big bucks because they have the antennae to pick up on customers' states of mind and provide the right information just when, or even better, just before prospects know they need it.

## *Who drives the customer?*
## *Engaging effectively*

In Chapter 4, I discuss control when you're setting the customer relationship tone for a first meeting. Take a look at Table 4-1 and think about what would create effective engagement in your own situation.

As you move from PRESENT to PROPOSE in Figure 3-1, consider this scenario: you've had a first conversation with a prospect that's in a fix, needs your services, has budget and is buying now. You did a great job of defining next actions and getting commitment from the prospect to co-operate in the process. The firm asks for a proposal. Yaay!

You have an appointment set for reviewing your proposal. Some new people from the prospect are going to be in the room/on the call/in the web meeting. Consider these questions:

- ✔ Who from your side is going to be in the meeting? What role do you want each to play?
- ✔ Are all players on your team in sync and do they fully understand the prospect's business problem, needs and proposed solution?
- ✔ Who are the prospect's people? What are their names and titles? Can you surmise their interest, their concerns, their questions, their objections?
- ✔ How are you going to introduce your company and what it does?
- ✔ How are you going to present your proposal?
- ✔ How are you going to field questions?
- ✔ How can you manage the time so that everything gets covered?
- ✔ How can you allow enough time for next actions and commitments to be confirmed?

The reality is that customer meetings can be rather different from your plan. I always prefer to do this second meeting to propose something in person, but only if I'm guaranteed that the decision-maker is going to attend. If not, I back out. That may seem a bit extreme to you, but it works – you really know whether the prospect's need is imperative and whether it's just fishing or is serious about talking to you. If it's serious, the prospect begs you to continue the discussion and bends over backwards to do what you ask.

You're in control. You don't have to play it the customer's way. You do yourself no harm by being firm, sticking to how you want the meeting to go. Customer engagement should be by design, not by accident. Make sure that the design is yours, not the customer's.

## Getting to the sale

Most people have been jilted: not a nice feeling. It leaves you angry, sad, diminished, even powerless. In selling, like in romance, it pays to jilt rather than be jilted. I don't mean that you leave your prospects feeling jilted. What I'm driving at is that you should be able to see it coming, often quite early on. If this marriage isn't likely to be a happy one, respectfully disengage, giving a genuine reason for doing so.

Assuming that all looks good, you've given the prospect a proposal and are waiting for a decision, do you just wait, hoping for the best? Maybe not.

Customers are flirtatious – they're dating others behind your back. To make that ultimate impression, you have to show some vulnerability so that they know you're the one.

When I review carefully how the last interaction with a prospect went, I always know that certain things were out of whack. It's a feeling that people want to sweep under the carpet with a 'nothing I can do about it now' resignation. Instead, try figuring out what didn't work and use it to your advantage:

- ✔ Did you feel that you 'lost' them at specific moments?
- ✔ Did they ask questions that you couldn't answer?
- ✔ Did they seem to want to tackle their need in a different way from your approach?
- ✔ Did they seem to like/trust you?

Take what didn't work and set up a call with the prospect. Let the person know that you have a few questions about whether you're a fit for the firm. Be direct in asking what the prospect is seeing – share what you identified that you think this individual may be unclear about.

This meeting may be your best opportunity to create alignment, value and trust, opening the way to serious consideration of your proposal.

It can also be a great opportunity to start seeding the customer's responsibilities – what the customer will be on the hook for during delivery. Carefully note and work these aspects into the contract. If you do lose, it won't be because you left some uncertainty at your last meeting – you gave it your best shot. If you win, it won't be in the face of niggling concerns. How good is that?

This meeting may also be where you discover an issue that's serious enough to derail your desire to work with this prospect. If so, sleep on it and then decide whether you want to withdraw your proposal. If you do, be courteous and appreciative of the customer's time and trouble. Make clear that you don't think you're the right fit, and why. Firms may accept your withdrawal (and if so you wouldn't have won anyway) or ask you to reconsider (in which case you're justified in talking to get any differences of opinion out of the way).

## Building your contract process

Firms sometimes approach contracting by throwing a document over the fence and waiting for it to come back, usually covered in red ink (customer changes to your contract). That approach gives up power to the customer. For powerful contracting, you need two things:

- ✔ **A great contract:** Don't short change yourself. The contract needs to represent what you're willing to enforce – what the customer must provide and in what timeframe, the consequences of non-compliance – as well as a clear statement of deliverables, milestones and payment schedule.

- ✔ **A process for presenting the contract:** Talk to the prospect, or craft a good email, and convey what's important to you. Offer to walk the person through the contract. Don't give way on your wants without getting something in return: for example, if you give up 15-day terms for payment, you can accept 30 days if the customer agrees to pay electronically. Give and take.

Read Chapter 14 for a deeper discussion on contracting and its importance as a pivotal moment in the process.

# Continuing Your Great Work beyond the Sale

After your contract is signed, you need to sustain the early trust and control that you've established. This section discusses how you interact with the customer as you transition into DELIVER. (Chapter 4 describes moving into the second part of the lifecycle.)

## Understanding the importance of relationships

In practice, a customer relationship is a number of connections between your company and the customer's company that exist for a specific purpose (mutual or unilateral). These connections and how they're used, create a customer relationship that works (or doesn't).

You need to do a bit of *account planning* (for your relationship with your customer and how you want to drive results over time) to identify the key relationships that you need and actively pursue getting them. Initially, these relationships are the ones you require to keep the work going forward, as shown in Table 5-1. Note that if the customer's business is much larger than yours and has an army of people, the roles in the left column may be all one person wearing lots of different hats!

| Table 5-1 | Relationships You Need | |
|---|---|---|
| *You* | *Your Customer* | *Why?* |
| CEO | CEO or other executive | Establishing a level of partnership over and above the specific work being done |
| Account manager | Project sponsor (most senior person responsible for the outcome of the project) | Strategic direction/advice/conversations |
| | | Escalation point if things aren't working as they should |
| | | Identifying new opportunities |
| Project manager | Project manager | Day-to-day management of the work, including timeline, quality of work, reviews, sign-offs and communications |
| Account manager | Procurement, legal | Keeping an eye on the contract |
| | | Processing change orders (amendments to the contracts) |
| | | Resolving disputes |
| Controller (or CFO, director of finance) | Accounting department | Managing the financial transaction written into the contract |
| Accounts receivable | Accounts payable | Managing invoicing and on-time payment |
| Delivery team | Stakeholder group (people with authority to provide direction or make decisions) | One-on-one relationships that grow the customer's respect and appreciation for the quality and value of the work |

Developing the key customer relationships shown in the table early on allows you to achieve the following goals:

- ✔ Start the work on a solid foundation of relationships
- ✔ Set expectations
- ✔ Establish responsibilities
- ✔ Define how to track the project and sign-off work
- ✔ Decide how invoicing is done, what level of detail is needed, who invoices go to and who to call when payments are late
- ✔ Get paid on time
- ✔ Have escalation points to people who get involved with a concern or dispute
- ✔ Earn the right to speak to senior people any time you have something useful to say

Ensure that part of your plan is to get these relationships started and actively managed throughout the lifecycle. Use them when you need them, but don't be neglectful. If a customer pays on time, call the person responsible and thank her. Take the project manager to lunch when a milestone is reached. Water these relationships or they die on the vine.

For now, you have enough relationships to keep the work moving forward as well as managing the inevitable upsets, miscommunications and issues: dealing powerfully with them is what matters.

In Part V, I go into customer management in a lot more detail and expand on this idea of the key relationships that go beyond the specific customer project you're working on right now.

## Completing the work

If you've established your key relationships and worked with your customer for a while, things can get very comfortable. However, you're about to transition to a new stage: COMPLETE (refer to Figure 3-1). As your work nears conclusion, be clear how you're going to get the customer to agree that you're 'done'. Getting this agreement can be a thorny issue in many services situations where the deliverable is vague around the edges.

Distinguishing between DELIVER from COMPLETE is important, because you need to be clear with the customer that you're 'done' (from your point of view) when you get to the end of the DELIVER stage. The COMPLETE stage allows you to get sign-off, not only on final deliverables, but also on the fact that the contracted work is completed and to secure final payment. You also may want to position any follow-up work or support contract.

Customers often try to get extra services for nothing in the final days of the work, sometimes earlier (I call this *scope creep*). This problem is difficult to resist if your contract isn't clear or your process for getting to 'done' is loose and ambiguous. You can work on these areas over time, incrementally tightening them up – because if not handled really well, they can eat into your profits big time.

Here are the things you need to do to prepare for 'done':

- ✔ **Get down on paper what 'done' means for this customer.** You typically have a list of final deliverables, when they're completed, what the customer needs to do and how sign-off happens. You can also add what comes next – final invoice and payment, feedback interview, potential transition to a new piece of work or ongoing services or support.

- ✔ **Share the sign-off conditions with the customer, along with the timeline and activities for the final stages (days or weeks) of the contract.** Do this well ahead of time so that the customer's prepared.

- ✔ **Prepare a sign-off document.** Show it to the customer before the signing.

- ✔ **Tackle any of the customer's 'we-need-you-to . . .' items (such as 'I thought we were getting this as well').** Look at your contract and decide whether you can push back or suggest a change order, or whether you just have to suck up and do the work because the customer has some justification for asking.

Get the account manager and project manager to do these steps together during DELIVER. Doing so helps the project manager to get the desired result, namely satisfactory closure on the project in the form of a sign-off by the customer, and the account manager can handle the transition to the EVALUATE stage (see the next section). The project manager is probably in regular contact with the customer and so often knows what opportunities may be available.

You can also use these steps on longer/larger projects at specific milestones, which trains the client on how you operate, so that when you get to the COMPLETE stage (see Figure 3-1), the progress goes smoothly.

Completion involves finishing the work, getting sign-off and getting paid. Make sure that you can check all those steps every time.

# *Learning from Your Customers*

The EVALUATE stage of the lifecycle (see Figure 3-1) is a formal opportunity to review how things went on a specific customer project and take a wider look at how well the business is performing. Tweaks to who you sell to, do work for and how you complete with customers benefit everyone. You can spot small gaps in how you're working and plug them.

Periodically, you spot signs of bigger breakdowns in your process – such as customers reporting that they weren't communicated with enough during the project, or you had regular issues getting paid, or the customer work is only breaking even or losing money. You can probably think of a dozen more breakdowns in your own business (I discuss breakdowns in the earlier section 'Ensuring that you're giving the market what it needs'). This is the time to gather your feedback more holistically and to reinvent what you're doing and how you're doing it. The specifics of what you need to reinvent depend on the issues you're seeing.

## Gathering intelligence: The importance of data

Before I get to reinvention, I want to discuss what data you need to be gathering and from where. You obtain data from three direct sources:

- ✔ **Your customers:** Use the customer feedback session, as well as any interaction during the lifecycle, to tell you something about how things are going. Include ratings (quantifiable measures) and anecdotes (qualitative feedback) in your feedback process. In simple terms, get a score and get specific examples. Use Chapter 16 to design your process for customer feedback.

- ✔ **Your team members:** Take a walk through the project with them in a review meeting and capture their feedback. This feedback includes the pre-contract team too – your marketing and sales functions.

- ✔ **Your business:** Gather information on how your projects are performing. Are they getting done on time, within the budget? Is your use of staff managed in a way that has projects be profitable? Are some projects more profitable than others?

You're the best person to choose how to measure the performance of your business, but if you want to grow, you need to be on a solid foundation. As you become skillful in designing good measures and then using them to check the health of your business, the picture of where the issues are starts to emerge. You're able to assess a project at the end using the quantitative measures you've designed. You only need to inspect more deeply if a problem exists with the numbers.

When you evaluate your work, you're closing the circle on the lifecycle. Starting this practice while you're still small pays huge dividends when you establish it as 'normal' and as you grow. Evaluation is the difference between managing order or chaos.

Beyond data from your lifecycle performance, you can also use other sources if you decide that you need to do some reinvention. See Table 3-3 for a few places you can go to get external data.

Where do you put all this intelligence coming in? I have three guidelines:

- ✔ Keep data simple.
- ✔ Keep data accessible – use an appropriate system to store customer data and market intelligence (advice on choosing the right tools is in Chapter 13).
- ✔ Make sure that your team contributes and uses the data.

Of course, some data has to be kept confidential. You may not want to share data about individual performances or salaries or even customer invoices. The more transparent you are about performance, the more willingly your team is to work to get to the right results, as shown by your key metrics. Where you start to suspect that an individual is underperforming, you're in difficult territory and so go to your HR support to handle it. This kind of situation is not for sharing.

## Evaluating your offer

When you combine market intelligence with feedback from your team and your customers, you have solid data for a regular evaluation of your offer. Here are the key questions to ask yourself:

- ✔ Is your offer still a fit for what customers need?
- ✔ Are you providing high levels of customer satisfaction?
- ✔ Are you incorporating best practices, including being up-to-date and using a solid methodology for your work with clients.
- ✔ Are you competitive – as good as or better than your competition? Are you highly valuable to your customers?
- ✔ Are you less flexible than you need to be?
- ✔ Is your offer under threat of replacement by a new solution/product?

The ultimate question is 'Do we need to make a shift in our offer?'. If you do, this chapter is a good foundation for the process you need to go through, as are Chapters 6 and 7. If something dramatic happens in your space, such as the emergence of a completely new and less costly way of doing what you do, you'd be foolish not to attend to it right away. But, at least, check the currency of your offer at least once a year: in other words, check that your offer is still what the market currently needs.

Unlike your work with a customer, business development is never finished, because your business is an ever-evolving entity. Your business development practices, including using the lifecycle to think about, design, manage and deliver on your business goals, are ways of bringing systematic management to your business.

# Chapter 6

# Building Your Business Development Plan

*In This Chapter*

▶ Considering the essential role of planning

▶ Formulating your successful plan

*I*f you've ever run a marathon, got married or settled down in front of the TV to binge on *Breaking Bad* DVD box sets, you know that these activities don't turn out well if you leave things to chance. You need to prepare, plan and execute properly to succeed. Every so often, you look at the plan and ask yourself how you're doing: 'Was my 15-mile run on pace?'; 'Did the cake get ordered last week?'; 'Do I have enough beers in the mini-fridge?'

Without a plan and a way to monitor how you're doing, you're likely to lose the game. And running a business is like a game, with a purpose, rules, scoring, challenges and other competitors: lose some, win some, but become the best team you can.

In Chapter 5, I lead you through developing your offer. When your offer's ready, you can start to build your business development plan. Here I help you focus on the areas most important to your success, so that you can build a plan specific to your business, starting from where you are today and where you want to be one year from now. It's a short-term plan, because that makes it about real action, not 'head in the clouds' long-term visions. Nothing wrong with those, but you want to be doing things today.

By the end of this chapter, you have a high-level plan in your hands that allows you to measure how you're doing, track progress against goals and know what's working and what isn't. Your plan is going to be about *managing* business development.

On the ground, you use specific strategies to get results and choose the best approaches for you. To flesh out your tactics in detail, jump to Chapter 10 (on marketing), Chapter 13 (sales), Chapter 16 (customer management) or Chapter 20 (partnerships), where I cover the specifics for these different areas.

# Planning for Business Development Success

Before you start the planning, I want to reiterate the role that business development has in helping you to attain your *goals* (your 'big' objectives):

> Business development is the process required to achieve growth through the acquisition of profitable net new customers and expansion of existing customers.

Business development is essentially forward-looking. You require discipline to prioritize tasks that bring longer-term benefits, rather than immediate gratification, and to work on activities that can wait until tomorrow – while dealing with today's priorities, including the crisis of the moment. After all if you can push business development activities to tomorrow, why not next week or next month?

No, for your business to succeed you have to plan properly, develop clear goals and work daily to achieve them.

## Winging business development doesn't work

You have to find a way to make business development a priority and also make space for the work that needs to be done every day, systematically, by you or by your team members. Business development work needs to be imperative; you have to start measuring so that you can sustain the forward action.

You have to shift 'What next?' to 'What's going to get me to my goal?' (which I cover in the next section).

Your business development plan needs to include:

- ✔ **Goals:** Broken down into *milestones* (intermediate goals): 'Where do I want to be in 12 months?' and 'Where do I need to be this month?'
- ✔ **Metrics:** Numbers that measure the health of your business (see the later section 'Working on metrics' for more).
- ✔ **Targets:** Specific numbers that individuals are aiming to reach. Targets ensure that the metric is in a healthy state.
- ✔ **Measures:** How you count progress towards a target.
- ✔ **Tactics:** Major groups of activities that contribute to the above points.

If you have all these items, great: you're building by design, not by accident. Your plan helps you know what to do next, prioritize what's important, avoid busy work (activities that make no difference to your goals) and see which tactics are working and which aren't.

In addition, your plan (as I develop it in this chapter) includes:

- **Communication strategies:** How do I enroll others in my plan? (Flip to Chapter 7 for details.)
- **Risk management:** What risks may I need to plan for? (Again, check out Chapter 7.)

Although businesses can grow without a plan, they require a hefty dose of luck: like showing up at the train station knowing that you have to get to Sometown, but you don't know the timetable, the connections or the cost. Maybe you get there, most likely you don't. Perhaps planning the journey would've been a good idea.

## *Knowing where you're going*

Worse still, imagine turning up at the train station without even knowing your destination. You know that you need to be somewhere, just not precisely where. That's why you need near-term goals as part of your plan. I'm talking here about the type of goals you can measure and use to drive results quickly.

Different types of goals exist, of course. For example:

- Total revenue
- EBITDA (earnings before interest, taxes, depreciation and amortization – it's a mouthful so just think 'profit')
- Number of employees
- Number of customers

I mention EBITDA because if you ever happen to want to sell your firm, it's a measure in which the accountants take an interest when they value your business.

Make your goals measurable – ideally they're *quantitative* (numbers such as revenue, number of staff, number of customers, size of pipeline), so that when you check your performance, you can say 'we did it' (hurrah!) or 'we didn't make it' (ouch!). Avoid goals such as 'improve the methodology' (which is *qualitative*) and instead try the measurable 'all staff members have been trained on the new methodology by [date]'.

You can all too easily confuse *goals* (where you want to be further down the road) with *metrics* (numbers that tell you whether your business is healthy). One trick is to check whether you can break down the goal you're thinking of into milestones – such as, 'If I get to here by the end of June, I'm on track.'

# Creating Your Winning Plan

In this section on creating your business development plan, I use a total revenue goal as illustration, but you can substitute your own goals, of course.

Your goals don't have to be numbers. They can be other types of objectives, such as, 'create a productive partnership with XYZ Co'. However, when you move from goal to metric, you tease out the measurable aspects of your goal, such as, 'eight joint presentations this year with XYZ Co' and then create targets for each month or quarter.

Back to revenue. Your plan is going to be for one year and broken down into monthly revenue milestones. If you hit each milestone, you reach the goal. With goals, milestones, metrics (the numbers) and sources of new opportunities to hand, you can then use Chapter 7 to manage your tactics and help you reach the overall goal.

Be realistic with your goals: make them attainable but with a bit of stretch added in, just a little more than you think you can do. Revenue is a good goal to work on (no surprise there). After all, if the money side works, so does the business. I also strongly suggest you track profit, gross or net.

I design the planning exercise in this chapter to help you track revenue from net new customers and expansion of existing ones and to look for areas to improve performance in both. This planning exercise is a tool for your management team to see how you're doing.

Your planning is certain to be influenced by factors I don't know about. If you have large, stable long-term customers, your plan is sure to look different from someone with smaller, short-term customers: simply adapt your plan as necessary.

If numbers aren't your thing, and they're not everyone's cup of Java, you need to get comfortable with only a few simple measures. Then you can delegate the tough stuff to someone else. Just don't do an ostrich on me!

## *Choosing where to start planning*

You can't build a plan for the next 12 months unless you know where you are today. Whether or not you have your reporting act together, you're going to need data that allows you to check how you're doing against the plan.

At the simplest level, you need to do the following:

- Look at your last 12 months' results.
- Set a goal for the next 12 months.
- Project numbers out month-by-month for 12 months.

Take your revenue for the last 12 months and up it by an appropriate percentage. You want a minimum of 15–20 per cent growth year on year. Go back over the past few years, if you've been going that long, and see what your growth rate has been – and that includes downs as well as ups. If you think that you can do 25 per cent growth next year, conservatively, push it to 30 per cent. Frighten yourself a little – good for the circulation.

In the early years, you can see growth percentages of 100 per cent, 500 per cent or more. As you get larger, this percentage declines, which is fine if your revenue is still growing at a respectable rate. You can't keep up astronomical growth in services, because your revenue is highly dependent on people and a limit applies to how fast you can assimilate customers and hire new staff without impacting quality (unless you start into acquisitions, for example, and that's a whole other ball game).

I assume that your year-end is 31 December. Most likely it's not December as you're reading this chapter right now, so use this guide:

- **September–December:** Plan for the rest of this year and all next year.
- **June–August:** Plan through to the end of next June. Revisit in January of next year and plan the rest of the year.
- **January–May:** Plan the rest of this year, and in December plan for next year.

You can find a planning spreadsheet at www.dummies.com/go/businessdevelopment.

Assume that it's April right now. Figure 6-1 shows a part of your plan where the revenue from last year was $500,000 (£315,000) and the goal for this year is set at $950,000 (£598,500). Big growth coming!

| | A | B | E | F | G | H | I | J | K | L | M | N | O | P | Q |
|---|---|---|---|---|---|---|---|---|---|---|---|---|---|---|---|
| 1 | | | | | | | | | | | | | | | |
| 2 | | **TOTALS** | | | | White cells are booked/firm. Gray cells are projections | | | | | | | | | |
| 3 | | **Current month : APRIL** | | | | | | | GOAL FOR THE YEAR IS $950k | | | | | | |
| 4 | | | Month 1 | Month 2 | Month 3 | Month 4 | Month 5 | Month 6 | Month 7 | Month 8 | Month 9 | Month 10 | Month 11 | Month 12 | TOTAL |
| 5 | | 2014 Goal and Milestones | $32,500 | $32,500 | $47,500 | $47,500 | $47,500 | $50,000 | $75,000 | $110,000 | $120,000 | $120,000 | $120,000 | $120,000 | $922,500 |

**Figure 6-1:**
Goal
projection.

Fill your plan with projected numbers and add actuals when you have them. In the case in the table, January–March are actuals and April is looking good, but not finalized until invoices go out. The rest of the cells are gray (projections).

Have no less than six months of projected revenues. Think of those monthly projections as your milestones on the way to your goal.

Now break down where that revenue is going to come from: your existing customers and your *pipeline* (your list of prospective customers and where they are in the process of buying services). I tackle these two revenue sources one at a time.

### Existing customers

Customers are in the DELIVER or COMPLETE stages of the lifecycle (check out Figure 3-1); otherwise they're past customers.

List your existing contracts. Then think about each customer and whether more work is likely to come from them. As far as possible, predict revenue across the months from existing customers when you're secure that you:

- Have a contract
- Have specific new *opportunities* (prospective contracts, statements of work or change orders)
- Can reliably base your expectations on prior performance

Enter individual contracts and opportunities on separate rows. Also, don't forget to add any historical customers that you may not be doing work with today but have new opportunities with.

Figure 6-2 shows the forecast of where (which months) the revenue will hit for booked business and new potential. Note that the figure doesn't yet show prospects (net new customers). That's coming next.

For the purpose of goal-setting, tracking customer opportunities with your booked business keeps responsibility for the goal with the customer management team. In terms of your pipeline management day to day, you can definitely include these opportunities with your prospective new customers, for sales tracking purposes (see Chapter 13 for more on this topic).

### Prospective customers

The next thing you bring to this plan is your pipeline – the list of prospects that are considering your services: in other words, they're in the PRESENT/ PROPOSE or even CONTRACT stages of the lifecycle (see Figure 3-1).

**Figure 6-2:** Customer revenue projection.

| | A | B | C | D | E | F | G | H | I | J | K | L | M | N | O | P | Q | R |
|---|---|---|---|---|---|---|---|---|---|---|---|---|---|---|---|---|---|---|
| 1–2 | | **BACKLOG of current clients** | **Current month:** | **APRIL** | **White cells are booked business. Gray cells are projections** | | | | | | | | | | | | | |
| 3 | | **Customer Name** | **Start date of billable work** | **Current deal size** | **Month 1** | **Month 2** | **Month 3** | **Month 4** | **Month 5** | **Month 6** | **Month 7** | **Month 8** | **Month 9** | **Month 10** | **Month 11** | **Month 12** | **TOTAL** | **GAP!** |
| 4 | 1 | ABC Company | 1/2/2014 | $100,000 | $25,500 | $25,500 | $25,000 | $25,000 | | | | | | | | | $100,000 | $0 |
| 5 | 2 | ABC Company | 5/1/2014 | | | | | | $10,000 | $10,000 | $10,000 | $30,000 | $30,000 | $30,000 | $30,000 | $15,000 | $165,000 | $165,000 |
| 6 | 3 | PQR Company | 3/1/2014 | $45,000 | | | $15,000 | $15,000 | $15,000 | | | | | | | | $45,000 | $0 |
| 7 | 4 | PQR Company | 8/1/2014 | | | | | | | | | $20,000 | $20,000 | | | | $40,000 | $40,000 |
| 8 | 5 | XYZ Company | 1/1/2014 | $90,000 | $7,500 | $7,500 | $7,500 | $7,500 | $7,500 | $7,500 | $7,500 | $7,500 | $7,500 | $7,500 | $7,500 | $7,500 | $90,000 | $0 |
| 9 | | Total | | $235,000 | $32,500 | $32,500 | $47,500 | $47,500 | $32,500 | $17,500 | $17,500 | $57,500 | $57,500 | $37,500 | $37,500 | $22,500 | $440,000 | $205,000 |

If you already have a system for managing your pipeline, for example, a spreadsheet, or a sales management system such as Salesforce, you can use the data from those sources. If your pipeline is in your head, or someone else's, you need to stop relying entirely on your brain.

Pipelines usually show the overall project budget, but they don't necessarily spread that budget out into the months when you expect the work to be done. So as well as the total fees for each prospect, you need to estimate two other things:

- ✔ **When the work will happen:** Project revenue out into those month(s).

- ✔ **A percentage probability against each opportunity:** The likelihood that the deal will close (percentage goes up the closer you get to a sale).

Figure 6-3 shows the prospect part of your planning spreadsheet in two parts: at the top are the projected numbers; at the bottom, the monthly projections have been *weighted* (reduced by multiplying the revenue numbers, both total and monthly, by the percentage probability of closure). The reason for weighting is that as you win and lose deals, your actual revenue roughly matches your original weighted prediction. Over time, your skill at projecting future revenue becomes more and more accurate.

If you're wondering why the total value of opportunities and projected revenue for the year are different in the top half of the table, the reason is that one of the contracts goes beyond the end of this year.

So, with goals, milestones, customer projections and prospect projections, you get to see the whole picture. Figure 6-4 shows your totals only.

Think of it as your dashboard and watch it closely.

### Mind the gap!

As you track your total projected revenue from customers and prospects, you almost certainly have a gap if you're looking forward 12 months:

Goal – Customer Business – Weighted Prospects = Gap

Figure 6-4 shows a gap of $200,500 (£126,315) in the prospect list, which requires completely new sales opportunities to fill it.

You shouldn't have a gap for the current month. If you have a gap for next month or the one after (as in row 6 of Figure 6-4), you have a problem (pop to Chapter 13 for how to 'panic now'!).

**Figure 6-3:** Prospect revenue projection: unweighted (top) and weighted (bottom).

**PIPELINE — Current moth: APRIL**

| | Prospect name | Opportunity name | Amount ($) | Close Date | Probability(%) | Month 1 | Month 2 | Month 3 | Month 4 | Month 5 | Month 6 | Month 7 | Month 8 | Month 9 | Month 10 | Month 11 | Month 12 | TOTAL |
|---|---|---|---|---|---|---|---|---|---|---|---|---|---|---|---|---|---|---|
| 1 | Jingle Inc | Annual retainer | $144,000.00 | 4/31/2014 | 75% | | | | | $12,000 | $12,000 | $12,000 | $12,000 | $12,000 | $12,000 | $12,000 | $12,000 | $96,000 |
| 2 | Jangle LLC | Strategic consulting | $30,000.00 | 5/31/2014 | 25% | | | | | | $10,000 | $15,000 | $5,000 | | | | | $30,000 |
| 3 | Jumble Corp | New build | $250,000.00 | 5/31/2014 | 50% | | | | | | $15,000 | $45,000 | $45,000 | $45,000 | $45,000 | $45,000 | $10,000 | $250,000 |
| | | | | | | | | | | | | | | | | | | $0 |
| | | | | | | | | | | | | | | | | | | $0 |
| | | | | | | | | | | | | | | | | | | $0 |
| | | | | | | | | | | | | | | | | | | $0 |
| TOTAL | | | $424,000 | | | $0 | $0 | $0 | $0 | $12,000 | $37,000 | $72,000 | $62,000 | $57,000 | $57,000 | $57,000 | $22,000 | $376,000 |

**WEIGHTED PIPELINE — Current moth: APRIL**

| | Prospect name | Opportunity name | Amount ($) | Close Date | Probability(%) | Month 1 | Month 2 | Month 3 | Month 4 | Month 5 | Month 6 | Month 7 | Month 8 | Month 9 | Month 10 | Month 11 | Month 12 | TOTAL |
|---|---|---|---|---|---|---|---|---|---|---|---|---|---|---|---|---|---|---|
| 1 | Jingle Inc | Annual retainer | $144,000.00 | 4/31/2014 | 75% | | | | | $9,000 | $9,000 | $9,000 | $9,000 | $9,000 | $9,000 | $9,000 | $9,000 | $72,000 |
| 2 | Jangle LLC | Strategic consulting | $30,000.00 | 5/31/2014 | 25% | | | | | | $2,500 | $3,750 | $1,250 | | | | | $7,500 |
| 3 | Jumble Corp | New build | $250,000.00 | 5/31/2014 | 50% | | | | | | $7,500 | $22,500 | $22,500 | $22,500 | $22,500 | $22,500 | $5,000 | $125,000 |
| | | | | | | | | | | | | | | | | | | $0 |
| | | | | | | | | | | | | | | | | | | $0 |
| | | | | | | | | | | | | | | | | | | $0 |
| | | | | | | | | | | | | | | | | | | $0 |
| TOTAL | | | | | | $0 | $0 | $0 | $0 | $9,000 | $19,000 | $35,250 | $32,750 | $31,500 | $31,500 | $31,500 | $14,000 | $204,500 |

**Figure 6-4:** Summary revenue projection.

| | Month 1 | Month 2 | Month 3 | Month 4 | Month 5 | Month 6 | Month 7 | Month 8 | Month 9 | Month 10 | Month 11 | Month 12 | TOTAL |
|---|---|---|---|---|---|---|---|---|---|---|---|---|---|
| **TOTALS** | | | | White cells are booked/firm. Gray cells are projections | | | | | | | | | |
| **Current month : APRIL** | | | | | | | GOAL FOR THE YEAR IS $950K | | | | | | |
| 2014 Goal and Milestones | $32,500 | $32,500 | $47,500 | $47,500 | $47,500 | $50,000 | $75,000 | $110,000 | $120,000 | $120,000 | $120,000 | $120,000 | **$922,500** |
| MIND THE GAP! | $0 | $0 | $0 | $0 | $6,000 | $13,500 | $22,250 | $19,750 | $31,000 | $51,000 | $51,000 | $83,500 | $278,000 |
| Customers-booked and projected | $32,500 | $32,500 | $47,500 | $47,500 | $32,500 | $17,500 | $17,500 | $57,500 | $57,500 | $37,500 | $37,500 | $22,500 | $440,000 |
| Prospects projected | $0 | $0 | $0 | $0 | $9,000 | $19,000 | $35,250 | $32,750 | $31,500 | $31,500 | $31,500 | $14,000 | $204,500 |
| **Grand TOTAL** | $32,500 | $32,500 | $47,500 | $47,500 | $41,500 | $36,500 | $52,750 | $90,250 | $89,000 | $69,000 | $69,000 | $36,500 | $844,500 |

The gap is important because it represents the completely new business that your marketing and sales efforts have to produce. The gap should be pretty small for the next three months – unless a miracle happens, you can't fill such a near-term gap, unless your sales cycle is very short indeed.

Your task, if you choose to accept it, is systematically to fill your pipeline over time to reduce the gap as the months roll by and to convert opportunities into customer revenue.

Here are a few things to note:

- ✔ **Don't flatline your revenue.** Just like you're looking for year-to-year growth, you should also be looking for month-to-month growth.

- ✔ **Look carefully at the revenue patterns of the past couple of years.** For example, if your business is seasonal, namely with predictable trends as to when in the year you're particularly busy and when you have some slack, build those peaks and troughs into your planned numbers.

- ✔ **Try to estimate the length of your sales cycle.** If you start projecting for miraculous sales, you may fall behind, so allow time for sales to catch up with your vision.

- ✔ **Be ambitious with your goals and conservative with your projections.** The gap drives a sense of urgency. Don't underestimate the importance of minding the gap.

At this point, you may be elated at the possibility of projected growth, in despair about how you're going to achieve it or somewhere in the middle. Just remember that in future you're going to know how you're doing and knowing is the first step to impacting the outcome. *Courage, mon brave.*

For this illustration I use revenue as a goal, which you can also convert to a metric. An actual revenue number is a goal; the percentage of actual to plan (projected revenue) is a metric (see the next section).

## Working on metrics

*Metrics* are real numbers that tell you about the health of your business. You best set them as ideals – in that you expect to trend towards them but not meet them right away (distinct from goals, which you expect to reach).

A metric is a measure of business health. It's usually a percentage or a ratio (such as your win rate or the percentage of customers giving you five marks out of five). If you can break a number down into discrete milestones, it's probably a goal rather than a metric. For example, increasing your staff by 10 this year is a goal; increasing by 25 per cent is a metric that can stand for a longer time as a measure of growth. Goals change from year to year, metrics have longevity.

Table 6-1 shows some typical metrics and how to track them.

| Table 6-1 | How to Track Metrics | |
|---|---|---|
| *Metric* | *How to Track* | *Which Way Should It Go* |
| Revenue: Percentage of goal reached | Set a monthly projection for 12 months ahead and track the actuals as they come in. | You want to attain 100 per cent. In other words, your revenue projections should be as close to spot on as possible. |
| Gross Margin: Revenue minus cost of delivering the business | Have a target percentage, probably in the range 25–50 per cent. Note: don't include operational/fixed expenses. | Upwards! Most services businesses can't surpass 50 per cent, though a few do. The goal is to push it higher by charging more and/or increasing the efficiency of delivery. |
| Average deal size in the pipeline | Check what it currently is and set an average deal size that's 20 per cent. | Upwards! Larger deals allow you to reduce the number of customers, focusing on each with more depth and diligence. It doesn't always mean a lot more work – just the ability to deliver higher value. |
| Win percentage: Wins divided by total number of opportunities that reach a decision | Check what it currently is and increase by 1 in 10. It makes a huge difference. | Upwards! Be realistic, though. Losing is not always failure – it can be a sign that you're stretching yourself. Note: if you track your win percentage, you're also tracking your loss percentage and seeking to reduce it. |
| Pipeline to add | The total project value that your sales activity needs to add to the pipeline this quarter (or next) | Upwards to track with your growth goals. |

*(continued)*

**Table 6-1** *(continued)*

| Metric | How to Track | Which Way Should It Go |
|--------|--------------|------------------------|
| Customer satisfaction measured by customer reviews | You're aiming for five out of five (see Chapter 16 for a review format). | Upwards! Happy customers are a significant contribution to you, your business and your future success. |
| DSO (days sales outstanding): Measure of how fast you get paid DSO = accounts receivable divided by (annual sales/365 days) | Create a target that no customer is later than seven days beyond the invoice due date. Train customers by reminding them that their invoice is due and call them as soon as they're late. | Downwards or holding steady! Calculate your DSO on the same day each month (perhaps the last day and before you send out invoices). Check your DSO each month to see whether it's coming down. |
| Lead conversion per cent: Number of leads converted divided by total number of new leads | Set a percentage – if currently 1 or 2 per cent, set the goal at 3 per cent. Track how many leads convert to an opportunity. | Predictability is important. The cost of converting needs to produce a result that justifies the investment. |

The table simply contains example metrics – you can use many more. Pick the ones that work for you and make them public. Have everyone committed to driving results in the right direction.

## Components of your plan: Creating the blueprint

Where, I hear you ask, are my prospects going to come from to fill the spreadsheet in the preceding section? You're going to use your business development plans to drive your engine, the high-level one in this chapter and the detailed plans for marketing (Chapter 10), sales (Chapter 12), customer management (Chapter 16) and partnerships (Chapter 20).

You're doing business today, of course, but perhaps you're not measuring what you should to be really sure of where you are. Taking the one step of creating metrics and measuring with diligence is the single most effective tool for growing your business: it changes everyone's behavior. But I know that you want to get started right away, so here I outline how to produce a simple 3–6 month plan. You can create a longer-term strategy when your short-term plan is underway.

### First question: *Where do your customers come from?*

Review your customer list from the past couple of years and see where your customers come from:

- ✔ Your own network?
- ✔ A referral from a customer, employee or partner?
- ✔ An event?
- ✔ Online (search engine optimization (SEO), ads, blog posts, social media, your website)?
- ✔ Mailing or emailing?
- ✔ A cold call?

If you can, do the same for your losses. If you don't have the data on prospects, don't sweat it. Just start gathering that information in the future. For now, the most important thing is to know where your successes came from and, in the short term, focus effort on the most productive sources.

The sources that have been effective for you in the past may not sustain your growth longer term. Focus on your top sources in the short term, say this year, while you start to experiment with other channels.

---

## Doing the right things to get customers

Are you using the right tactics for getting new customers? You can encounter surprises when you look closely at where your business is coming from (your wins) and where not (your losses). For example, I see companies spending lots of money on SEO to drive people to their websites so that they can sign up to be contacted (I'm oversimplifying here to make the point).

In many cases, none of those so-called leads convert into business; as well as the cost of SEO, someone spent time calling, qualifying and trying to progress the relationship for no benefit.

I'm not suggesting you don't use SEO – it can be a powerful tool – just make sure that the channels you use are producing wins, not just noise in your pipeline (sounds painful, and is!).

To counter that thought, some activities, such as brand-building and recognition, become more important as you start to grow, say from $10 to $20 million and beyond. You need a stronger identity in the marketplace than you require when you're small. Not all your tactics have to be designed to produce wins – other goals are perfectly valid.

### *Second question: What percentage of your business comes from the sources you've identified?*

You need to work this percentage out based on the customers that come from each source. Count the revenue from each source (not the number of customers). Plan out what your future investment in those sources is going to be.

For example, if 75 per cent of your business comes from your network (business contacts referring prospects to you), in the short term court those contacts and add new ones (I call them 'friends and family') in a systematic manner. Thank them for helping you. Take them out to lunch. Send them a gift card when they give you a referral. Educate them as to the sort of leads you're looking for.

I provide a couple more examples in Table 6-2. Follow this model for all your sources and confirm or replan your investment of time and/or money.

| Table 6-2 | Sources of Your Wins (Tactics You Use) | |
|---|---|---|
| *Source* | *Percentage of Revenue From This Source* | *Future Investment/Tactic* |
| Employee referral | 5 per cent | Institute a prospect referral bonus for employees, which pays out if the customer signs a contract. See whether you can boost this source with little effort beyond having your employees understand what you're looking for. |
| Partner referral | 60 per cent | Spend a lot of time with partners, court them, make sure that they know your successes so they can share them, ask them what would have them send you more referrals: work as closely with them as possible on new opportunities, schedule regular pipeline review meetings, look for ways to reciprocate. Set a budget to nurture this stream. |

Upselling to an existing customer is always easier than selling to a new one, as is selling to a referral rather than to a cold lead. Spend time figuring out where to spend your time and when you decide, stick with it. Avoid knee-jerk reactions if you don't see a deal in a couple of weeks.

By all means get creative and play with ideas. Don't entirely neglect sources that provide lots of leads, just not the right size. Explain what you're looking for and why. If you decide to try a new source and new tactic, treat it as a pilot and monitor it closely to see whether it produces a result, such as an increase in the number of prospects/wins.

At the end of this exercise, you have a plan to do the following:

- ✔ Eliminate or minimize non-producing sources.

- ✔ Optimize low-producing sources.

- ✔ Maximize and enhance high-producing sources.

- ✔ Introduce new sources and track how they perform.

Use your revenue plan to determine the effort that needs to go into upselling existing customers (or asking for referrals or expanding into another department or division of their business) as against the effort that needs to go into net new sales.

If you include a wild new idea, that's great, just don't put all your eggs in that basket. If a quick fix existed, everyone would be doing it. Don't let a company sell you a service it says gets you an instant pipeline. Be sceptical – ask a lot of questions of your friends and family before you jump into something completely new.

## *Monitoring progress*

The numbers are your clue as to whether your team's performance is going to deliver the goods. The best way to get at those numbers is to have systems that can provide you with reports, with no more than 30 minutes effort per week. Your finance system and your SFA/CRM (sales force automation/customer relationship management system) should be able to provide most of what you need. Simple spreadsheets can do the rest.

Tracking the performance of a specific tactic provides the following:

- ✔ You get clear evidence of whether you're on track.

- ✔ You can *inspect* – namely you can examine each tactic and ask for specifics that underlie the numbers (see Chapter 7).

- ✔ You can see whether the tactic is working (see Chapter 10 for more on measuring marketing tactics and Chapter 13 for measuring sales tactics).

If you don't track, you have less accountability, staff members are less driven to be active in their efforts and results decline or even disappear into thin air. No matter how diligent you are, few people are wired to be on their game all day every day.

Consider adding an incentive (often called a *spiff*) for a target reached. The combination of metric and incentive is your stick and carrot. Use both if you can. Also, consider paying for performance, not for time. Although people can and do lie about their activities, if you're tracking properly and inspecting rigorously, they get found out.

Based on your chosen tactics, select what to track. Use Chapter 7 to guide you in designing simple tools and processes – and then enforce them. Think about tracking the following:

- ✔ Revenue
- ✔ Cold calls – number of calls, conversations and conversions from lead to prospect
- ✔ Pipeline – number of opportunities, average size of deals and wins

Consider having a visible dashboard, a physical board or a virtual one (online), to give the whole company a transparent view of how things are going.

# Chapter 7

# Putting Your Plan into Action

## In This Chapter

▶ Preparing for a successful launch

▶ Lifting off your business development plan

▶ Anticipating threats to your plan

*B*uilding something is satisfying (such as the business development plan you construct in Chapter 6), but you don't then want to leave it on the shelf gathering dust; where's the fun in that? No, like a child who's built a model airplane, you can't wait to race down to the local park and see it in action. But you need to prepare for that flight – so that the plane doesn't crash the first time out and spend the rest of its life dangling sadly from a high treetop. This chapter guides you through a successful launch of your plan.

Growing your business involves change: more customers, more staff, more revenue, higher levels of investment, more risk and tighter cash flow. Therefore, you need to change the plan from Chapter 6 as you experience each new challenge. Here I help you roll out your first (fairly simple) plan, guiding you through the key steps: carrying out initial activities concerned with communication and setup, and then some regular, reliable and measurable tasks for taking care of business development over time.

Where a team's involved, the start and roll-out are critical. You need to enrol team members in your vision so that everyone pulls in the same direction when the work gets going. Don't short-change these activities in your eagerness to get started. Effort upfront in communicating your plan maximizes your results down the road.

Get the wider company's employees onboard as well: your business growth is their guarantee of continued employment.

# Checking Your Plan before Lift-off

A business development plan is just a piece of paper with no life: it can certainly energize people, but alone it doesn't generate action. For that you need to state specific milestones and tactics, identify initial tasks to begin carrying out the plan, decide who's going to help and with what, and calculate your investment of time and money.

Your initial business development plan has to be fairly short term: plan for 12 months to keep you focused on near-term results and detail tactics for the first 3–6 months to keep your actions focused.

Ensure that your plan, at a minimum, comprises the following and that you're in good shape:

- ✔ **Goals:** Key measures of where you want to be in 12 months, such as revenue or number of customers.
- ✔ **Milestones:** Monthly targets to tell you whether you're on track for a goal.
- ✔ **Metrics:** Target numbers you track to ensure that activities are being done.
- ✔ **Tactics:** Specific activities to drive your customer and revenue acquisition.

If you don't yet have all these elements in place, read Chapter 6 to make sure that your plan is solid.

Don't go it alone. Even if your company is very small, or you're the only one doing any business development activities in it, remember that services is a team game: so go get yourself a team. If you're only accountable to yourself (or to the boss), you don't have the support structure you need to keep going when the going gets tough – as it surely will.

## Setting milestones, tactics and metrics

Your plan is founded – and indeed is dependent on – key goals. If you don't have a place to get to, how can you know what the journey should look like? Imagine that I want to drive from Los Angeles to New York for a concert in ten days' time: that's my goal. My plan may include gas costs, hotel charges and meals, and a fellow driver or two, plus a few contingencies in case the car breaks down.

But without milestones (for example, actual hard mileage I need to drive every day) how can I know that my plan is feasible and, when I'm on the road, how can I tell whether I'm on track? With milestones in place, I can start detailing how to reach them, how much budget to allocate, who to have as co-drivers and how to get help if disaster strikes.

In Chapter 6, I focus mostly on the goal of revenue and where this revenue is going to come from, whereas here I discuss how to track the key goals that you choose for your plan, as you set up milestones and metrics. I provide examples and you can adapt the concepts to your plan. Meanwhile, think about who's accountable for those milestones and metrics.

### *Creating milestones*

Based on the goals you have in your plan, you need to set specific milestones to keep you on track. Typically, you measure milestones numerically. I give a few examples in addition to the ones in Chapter 6:

- **Profit per month:** You want to get a grip on your gross profit and your net profit on a monthly basis. *Gross profit* is the revenue minus the cost of sales (namely how much it costs you in staff and expenses to acquire and deliver the business). *Net profit* is the revenue minus all expenses (including overhead and fixed costs such as rent or computers).

- **Number of employees:** Similar to revenue, when will your plan call for additional staff? Spread the hiring across the year and set some metrics for how many staff you need to interview to fill your open positions.

- **Average revenue per customer:** Typically, you base this figure on completed projects and set a goal to increase the number. This approach works well if customer projects are short. Alternatively, you can use your 12-month projection, including actual customer revenue as the months progress, to compare to last year's actual result.

You can set and use all sorts of goals and milestones. Some of them apply to the first half of the lifecycle and some to the second (see Figure 3-1). Therefore, different people are involved in managing and measuring, that is, contributing to the goal. Of course, they're already contributing; you just want them to be responsible for the outcome. To do that, you have to make the goals and milestones overt.

Don't go overboard: start with two or three goals/milestones at most and include a small number of people to be in charge of them. You can always add more later.

### *Relating milestones and metrics*

Now you need to take the next step and set targets (metrics) for the tactics that are going to drive your goals. I focus on management tactics that apply in every business. Throughout this book, I discuss grass-roots tactics for choosing tactics that will deliver on your goals, but for now I'm assuming that you stick mostly with what you're doing today and start tweaking it to improve performance – by watching your numbers, delegating responsibility and introducing new approaches gradually.

I use the goal of revenue to drill down to some tactics, associated metrics and how to track progress. Table 7-1 shows some measures to help you maximize revenue.

| Table 7-1 | Milestones, Tactics and Metrics for REVENUE | |
|---|---|---|
| *Milestone* | *How Often to Measure* | *Metrics and How to Measure Them* |
| Customer booked revenue reaches the forecast | Monitor *customer projects* to make sure that things are on track for next month. Measure monthly.<br><br>Make each individual who's responsible for a project also responsible for driving the revenue number. | Customer revenue actuals are 100% of original projections for booked business. (Financial reporting.) |
| Customer opportunity revenue reaches the forecast | Review *new potential projects with existing customers* and check progress with securing those contracts. Measure monthly.<br><br>If someone's driving new sales to existing customers, make that person responsible for these results. | New sales to existing customers are 85% of original projections. |

| Milestone | How Often to Measure | Metrics and How to Measure Them |
|---|---|---|
| Prospect revenue reaches the forecast | Review *prospect pipeline* to track progress with deals. Measure weekly. | New sales to prospects are at 100% of weighted projections (see Figure 6-3). |
| | Task the person responsible for the accuracy and health of your pipeline with this metric. | |
| Average deal size reaches a specific target number | Monitor *average customer deal size*, actual for completed deals, estimates for projected deals. Measure monthly. | Increase in deal size by a specific percentage (say 10%) year over year. |
| | Monitor *average prospect deal size* monthly. | |
| | This task needs a leader — based on the size of contracts going through, you may need to look at your prospect acquisition: which prospects you choose to propose to (and which you don't). | |
| Win ratio increases by 1 point | For prospects, measuring the number of wins against the total number of decisions (win or loss). | Increase in wins from, say, 3 in 10 to 4 in 10 over 12 months. |
| | This target is for the sales team. Have them responsible for driving this increase. | |
| Add your own measures . . . | | |

## Monitoring tactics at grass-roots level

Part of driving up revenue (maybe an important part) comes from acquiring new customers. You can employ all sorts of tactics for driving prospects into your pipeline. Assume that you need eight prospects in the pipeline to close one new customer a month and that one of your tactics is cold calling (something companies often invest a lot of time and effort in for little result). How can you monitor its effectiveness? (By the way, I'm not advocating cold calling – it works in some businesses and not in others. If you do decide to try it, give it three months at least.)

Without historical data, establishing a target is hard, but you have to start somewhere. How many cold calls a day do you think are needed? How many conversations will occur from this number? How many will convert to a prospect (where the lead is interested and accepts a second call to dig deeper)? If you're not tracking the numbers, you can't predict how many calls get to a solid opportunity and eventually a win.

Ideally, you'd have a system that captures dials, where conversations are logged and conversions are captured, but who has that? Not many small companies, that's for sure. As an alternative, you need a simple logging tool (say a spreadsheet, with the numbers to be logged daily against a weekly target). Say you target 40 calls per day, 2 conversations per day and 2 conversions to a prospect per week. Make sure that your callers have a suitable calling list where they can make notes, check off every call made and record the results. At the end of the day, they count up and enter the numbers into the tracking spreadsheet. You, or one of your managers, needs to review the summary and inspect some of the detail every week.

If you're not getting the right average of conversations and conversions, something has to shift. Does the number of calls need to go up? Do you need to improve your calling strategy, your follow-through, your nurturing of these leads?

Some of these milestones and tactics relate to pre-contract goals, and some to the delivery phase of the lifecycle, spreading the responsibility across the organization.

Although Table 7-1 refers to a lot of reporting, the act of reviewing the numbers, noting high and low performance and whether you're on track, actually changes behavior. People start to ask, 'What caused that?', 'What should we do differently?', 'How can we repeat that success?' *That's* the underlying change you're trying to effect.

I'm going to include one example of a grass-roots tactic, so that you can refine your own ideas. Say you use cold calling to generate prospects. Table 7-2 shows what the table entry would look like.

| Table 7-2 | Table Entry for Cold Calling Example | |
|---|---|---|
| *Milestone* | *How Often to Measure* | *Metrics and How to Measure Them* |
| Lead conversion to prospects | Track cold calls weekly, with conversions to prospect status. | An average of two leads per week convert to a prospect. Ensure that your caller is capturing calls, conversations and conversions. |

To track performance, you need to establish a weekly report against a specific target number of calls/conversions. See the sidebar 'Monitoring tactics at grass-roots level' for a deeper dive into this example.

You can add to your on-the-ground tactics as well – Parts III to VI help you do that, as well as put them into action.

### Monitoring performance

Beyond the initial tactics and how to keep an eye on them, you need to build some grass-roots monitoring to get a handle on what works. Reporting is all very well (and useful): just make sure that you also *inspect* regularly, namely drill down into the numbers to the specific activities by a team member with a prospect or a customer. If you're concerned about people inflating their numbers, don't worry too much. If they promise and don't deliver, a deeper review becomes necessary. Your inspections are invaluable here.

Choose your milestone and metrics and work out how your tactic will meet them, how often you'll report and how to make sure that you reach the overall goal.

Pick a milestone or metric you think you may struggle with and map it out as shown in Table 7-1.

## Identifying initial tasks

As your business development plan deepens, you need to consider what first tasks to think about and work on. How much preparation you have to do depends on the extent to which you're shifting what you're doing already:

> ✓ **You're using the same basic approach as you did before, but adding some monitoring (goals, milestones, metrics gathering, inspection, adjustment).** Your initial tasks focus on designing your monitoring so that's it's easy to use and thinking about how to roll it out to the team.

✔ **Your approach is the same, but you need to add more people to the team.** As long as your monitoring is planned, your task is to design a process to get existing employees and/or new ones onboard. Outline what you think team members need to know about your business development approach, what to do and how to record what's being done. Consider setting up a mentoring program. Take your best business development team member(s) – maybe that's you – and set up a support structure for new team members. Give them an hour of your time every week for the first couple of months, and let them shadow you at events, on sales calls, in customer meetings. See Chapter 13 for a strategy for adding new sales people – the principles apply whatever the role of the newcomer.

✔ **You're streamlining your existing approach and trying one or two new ideas.** Of course, you need monitoring and everyone has to be trained, but when you start changing things, you may meet resistance. Give the team confidence by designing how the new idea will be implemented as fully as you can. Ask for and be willing to incorporate feedback. Dip into some other chapters for guidance on specific tactics – whether they be marketing (Part III), sales (Part IV), customer management (Part V) or partnership ideas (Part VI).

If you're trying to shift your practices significantly, prepare a high-level overview to share with your staff and your friends and family. Identify when you're going to roll out the different tactics; make sure that your plan is realistic and only go into the detail when doing so is timely. Change is a slow process and doing one or two things well is preferable to doing six things badly.

## *Calling on helpers*

Business development is a complex and wide-ranging process, as you see from Figure 3-1: no one person can be good at everything that needs to be done. The success of your business shouldn't rest on your shoulders alone. You need a support structure as a leader, people you can talk to and people you can delegate to:

✔ **You can't know everything.** Awesome as you are as a leader, others may have more experience, better insights, more objective thinking than you do in any given area.

✔ **Different tactics require different proficiencies and experiences.** Working with leads or prospects or customers, doing the finances, managing the office and leading the company, all rely on specific skills and talents. If you're in any doubt about that, consider your own background and preferences. What tasks are you good at? What tasks are you mediocre at? Take a look at the sidebar 'Personality and your business success'.

� **Your people really do want your business to succeed.** Modern business suffers so much from responsibility for the results all sitting at the top, from not allowing everyone to take their share of the goal and do their bit towards it. Go it alone and you end up doing everything and working 100 hours a week. Share it and you'll be leading and managing, and doing a lot less 'doing'.

Being in your own skin is like being a fish – you don't notice the water you swim in. Jump out of the lake and take a look around. Consider whether your own strengths and capabilities are coloring your perspective. Are you holding on too tight or are you willing to get help, share the load and grow the careers of others?

By all means stick to what you're good at, but be willing to have others lead the charge in the key areas that secure growth and in which they're better than you are.

---

# Personality and your business success

Owners, business leaders and others in services firms contribute to their companies in different ways, especially in business development. Two factors are the source of the differences:

▮ The personality and proclivities of the people

▮ The nature of the business and the subject-matter expertise

These factors are connected. Consider these two examples:

▮ Subject-matter experts, such as a management consultant, are well educated, probably great at winkling out inadequacies, getting to the bottom of them and proposing well thought-out solutions. They tend to be objective, not emotional, creative within their own sphere, but not artistic, interested rather more in facts than in opinions. They're confident in their own abilities, systematic and, typically, successful: maybe mildly contemptuous of the mess other mortals get themselves into. Not always natural team players, when they delegate things that don't get done in what they see as 'my way', or the 'right way', it can drive them crazy.

▮ Serial entrepreneurs are natural creators or enablers of new business ideas and naturally pursue growth. Their skill is in pulling together the right resources; they're usually good at having people buy-in to their ideas, go-getting and highly focused on where business is going to come from. They're not usually interested in detail, but in the broad sweep of things, and they're impatient of delays and roadblocks. They also think that things should be easier than they actually are, so they get irritated. They accept failures and they don't have to have everything fully baked to storm ahead. Things get done around serial entrepreneurs. They delegate readily, although others can't always see where they're heading.

As you can see, you need to account for people's strengths and weakness as you build your team. Asking them to change just doesn't work.

You can look for help in a number of places:

- **Barter for services:** If you need something tactical, perhaps you know someone who'd trade services. Say you're doing an office redesign for a law firm and you need legal advice. How about trading part of your fee for their services? Given that you're making good margins (you are, aren't you?), the hit to your profit may not be all that big.

- **Use independent contractors or a firm:** Without making a long-term commitment, you can engage a recommended contractor/firm to help you with a specific initiative. Just ensure that they understand your business well enough to be useful.

- **Think externally in your network:** Use your friends and family or other business contacts to provide you with support, ideas and advice. Doing so is never more important than when you've devised a new strategy. Who knows, they may even work on your plan, or another aspect of your business development, for free.

- **Look inside your organization:** People in your company come with a significant advantage – they know your business already and so can relatively quickly pick up a new responsibility or an update to your *methodology* or *process* (how you've been working up to now with customers and prospects). This source is best used for extending existing approaches, at least initially. See whether you have individuals who can step up to the plate and hit the ball out of the park. If you've got people like that, you already know who they are. Wait to see evidence of performance, and then promote them.

- **Engage new hires:** Your business growth needs new talent from time to time – initially, perhaps 'more of the same', such as a new project manager, a new salesperson, an assistant in finance. Later you may need different skills, new managers, people capable of managing larger clients, bringing in bigger deals and implementing sophisticated marketing.

Growth takes a lot of planning so make sure that you have trusted advisors as you transition from one form of help to another.

Start involving others, even if in a small way. Create a group that cares about the outcomes, has the right skills and innate talents, and is willing to help. At the very least, find a 'buddy' from outside the company – maybe someone in a services business with your role, or a trusted advisor – and see whether they're willing to have a monthly meeting with you to share experiences, results and challenges.

## Determining your investment

Before you decide where to invest, take a look at your plan – the revenue goals (including customers and prospects that you expect to serve), the tactics you want to use, the metrics you want to track – and consider what you're going to need to get to the goal:

✔ **Most of your cost in a services business is staff.** Whether you're looking for some short-term help or long-term employees, growth means spending money. That means you need a staffing plan, so that you can match your personnel needs to your goals and milestones.

✔ **Think about compensation plans carefully.** Be willing to pay a fair wage, but also build an incentive for performance – from commissions to bonus pools, be willing to share the wealth. Also don't forget that some people are going to incur expenses.

✔ **You may need new tools, so that you can optimize running your business development.** From tools that support specific tactics (such as lead qualification questionnaires to determine whether a new lead is one you should work on) through to systems (such as your customer relationship management (CRM) or accounting ones), growth requires a bit more formality.

✔ **If you're going to engage in any kind of marketing, you need a budget.** Some things are free (well not really, they take time, which is money), but online tactics, advertising, printing and sponsorship all require you to spend.

After you've assembled your investment ideas, scale your budgets to your growth. The more revenue you have coming in, the more you need to invest to sustain that level of revenue. Unless you're getting a cash infusion, the business is going to have to pay for all this investment.

Get help with creating your budgets if you can – a second pair of eyes (especially ones that don't wear rose-tinted spectacles) is useful: use your accountant, your finance person or your life partner to get a dose of reality.

Check out the simple spreadsheet on www.dummies.com/go/businessdevelopment as a starting point.

# Lift-Off! Launching Your Plan

In this section I cover the essential tasks of communicating your plan, getting and using feedback, and starting up your dream team. I don't advise on how to roll out your plan in detail here. Chapter 13 gives you ideas for rolling out a new sales team approach – you can use that as a model.

Flexibility is crucial at the launch stage. A contact from one of the largest software companies in the world told me:

> *People think we're like an ocean liner – a huge ship that takes time to change direction. We're not. We're like a small flotilla of yachts and rowboats. Someone says, 'I'm going this way', and we all say, 'Sure, let's do that. That looks like a good idea'.*

Whatever its size, no company should be an unwieldy ocean liner. In the early days, it needs to be nimble, opportunistic and able to respond to circumstances; with growth comes the challenge of being responsible for employees, payroll and competing priorities. Your people are like that flotilla of small boats. Point the way, show them what they can get out of it and watch them switch direction.

## Communicating your plan internally

You're at the core of directing your business as owner, management-team member or business-development leader, trying to change with changing circumstances. You need to communicate clearly and effectively your plan, your ideas and your thoughts on how to move forward to all who need to know.

If your plan has been living in your head, now's the time to start sharing it with others, for three reasons:

- ✔ **You need support:** Moral, expert and hands-on-deck. You have to extend your team to drive growth.

- ✔ **You need advice from others:** Especially those who've been there, done that, or who know a lot about a specific area in which you're not an expert. You require such input and counsel.

- ✔ **You need your people pulling in the same direction if you want your business to succeed:** Start getting others involved, sharing responsibility; use the skills and talents that you have around you.

You can implement with a spectacular Big Bang or go slow at a steady trickle. Either way, talk to people. Sharing your plan brings others into the picture and allows them to get excited about it and start contributing. I appreciate that doing so can feel threatening for you – raising troubling questions such as 'Will they like it?', 'Will they follow it?' or 'Will it work?' – but do it anyway.

In the final analysis, your people's concerns are individual: they're motivated by keeping their jobs, paying the rent/mortgage, feeding the family, having fun with friends and improving their lot in life.

People are made anxious when they don't know the following:

- ✔ Is the company doing well?
- ✔ Does the loss of a customer mean that they're going to be let go?
- ✔ Are they going to be moved to another project soon?
- ✔ Does their boss like them?

People perform better when they're kept informed, even more so in tough times, and when they think that they can influence the results for themselves and for the company. Part of business development is unifying your team around common goals, preferably where your staff can see a personal upside for their contribution/co-operation.

If you expect more than the above – such as staff jumping into new responsibilities/adding more work with no clear benefits for doing so – you're going to be disappointed. In the end, people have one question: how is this new business development plan going to impact me/benefit me? To be blunt, they don't really care about you and your plan! No, I take that back. They may like you, admire you and hope you do well too, but inevitably they have their own concerns. Therefore, when you communicate with this fact in mind, you see results. And no, I'm not a cynic, just a student of human behavior.

At the strategic level, consider closely how you plan to communicate to the whole company – take a second look to make sure that it floats like a balloon and won't fall flat like a pancake.

Give people enough of the vision to get them excited, but not so much detail that they start falling asleep. If you can, have other members of your management team, or new team members, present their parts of the plan. Make part of your communication the opportunity to get feedback (see the later section 'Making use of friendly feedback' for doing so effectively).

If you have underperformers in your company, you already know who they are. These people are highly resistant to change, especially to measurement because they don't want their underperformance discovered. Don't give them any responsibility for management of results; instead, make sure that they understand what *they* have to deliver and if they don't, follow through with the right procedures to move them out of your business. After all, they're most likely unhappy doing a job they're no good at. You need 'A' players at the top and 'B' or better on the wider team. In services, a 'C' doesn't hack it.

## Enrolling 'friends'

Leadership is lonely and hard. Everyone tends to think that you have power, when you don't. Everyone wants you to make decisions, so that they don't have to take responsibility. All too often, the situation can feel like management against workers, 'us' against 'them'. Even in the most democratic, structurally flat companies, when the going gets tough, you're the one people blame, especially if you have to dismiss them. Well, they blame you or the circumstances – they rarely point the finger at themselves.

So, by all means build your open, sharing, collaborative company, where everyone takes responsibility for the results, but in addition, get yourself some support that's worthy of *your* big game. Think of people you know who can be critical in a constructive way, who call you on your mistakes and who celebrate your successes with no agenda (other than feeling good that they helped).

Assemble a mix of the following people:

- ✔ **Coach/mentor:** Consider paying someone a modest sum for working with you. This person can help you design your goals, metrics and tactics. You want to be able to run ideas by this person, bring up issues for discussion and have her hold you accountable for your results.

- ✔ **Other business leaders:** Look for people who have expertise you don't, valuable market intelligence or experience greater than yours. Use them for an occasional lunch and free advice (you pay for lunch!).

- ✔ **Formal group of peers:** Some organizations offer this service (and some include formal coaching too). If they're too expensive for you, see whether you can start one. Maybe your coach/mentor would consider leading it. Just ensure that the group has structure and method – it shouldn't be just an opportunity for whining about your businesses.

You can admit failure and worries to these people; they uncover your deficiencies and flaws in your plan. Inside the company, you sometimes have to put a brave face on it. Outside, you should be able to be vulnerable and get some help. Actually, that's when you're at your most powerful – when you're willing to admit you don't know it all.

You can use these outsiders in any way you see fit – just ensure that how you use them makes a difference for you. Be clear about how, where and when you need their input. Create your support structure to provide what you need.

## *Making use of friendly feedback*

Your employees and your external support structure will have feedback when you share your initial business development plan with them. In Chapter 3, I look at feedback from customers, prospects and the team concerning your services work. In a similar way, the wider you go for feedback, the better. Take it with a pinch of salt, by all means, but take the gems onboard and incorporate them. Your plan isn't the Rosetta Stone – you can change it.

Structure your requests for feedback so that you can significantly increase the value of the responses. For example, try asking your management team and external advisors:

- Do you think that the plan is realistic?
- What do you think of my goals?
- Is the roll-out at a good pace or is it too fast?
- Can you see anything missing?
- Do you think that I can handle everything else that needs to happen alongside this plan?

You usually collect this feedback verbally – with this senior group, conversations allow for follow-up questions and digging deeper.

Split the employees into two categories: those involved in working the plan and those it impacts only indirectly. Start with the first group, one on one. Share your plan and explain where you need their help. Ask for feedback and for them to come back with their ideas.

This approach has a number of advantages:

- You test your plan with a few key people.
- You get a reaction (good or bad) that helps you tweak how to share it with the wider company.
- You obtain initial feedback from people who're going to be involved, which should make things easier to implement.
- You have at least a part of your staff on your side before the wider communication.

You also want general feedback from the second category of employees:

- What do they think?
- Is anything missing that they think is important? (If they suggest something, ask whether they're willing to take that on.)
- Do they have suggestions to improve the plan?
- What interests them? What part would they like to be involved in?

Often only vocal employees are forthcoming in general meetings; yet the more reticent may well have great insights. Consider having a suggestion box open for a week, or invite individuals to stop by your office or call you if they 'think of something later'.

Here are two things not to do:

- **Don't try and sell your plan as if the plan is rock solid.** Tell your people that you're making moves to prepare for growth and expansion and you're going to start introducing new tactics and measures to see how things go. Tell them that the next three months are going to be a pilot, that you're open to their feedback and ideas, and that the plan will be adjusted at the end of three months and further on.

- **Don't roll out an incentive or bonus plan until your tactics are established and starting to show initial results.** Tell people whether you're planning an incentive plan and that you'll share more information in three months' time.

## Getting the team going

Most people are excited and energized as a plan approaches implementation. Here are some things to do as you launch into action:

- Do a final update on your plan based on the feedback you've had.

- Choose pilot tactics/tasks wisely. They need to contribute directly to the goals and you need to run them for a minimum of six months, with a review at three to see whether anything needs adjusting.

- Make sure that all team members know what they're accountable for, what you're asking them to do, what they need to report on and when to ask for help or raise an alarm. Create a team culture of open communication and questioning: everyone is capable, everyone is an equal contributor; explain that your plan is a pilot and won't be perfect. 'Your company needs YOU!'

- Ensure that the tools are identified and going into place. You may need new spreadsheets, a shared area for files, other systems, better hardware (maybe get the team excited by giving them a new smartphone or tablet device). Little things can mean a lot. Above all, supply the team with the tools they ask for to do the job (within reason).

- Enforce monitoring. Everyone on the team and everyone who reports to them for this purpose *must* provide the data that you need to track how things are going. Your team members also need to inspect the work. Ask questions, provide advice and coach other staff. Start small and spend time making sure that you're doing it right. As you grow, these practices extend across the wider company – tweaking them later is easier.

✔ If something isn't working, deal with it right away. If a problem is ignored or a faulty practice is allowed to continue, it becomes 'how we do things' quickly. Don't let it become ingrained.

✔ If you're asking people to take on a lot more work (such as a designer to update your brochure or your senior project manager to do some serious number crunching every month), see what you can take off their shoulders, or set a deadline for when it will be done or when they'll get help (such as the end of the pilot). Many people willingly work harder and longer hours for a short while, but don't expect it consistently.

Within six months, you know where you are as a business and whether your numbers are on track. You've probably made some improvements that are ratcheting up your results and identified gaps and issues that you need to tackle in the next version of the plan.

Monitor your people. Over time, you come to rely on them more and more for your success. Make sure that they're enjoying what they're doing, feeling like they're contributing, and that they're valued and appropriately compensated. Give them progressively more responsibility. Your company isn't a pyramid scheme, but the more you trickle down the responsibility for results, the better you do personally.

## *Considering a few final thoughts as the plan takes off*

Keep your eye on the goals and milestones while implementing your plan (see the earlier section 'Setting milestones, tactics and metrics'). You built it to drive them and now you need to monitor your business and work the plan. The more you measure, the more you expose issues. That's a good thing because when you know they exist, you can handle them; if you don't, however, they grow with your business and cause a disaster later.

Business growth requires more than simply selling and delivering more projects: things don't work that way. Growth brings its own challenges and impacts every part of the business (see the sidebar 'Keeping ambitions realistic'). Be ambitious, yet cautious. Be willing to ask for help and get advice from people who've traveled this path before you.

You're starting with a modest plan, built on past performance and driving bigger results. What's good about this approach is that you're creating the foundation for a solid future while you start to extend your approach.

## Keeping ambitions realistic

Alan decided that small projects with low profitability were the root of his business problems. He had to work hard to get new customers, they paid relatively little and expected miracles. His clients were mostly small companies, but when he'd worked with larger companies in previous jobs, they were more realistic, less naïve and had deeper pockets.

He hired a sales person from a competitor to bring in bigger customers. Within three months, the new guy found an opportunity, worked with the team to create a proposal with a great big budget. They won the deal – it was five times larger than anything Alan's company had ever

done. Unfortunately, Alan soon discovered that how his team went about doing the work was too informal. The project was more complex, needing more planning upfront and more formal management all the way through. The project got done but was three months late, the profitability was low and the morale of the team was in the toilet.

He couldn't blame the sales guy – Alan got what he'd asked for, but if he'd stepped back on winning the deal and considered who to ask for advice, he might have thought things through and made the win a real win – for everyone.

# Managing Risk while Implementing Your Plan

You're not going to experience only 'ups' when putting your business development plan into action: ups at some moments inevitably mean downs at other times. Sometimes these downs are outside your control, but great companies succeed even in the face of setbacks.

Risks are unpredictable, but that doesn't mean that you can't begin to guess where problems can arise. Fortunately, thousands of businesses have trodden the path before you and you can discover a lot from their issues and mistakes. Planning for risks is an important business development activity and allows you to see problems coming, while you can do something about them. Well, sometimes.

## Thinking the unthinkable: What can possibly go wrong?

Lots of occurrences can cause problems with plan implementation, but at the core three things can throw you off course. Check out Table 7-3 for what to do.

**Table 7-3     Three Things that Can Throw Your Plan Off Balance**

| What Can Happen | Consider | What to Do |
|---|---|---|
| You have difficulty implementing your plan. | Is it too complex?<br><br>Are people resisting the work?<br><br>Are people resisting the measurement?<br><br>Are there just not enough hours in the day? | Ask team members what they think would make the plan easier. Then think about:<br><br>• Simplifying the plan<br><br>• Tweaking the tactics<br><br>• Streamlining the measurement<br><br>• Coaching/changing staff<br><br>• Eliminating non-essential activities |
| You don't see satisfactory performance and/ or improvement in your metrics. | Where is the underperformance?<br><br>Why is it happening?<br><br>Who's responsible?<br><br>What needs adjusting? | Strategize with your managers for solutions. Consider whether you have the right tactic, being delivered by the right person and being managed well. |
| Something disastrous happens (such as losing your biggest customer). | Learn from what happened. Apply 'panic now' tactics (see Chapter 13). Scale back your plan and goals. Make tough decisions. | Crisis is hard to deal with. Try to think clearly and keep communicating. Be a problem-solver. |

## *Dealing with large challenges*

Plenty of events can overwhelm a business: the economy, natural disaster, the competition, emerging technologies, customers being unpredictable.

To discover which of these challenges you really have no control over, consider these questions:

- ✔ Do you have a recession-proof offer?
- ✔ Do you have a disaster-recovery plan?

✔ Can you manage the competition?

✔ Can you keep on top of technology changes?

✔ Can you get the right customers?

You can plan around these challenges, although doing so takes time and you don't have a whole load of that. A day's retreat with the senior team can nail a couple of these issues, so that when/if they happen you know what to do.

The bottom-line question is how responsible are you willing to be to make your business a success? Everyone wants things to be easy, but sometimes they just ain't. How you respond when things are against you is what makes you a great leader.

Businesses are vulnerable in the early years and when revenue is low, so your top priority is to grow as fast as is reasonable to the point where you have a cushion against the big challenges.

# Part III
# Making the Most of Marketing

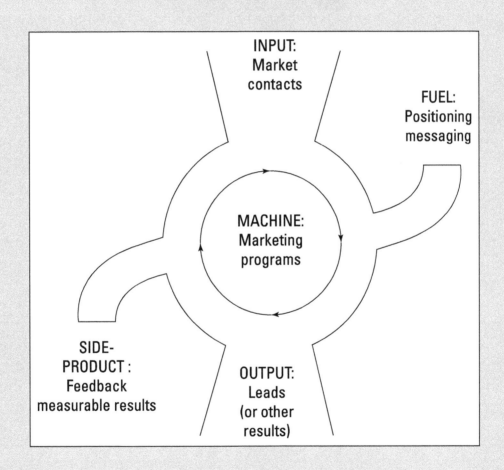

To read about the importance of building a powerful marketing operation, go to www. dummies.com/extras/businessdevelopment.

## In this part . . .

- ✔ Get your message out to the marketplace.
- ✔ Build a powerful marketing engine that covers traditional and innovative bases.
- ✔ Create an ideal marketing plan that meets all your needs.
- ✔ Discover and use demand-generation tools.
- ✔ Ensure that marketing and sales work together as a team.

# Chapter 8

# Appreciating the Benefits of Marketing for Your Business

*In This Chapter*

▶ Welcoming a new era of sales-orientated marketing

▶ Putting marketing to use as part of business development

▶ Considering whether you need branding

*N*ot that long ago, many people thought of marketing as being 'fluffy', of no real substance. When times were good, spending money on fluffy stuff was okay – but when money was tight, marketing staff were the first to go. But the times, they are a-changing.

At the root of that change is technology; at the epicenter is the connected individual. From my couch, I can log onto the web at the drop of a hat, finding out pretty much anything I want to know and then asking my private and business networks what they think. I bet you I can find a new apartment, view it, submit all the paperwork, order furniture, get services turned on and arrange a moving firm, all without leaving that couch. Well, maybe on moving day I'd have to haul my backside out of the chair.

But the Internet isn't only a massive information source – it's also where transactions happen and, increasingly, where prospective customers research services. Buyers expect to get to know your business online and they make judgments about it without ever talking to you.

Statistics vary as to how much of the business-to-business (B2B) buying cycle happens online these days, but for sure the percentage is certainly rising, with some estimates putting it as high as 60 per cent. That's why marketing matters and why you need to include it as part of your business development plan. In fact, your business really must engage in marketing if you don't want to get left behind.

In this chapter, I introduce you to practical and pragmatic marketing for a services firm, as well as describe the wide variety of marketing channels available that are relevant to services firms. I also demystify the mysterious concept of branding – businesses that is, you'll be glad to know, not livestock.

# Working Together in Harmony: Marketing and Sales

A myth exists that business development *is* sales (Chapter 1 explains why that's so widely off the mark). Business development concerns itself with the *entire* customer experience and more (check out Figure 2-1 for the customer side and Figure 3-1 for the business development lifecycle).

Marketing deals with buyers who're considering *whether* to buy, sales deals with buyers who know that they *will* buy. Therefore, marketing is the public face of your company. It creates the message of who you are, what you do to solve business problems and the value that you offer to your customers. In addition, marketing influences the pre-contract phase a lot, including making sales much easier, while feeding from the post-contract phase. Therefore, as I discuss in this section, marketing needs to work alongside and in collaboration with sales.

With your marketing spectacles on for a moment (check in the mirror that they're flattering, of course!), view the lifecycle through the eyes of marketing using Figure 8-1. Consider what marketing is thinking at each stage.

The job of marketing is to provide the messaging that goes out to the market, no matter what the *channel* (the vehicle that you use to communicate with the market and to generate leads). That messaging includes your firm's:

- Website
- Collateral (brochures and other stuff like that)
- Events
- Sales presentations
- Mass emails
- Advertising (offline and online)
- Image, wherever you show up in person

If marketing is doing its job, the work of sales is easier, more focused, more streamlined and more effective.

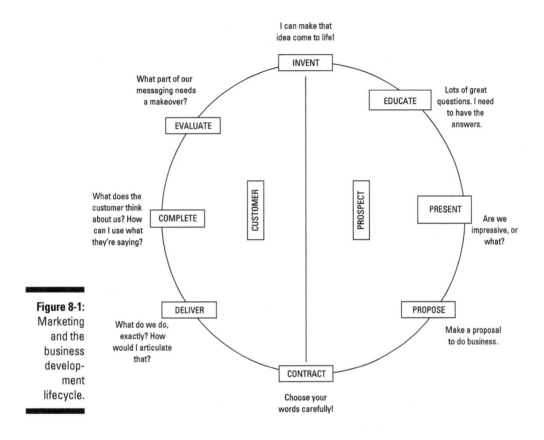

**Figure 8-1:** Marketing and the business development lifecycle.

# *Enjoying the perfect relationship (not!): Marketing and sales*

Marketing and sales typically have plenty to say about each other. Marketing says:

> *Sales is 'flying by the seat of their pants'. They make it up as they go along. They go 'off brand' all the time. They keep shoving things down the customer's throat before they're ready. They'll say anything to get a deal. It's like the Wild West out there.*

Sales says:

> *I need leads that are ready to buy. Where are they? What's marketing doing? 'Fannying around with the press releases' [to quote Bridget Jones's Diary, The Movie]. Nurturing, my eye – what's the point of that?*

The relationship has been confrontational for a long time. One of the reasons is that marketing isn't a quick fix and sales wants quick fixes. In reality, whether you think you're doing marketing today or not (in other words, whether you do or don't have a formal marketing role in your company), sales is spending time writing stuff so that the company can present itself credibly. Sometimes what sales creates is okay, sometimes really bad. Almost always the copy is created on an as-needed basis and thought of by sales as a necessary evil. Either way, sales doesn't have time for 'real' marketing.

Aligning sales and marketing is a common thread in really successful services firms. Doing so is not an option, but a necessity.

## Making your marketing sales-oriented

I think that everyone agrees that you can't grow your business without sales. Small firms have to fight for every deal, and being a salesperson is a really thankless job. I put it in the 'what have you done for me today?' category. You're not even as good as your last deal – you're only as good as the one you're about to close.

As the company grows, you want to shift to a 'large and thriving' position that looks like Table 8-1.

| Table 8-1 | Market View of Smaller and Larger Firms |
|---|---|
| *Small, Stable and Fighting* | *Large and Thriving* |
| Not well known. | People have heard of you. |
| The list of past customers may be small (evidence of competence is thin). | You have an impressive portfolio. |
| The phone isn't ringing. | Prospects are calling you. |

Marketing is the function that gets you from column 1 to column 2 in the table (and gives the salespeople a look in: yes, they're important too!). The point is that sales has great difficulty selling while simultaneously driving the company's business in the right direction. In the most enlightened organizations, marketing has a place at the top table, because marketing is the function that takes the business strategy and turns it into real actions that build your firm's recognition and reputation in the marketplace.

### Reaching parts that sales alone can't reach

Here's a back-of-the-envelope exercise that is nevertheless very useful. Take a look at Table 8-2, which extends the idea of growing from a smaller to a larger firm (say, $2 million (£1.26 million) to $20 million (£12.6 million), but by all means make up your own numbers). My model is simplistic: you get a customer, you do your work and you pile up revenue. Your projects are one-time and you have to replace your business every year with new customers. So, to grow you just have to scale the numbers, right? Note the challenges you see in moving from small to large.

| Table 8-2 | **Moving From Small Firm to Large** |
|---|---|
| *Small ($2 Million/£1.26 million)* | *Large ($20 Million/£12.6 Million)* |
| Average deal size is $100,000 (£63,000). | Average deal size is $100,000 (£63,000). |
| Number of projects per year = 20. | Number of projects per year = 200. |
| Most of your customers are existing contacts (your network) or referrals. | Most of your customers are 'strangers'. |
| Investment in business development is $100,000 (£63,000) (5% of revenue). | Investment in business development is $1.5 million (£945,000) (7.5% of revenue). |
| Number of salespeople = 1. Commission rate is 3%. | Number of salespeople = 10. Commission rate is 5%. |
| Vice President of Sales? No. | Vice President of Sales? Yes (someone has to manage all those salespeople). |

Here are some questions that may well have occurred to you:

- Handling 200 projects a year while maintaining quality? Yikes!
- Ten salespeople? Is that much business out there? Will they meet their sales targets?
- How do I find time to keep an eye on all those *metrics* (the target numbers you track to make sure that activities are being done)?

You may conclude that doing more of the same (scaling up) doesn't work. I agree. You end up with an unmanageable organization or you plateau at a certain revenue.

Alternatively, you can expand your geographic reach (that is, increase the size of your marketplace), increase your deal size, or try to get more sales of higher revenue with fewer salespeople. You can consider any of or all these options.

Without doubt, marketing can action your strategy, increasing your reach, recognition and revenue compared to using sales alone.

Here's why:

- ✔ Salespeople can only do so much in a day.
- ✔ Marketing can use high-volume tactics to get out in front of more people.
- ✔ Marketing can nurture leads that may become prospects but are currently some months, even years, from buying.

Sales needs to cozy up to marketing and look to them to work a few well-chosen channels and help produce a healthy stream of leads. Chapter 9 focuses in more detail on how effective marketing helps sales and can act as a fundamental driver to the growth of your business.

### Funnelling more leads with marketing

Marketing is clearly no longer all fluff and no substance – not these days. Modern marketing is in the business of driving leads: in the end, the staff are on the hook for a result, just like sales. Their job is to attract the market to the company, wrap themselves around sales and make sales as efficient as possible.

How does marketing do this? Imagine that a salesperson can handle 20 opportunities simultaneously and has to have conversations with a minimum of 100 contacts in his network, or from referrals or any other lead sources he currently uses, to get those 20 opportunities. The salesperson's view of his job is like Figure 8-2: constantly working to convert leads into prospects at the top of the funnel and then to push them down the funnel to a close. Read the sidebar 'To funnel or not to funnel' for some views on this funnel model.

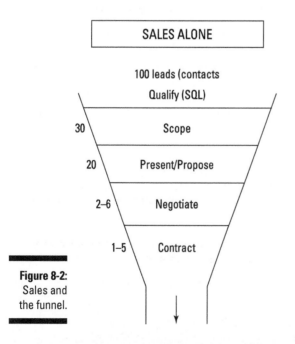

**Figure 8-2:** Sales and the funnel.

From Figures 8-2 and 8-3, what marketing calls a lead (an MQL or marketing-qualified lead) may not align with what sales thinks a lead looks like (SQL or sales-qualified lead). Expect sales to throw back some leads as not 'sales ready'. Sales is looking for leads (SQLs) that are ready to buy within a reasonably short timeframe; marketing is scoring leads based on how they're interacting with marketing campaigns. These different criteria explain the gap.

Salespeople typically use channels such as attending local events, calling on their network from prior jobs, asking people for referrals, working with partners, using social media to get introductions, cold calling local companies – all to produce leads that they can convert into prospects.

Marketing can use more channels, more technology and more automation to reach much wider, as in Figure 8-3.

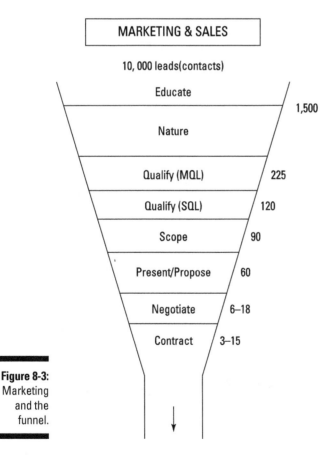

| MARKETING & SALES |
| --- |

10, 000 leads(contacts)

Educate

1,500

Nature

Qualify (MQL) — 225

Qualify (SQL) — 120

Scope — 90

Present/Propose — 60

Negotiate — 6–18

Contract — 3–15

**Figure 8-3:**
Marketing
and the
funnel.

### To funnel or not to funnel

The funnel model has been around for nearly 100 years and not everyone subscribes to it anymore. The problem is that it treats the customer-buying journey as if it's consistent or linear, whereas these days it seems much more erratic, with customers jumping from social media to websites to webinars to blogs and being in the middle of the funnel when they first encounter you. What they're doing, though, remains consistent with the stage in the buying cycle that they're at – they just happen to have a lot more channels available to get information.

To my mind, therefore, the funnel is still a worthwhile model – at least until someone comes up with a really good replacement. The debate rages online if you're interested: just Google 'is the sales funnel dead'.

Now you've enough leads for three salespeople. You've a great big funnel on top of a narrower one, with a steady stream of leads (those marketing qualified leads) to the sales team. For more on how this is done in practice, check out Chapters 11 and 12.

Historically, in business-to-business sales, marketing has been seen as nice to have, rather than the necessity is actually is. *Mad Men* adverts for the latest perfume are all very well – that's consumer marketing. These days, though, marketing has the technical power to become part of the engine of growth: and this power is happening right now. Make sure that you understand marketing so that you can use it when the time is right and not get left behind (Chapter 11 has loads more information).

When is the right time to start serious marketing? You may think that the answer is when your sales tactics can no longer keep up with your hunger for prospects, but actually the right time is about a year before that. Marketing isn't a quick fix – marketing is a long-term strategy and a key function of business development. You need to invest before you see returns. Having said that, you can take some early marketing steps before you get all sophisticated, some of which I describe in the next section, to get you jump-started.

# Setting Out Your Stall: Marketing for Services Firms

Marketing is a daily experience for people these days. Every day, you're bombarded with messages intended to influence you into making a purchase. It can be extremely subtle – savvy marketing can sell you something without you knowing you're being sold to. As a consumer, if you're buying something complex or high-ticket (such as a car or the latest tablet device), the retailer typically needs salespeople to help you make the right choice. With smaller purchases, you don't always need salespeople. Marketing can do the whole job, from the first twinkle in the eye to the final purchase. QED.

When a customer buys for his company, the money isn't his own and the consequences of getting it wrong can be serious. The B2B buying cycle is often long, with many people contributing to the decision. In B2B, the sale is just more complex.

The same applies – only more so – for services. In B2B product sales, the process can be much more like B2C (business-to-consumer), unless the product is also very complex or needs a hefty dose of services to implement.

In this section I cover marketing basics to consider as part of your business development, such as choosing techniques that work for you, creating a successful team, understanding the vitally important role of technology and the importance of using your contacts and building partnerships.

## *Selecting the best marketing techniques for you*

You spend a lot of time enticing customers to buy, and so you'd better invest your time and money in the right marketing tactics and channels for you and your company.

Start by working out:

- ✔ Where your customers are to be found
- ✔ What information they need
- ✔ Why they need it
- ✔ Where they go to get answers (publications, events, websites, influencers and so on)

Use your customer profile, your research from Chapters 3 and 4, and your (thoughtful) analysis of their needs and your offer from Chapter 5. You're then well prepared to start thinking about how to use marketing.

You have to have the foundation before you can build the marketing bridge that contacts can walk across to become leads and then serious prospects/customers. At the very minimum, you need the pillars in Figure 8-4.

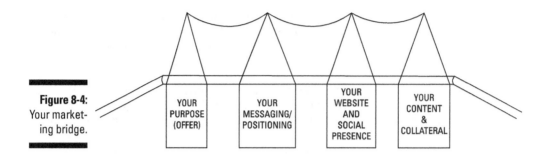

**Figure 8-4:**
Your market-
ing bridge.

Your four pillars are:

- ✔ Clarity about what problems you solve and what you offer
- ✔ A consistent way of talking about your offer and services
- ✔ A website that tells your story more fully – in other words that's clear about what you do and helps customers understand why they may need you
- ✔ Some basic collateral and possibly broader content, such as a brochure, services sheets (if you've more than one service or serve different industries), testimonials/customer stories (case studies), white papers and ebooks

You may have all these and more. Even so, step back and ask yourself whether your foundational pieces are actually talking to the customer and making clear how you can fulfill the customer's need.

## Energizing your team

If you need to do work on your foundational pieces (see the preceding section), or if you don't know where to start, go to your internal team. Assemble people from all around the business development lifecycle: representatives of leadership, marketing, sales, delivery, quality and administration all have something to say.

Prepare for your meeting as follows:

- ✔ **Create a title for your meeting:** For example, 'The Health of Our Marketing'.
- ✔ **Set a clear brief for marketing:** For example, 'To position our company, educate, inform and communicate with our market, inspire and support our leads, prospects, customers and employees'.

✔ **Create an agenda:** Consider what customers need at each stage of the lifecycle (that marketing can deliver):

– When they're educating themselves

– When they first talk to us

– When we're giving them a proposal

– When we're at contract stage

– When we're delivering the work

– When we're completing the work

You'll be amazed at what comes up at the meeting.

Bill was trying to improve upselling to his customers. When he sold a specific service, he tended to get 'pigeonholed', that is, the customers didn't know that his company did anything else. When he consulted with his team, his delivery folks suggested two things:

1. **To get really good case studies (the salespeople get them, why don't we?).**

2. **To put customers on an email list for a newsletter to tell them more about the company, our ideas, all the things we do, how we help.**

Bill passed case studies to his delivery team right away and had his assistant start working on a newsletter format and list. Within two months, he'd sold a new service to two of his existing customers.

Get feedback from your team and use it to set some immediate priorities (because you'll have more ideas than you know what to do with). Make the ongoing effort a two-way street – get your team to send you anything that the customer says or puts in an email about your company, what it needs next, who it likes working with and so on. Marketing, like Number 5 in the film *Short Circuit,* needs *input.* Your customers can provide that input:

✔ Testimonials

✔ Accolades for individual staff members or the whole team

✔ Case studies

✔ Opportunities for more business

Think about what's needed for your customers to do more business with you. Also, consider what would make it easy for your customers to refer you to other prospects in their network? A little stack of postcards with your information? An email or newsletter they can forward to someone else? Don't be shy to ask for their help.

If a team get-together is impractical, you can do your own brainstorming. You need to take every point around the lifecycle into account, thinking from your team members' perspectives.

## *Using your network*

I mention the importance of your contacts in a number of places throughout this book. From a marketing perspective, your network and the networks of your whole company – and the network of all those networks combined – is your secret marketing weapon. So how do you leverage that extended community?

To start, you want to analyze what your network looks like. I hope you're on LinkedIn and that you're connected to everyone you know in your business community (and probably to some people you don't know too).

If you're not on LinkedIn yet, get a copy of *LinkedIn For Dummies* by Joel Elad (Wiley) or consult the LinkedIn Cheat Sheet at www.dummies.com/cheatsheet/linkedin and get set up within the next seven days. Take a look at other companies like yours and see what they're saying about themselves. Then look at some larger companies in your space or close by (I call them 'aspirational'). Craft your company profile and your personal profile. Start searching for people to connect with (LinkedIn has ways of making connecting easy). Look for some groups to join. You can do the same steps for other social networks later, but LinkedIn is the most important and most likely to lead to results faster. If you've no idea where to start, collar a 20-something and ask for help – that's if they've a collar handy.

Start reviewing the people and firms that you're connected to, whether online or offline, and see which contacts are most promising as potential marketers for your services. They're the ones who:

- ✔ Have a lot of connections who may be prospects for you
- ✔ Would be willing to share your information with others in their network

Your message has to be pretty compelling (that is, it has to pass the 'Really? You do that?' test). If you think that your message is not yet quite that gripping, check out Chapter 5 and get it honed to a sharp edge.

Narrow your network down to 5–10 people who are active, well connected and respected. You may want a mix of:

- ✔ *Mavens,* namely experts in their fields known for sharing knowledge
- ✔ Companies you need services from and may be able to provide service to

✔ People with the job titles you want to connect to

✔ High-profile speakers and business networkers

Ask them for some of their time. Tell them about your business expansion plans and your latest clients. Ask about theirs. Ask what they think you should do. Ask what you can do to help them.

Go to a networking meeting with them and get into their network – always follow up if they give you a referral and thank them if they help you. Work these 5–10 contacts for 3–6 months; at that point, you'll have witnessed some great practices from these leaders (and some things not to do), and you're ready for social marketing (see Chapter 10 to plan that).

Including companies you may need services from allows you the potential to barter for services as long as they need something you offer. Try to include a good marketing firm that's worked with companies like yours, if you can. Just be sure that the contact you're using is one you know and trust not to try to sell you something you can't afford right now.

## Forming partnerships and alliances

Some of your network (see the preceding section) may include partners or alliances. Partnerships typically fall into two categories as shown in Table 8-3.

| Table 8-3 | Why Partnerships Are Valuable |
|---|---|
| *Category of Partnership* | *Benefits* |
| Companies who do something adjacent to what you do, but are minimally competitive with you. Perhaps they sell services that have to be done before (or alongside, or after) yours. | You can potentially sell bigger deals together. You can refer work to each other. |
| They offer a product that you implement or that you're considering implementing to extend your services. | They're a source of leads (or can be). They may promote you or have marketing dollars to allocate to you so that you can promote yourself. |

Select 1–2 of your top partners to court and nurture, and seriously work the relationships – partnerships are about the people, not about whole companies. Use what they have (ethically) where you can – their network, their database

of contacts, their marketing and their collateral. With partners, you're going for a win-win, and so engaging with them isn't too hard. You can bet a lot of other firms are waiting around for leads, but not being proactive with their partnerships.

*Alliances* are business relationships that often started as a partnership, but deepened into a more formal agreement. Where you detect a desire to improve customer service, share costs, do work together on a regular basis or leverage each other's assets, an alliance, which often has a formal legal basis, can be a good move. They're more common with larger companies where the parties have something highly valuable to offer each other.

I devote Part VI of this book to partnerships, so that's the place to look if the issue of partnerships is an important channel for you.

Some companies are very resistant to partnerships where they have to 'give away' business. They want to keep all the goodies for themselves, even if that means trying to do work they're not best qualified to do. My experience is that companies that share work, partner and expand their networks with a willingness to contribute to others, with no agenda, are the ones that expand. After all, if someone points you to a large lucrative contract, wouldn't you try and see what you can do in return? Give someone something and you put them under an obligation to reciprocate. Believe me, they'll want to.

## *Understanding technology and the online dimension*

More and more people are using the Internet to make purchasing transactions. Right down to your pizza for Friday night, you're probably spending time online as part of that process. In addition, prospective customers are increasingly researching services online.

Statistics indicate that most prospects are 66 percent of their way through the buying process by the time they connect with you other than in cyberspace – leaving you with a 33 percent window to make the sale.

Marketing departments have figured out that if they can get at the buyers in the 66 percent, give them what they're looking for and build trust at a one-to-one level, the value of marketing to the organization skyrockets.

A short time ago, marketing was fairly simple: you had your website, banner advertisements, search results, blogs and webinars. Now the online map is very complex and online/offline are integrating in highly creative ways. Figure 8-5 shows a highly simplified online map.

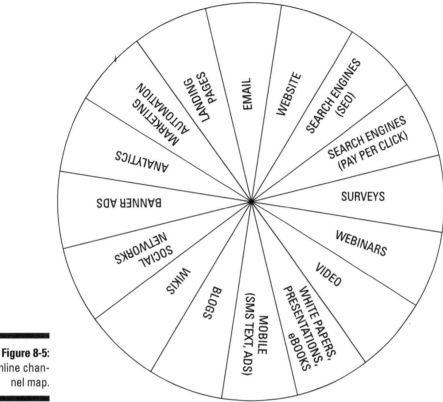

**Figure 8-5:**
Online chan-
nel map.

Now that you're officially overwhelmed (I get that way every time I look at a diagram, even one as highly simplified as this one), you need to get to the basics and figure out where online your prospects hang out, your competitors engage and your partners show up:

✔ Use LinkedIn (see the earlier section 'Using your network'), and maybe Twitter too, to track individuals and see what groups they belong to, who/what they're following, how active they are.

✔ Search to find out what forums, publishing sites and blogs they're likely to be reading/contributing to.

✔ Search to find out where prospects may be going when they're trying to fix their problem (the one you solve). Which websites, blogs and forums, LinkedIn groups do they visit and what are they reading?

Create your own online map. It may look something like Figure 8-6. Note that I've added an offline dimension too, because offline channels are online now too! Go find them. For example, if you have a local Chamber of Commerce, is it a potential channel for you? What is it doing online?

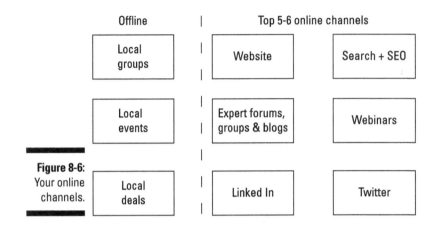

**Figure 8-6:**
Your online
channels.

Choose three to six online channels that you think may have potential for you, now or down the road. Explore what's happening in your local community too – such as perhaps joining local groups, attending local events or offering special deals to local customers. In the US, the boards of non-profit companies are also a great place to meet and nurture local contacts of note.

As with LinkedIn, *For Dummies* has a book and cheat sheet for Twitter too. If hash tags have you all confused, get a copy of *Twitter For Dummies* by Laura Fitton, Michael E Gruen and Leslie Poston or *Twitter Marketing For Dummies* by Kyle Lacy (both Wiley).

## Finding some quick wins in marketing

Planning marketing is definitely a challenge for people who didn't study it in college or university. But you can score quick wins in some areas without reading umpteen books or spending a lot of money. Here are three areas to look at:

- ✔ **Getting some outbound emails going:** Take a look at incoming marketing emails for a period of time. What do you instantly delete? What do you bother to read? Get registered with an email service such as Constant Contact, iContact or MailChimp. Create a simple newsletter (it can simply take the form of an update from you – just make sure that the content is likely to be interesting to your audience). Compile a customer email list and start by sending something out to customers every couple of months. Chances are that you get some reaction from a few of them – while you're building your confidence about using the email system. You'll need to be very confident in using email marketing later.

✓ **Creating some content that can be useful to sales immediately:** When you have a prospect, what's going to help push the sale along? Do you have great questionnaires for gathering the prospect's details? Do you have industry specific stories that you can write? Have you done things for specific prospects as a one-off that may be worth creating as a template (such as a return-on-investment calculator). These customer-centered sales aids are pieces that marketing should prepare, or at least help sales with.

✓ **Boosting your LinkedIn visibility:** People respond to LinkedIn emails much more than they do to regular email. You just need to get connected:

– Get well established on LinkedIn (your own and company profiles). If you need help, check out the earlier section 'Using your network'.

– Start building your network. Be choosy; don't just connect to everyone.

– Use LinkedIn to research every contact you're about to talk to or meet in person. Connect to them just before meeting them or immediately afterwards.

– Move to doing occasional status updates on your own profile or your company profile, maybe weekly or every other week.

– Join some groups. Stay focused and keep things light to start with. Get a sense of which groups are worth the time before you start contributing.

– Create standard email text for request-to-connect messages and for InMail emails (LinkedIn's own internal email system).

– Elevate your account to a paid level – you see much more information and can go beyond your direct network.

Like any tactics, these ones work only if you follow through and do them rigorously.

With any electronic communication, make sure that you follow the rules. LinkedIn, Twitter and email communications all have their own etiquette and legal restrictions, so read those terms and conditions before you jump in with both feet.

If the three approaches in the list aren't for you, choose some others. One thing's for sure – plenty of options are out there!

# Deciding whether Your Firm Needs Branding

For a lot of small businesses, the idea of even considering 'brand' as a concept may seem laughable. After all, don't only big companies spend lots of money creating a brand?

If you're unsure whether you need to think about your brand as part of business development, consider that an important responsibility as your business grows is to take care of your positioning in the marketplace. When the market isn't clear about your offer, you have a problem. You end up talking to a lot of people who want something like your services, but not exactly your services, or end up delivering what you thought customers wanted when they were expecting something else.

In this section, I help you decide whether branding is for you.

## Understanding the importance of brands

In Chapter 5, I suggest that when customers buy your services, they're buying a lot more than their immediate or obvious need dictates. An emotional/psychological dimension is always attached to a purchase, and usually this dimension is hidden.

I see brand as creating emotional associations between you and your customers. You can find a lot of definitions, but here's one that works well:

> *Brand is a promise. By identifying and authenticating a product or service it delivers a pledge of satisfaction and quality.*
>
> — *Walter Landor*

Of course, identifying the promise behind a burger or a car, a spa massage or a visit to Disneyland is fairly easy. Identifying the promise of a service to a business can be a bit trickier, but it's a valuable exercise nevertheless.

Whether you need to worry about brand today, or in the future, depends on where you are in your business's evolution. For a young company (say less than three years old), you don't have enough track record, enough consistency, to build a reliable brand, unless your services are very straightforward and the value is very easy to articulate. As you mature, you should be better able put into words what you stand for.

Working on your brand becomes important when you start extending the awareness of your company, to partners, local and national business leaders, and when you start speaking at local events, advertising, creating and developing your online presence.

## Identifying yourself with a brand

A brand needs to convey utility and be emotionally fulfilling at the same time. It needs to represent company ethos, values, capabilities and ways of doing things. Above all, it needs to communicate to customers an honest representation of who you are.

If, when your company name comes up in conversation, people say, 'Never heard of them; what do they do?', you've a blank slate for creating your brand. Your customers and a few prior prospects know who you are and that's about it. If pre-conceived notions exist about who you are, things are a little harder but shifting ideas is always possible.

In creating your brand, you're trying to shift the conversation from 'I've never heard of them' to 'They're the company that . . . ' to 'I've heard they're really good at . . . '.

Jan's company is known for exemplary services to its customers. The delivery team makes sure that customers have a great experience. Deep in the ethic of the company is that the firm bends over backwards to make customers happy, so when it created the brand message, it was encapsulated in 'A better experience'. The company can honestly say that it delivers that in every aspect of its services. Nine out of ten of the firm's customers give it referrals that turn into new customers. Now that's a powerful brand.

I can't do justice to brand building in a couple of pages, but a *For Dummies* book does. Although dealing primarily with consumer-facing brands, *Branding For Dummies* by Bill Chiaravalle and Barbara Findlay Schenck (Wiley) walks you through everything you need to know about brand building.

## Marketing your brand

Ultimately, everything that goes out into the marketplace with your name on it needs to be consistent with your brand. You also have to live up to the promise of your brand in everything you do:

✔ **Do:** Get everyone inside the company to buy into the brand promise and to uphold it in everything they do.

✔ **Don't:** Tinker with it. When you have a brand, stick with it.

Creating a brand normally requires some outside help, so expect to spend several tens of thousands of dollars on that help.

# Chapter 9

# Driving Sales Success with Effective Marketing

*G*etting results for your business requires an alignment with your customers around the customer experience, as in Figure 2-1. Problem is, in the early stages, you don't know them well – so how can you know what they're thinking; what do you put in front of them; and what do you say to them? Fortunately, two well-developed disciplines can help you answer these questions: marketing and sales. Like two sides of a coin, they're inextricably joined.

In small businesses, one person often executes marketing and sales – initially the owner, maybe later on a head of sales. Such firms may not even use the word marketing, but that's what they're doing a lot of the time. In fact, often businesses hire a salesperson long before considering hiring a marketing person. Unfortunately, this sequence has the potential to set up marketing as the unwanted child, always playing second fiddle to sales.

With business growth, the sales and marketing departments tend to get separated in an organization and sometimes don't communicate as well as they should. In the worst case, they don't talk the same language, they don't have the same goals, they have (often inaccurate) opinions about each other and they fight over who's really driving the results. I describe strategies for handling this problem in Chapter 12 – as you can imagine, the problem is important enough to deserve a chapter of its own.

In this chapter, I distinguish sales and marketing and focus on what marketing can do to make sales a hero. I look at how marketing and sales ideally relate to the customer lifecycle and the value that marketing can provide to sales and to your business as a whole.

# Revving up the Marketing Engine

The ultimate goal of marketing, as with any aspect of business development, is to drive revenue. Marketing contributes to that goal by taking responsibility for the following five key areas:

- **Market intelligence:** Investigating what's happening in the marketplace; who's buying what, when and how; the trends in your space; and what the marketplace is saying about your area of work.

- **Customer intelligence:** Gathering intelligence from your customers and prospects as a feedback loop.

- **Positioning and messaging:** Ensuring consistent, powerful and relevant positioning and messaging to the marketplace. Marketing is the guardian of your 'brand', whether this brand is fully developed or an internally agreed set of promises. Chapter 8 has more on branding.

- **Marketing programs:** Marketing develops and runs specific marketing *programs,* namely overarching marketing initiatives to fulfill on a specific strategy; and *campaigns,* namely individual marketing activities (such as email campaigns) that are part of the larger program. Marketing programs are initiatives designed from information gleaned from the three areas above that, when launched, reach out to the marketplace. They push out messaging, create awareness and create demand (namely leads).

- **Lead generation:** From marketing programs, sales gets qualified leads that it can develop into closed deals.

The first four areas above are the foundation for generating successful leads. Marketing needs to divide its time between these areas – neglect any one and the results are going to be less effective.

Marketing doesn't work in isolation: it's dependent on intelligence from a number of sources and feedback from programs to refine the approach constantly. Ultimately, if marketing isn't driving leads, whether directly or indirectly, it's not doing its job.

In this section I clarify the different, though complementary, roles of sales and marketing, how successful marketing works and what it requires to function at top efficiency.

## *Appreciating the differences between sales and marketing*

Whether marketing is being effective in generating leads is a complex issue. All too often, salespeople don't trust marketing to make a significant contribution to company results – they think that marketing is a waste of money. Marketing doesn't always appreciate that salespeople are on the hook for results.

As your business grows, you need to make sure that:

✔ Marketing and sales collaborate and communicate.

✔ Marketing and sales have shared goals and are clear as to individual accountabilities that contribute to the goal. That means having specific metrics, such as number of leads expected per month, conversions into opportunities and won deals.

✔ Marketing and sales each take responsibility for its portion of the results, which means being accountable and measurable. Sales is used to that – marketing less so. You're responsible for ensuring that it happens. Check out the later section "How will I know that marketing is achieving its goals?' Measuring marketing' for more.

Table 9-1 illustrates a few differences between marketing and sales that you need to take into account.

| Table 9-1 | Marketing and Sales – Key Differences |
| --- | --- |
| **Marketing** | **Sales** |
| Thinking is high-level and strategic, but becomes detail-oriented when executed | Tends to be detail-oriented |
| | Focused on individual opportunities, buyers and deals |
| Patient, thoughtful and willing to shift tactics gradually based on results | Impatient and nimble, with a tendency to create one-off approaches to get the result |
| Takes time to drive results – anticipate at least 12 months | Can drive quick results based on the salesperson's network |
| Wants broad input to design tactics | Responds to what's happening in the moment |
| When up and running, the marketing engine can perform consistently, producing leads for sales | After an early rush can tend to run out of opportunities unless additional channels are developed |
| Can scale to reach significant numbers of prospective customers | Can't scale and still do a thorough job on each opportunity |

If you're thinking that marketing and sales people have different personalities, you're right. Those personalities 'sell' their value rather differently. Salespeople tend to be particularly good at selling themselves – no surprise there! So beware: they can drown marketing's voice and opinions. Give marketing a chance to put its point of view – marketing people are worth listening to.

Marketing and sales are highly valuable disciplines, and when they appreciate each other's strengths and capabilities they can jointly produce significant results. But don't take my word for it: here are two expert quotes from the Sales Benchmark Index blog 'Top 5 priorities for CMO-CSO Alignment', January 2014 (CMO is chief marketing officer and in this context CSO is chief sales officer). According to the Aberdeen Group:

> *Highly aligned organizations achieved an average of 32% annual revenue growth – while less well-aligned companies reported an average 7% decline in revenue.*

Sirius Decision research reports similar findings:

> *B2B organizations with tightly aligned sales and marketing operations achieved 24% faster three-year revenue growth and 27% faster three-year profit growth.*

So the clear message is: get marketing and sales to work together. To start, clarify what marketing should be doing and how you're going to measure it. In Figure 8-1 I show how marketing thinks about the business development lifecycle – take a quick look at that figure.

Now check out Figure 9-1, a mini-lifecycle for marketing and sales. Marketing communicates with the whole marketplace (your prospective customers, partners and other parties that need to be aware of your business). Marketing's goal is to generate marketing-qualified leads (MQLs) to hand over to sales. Sales takes those leads and either works on converting them to prospects (that is, they qualify as sales-qualified leads, or SQLs) and then become customers) or hands them back to marketing as being not quite mature enough yet – I discuss this issue in Chapter 12.

Naturally, this description is a gross simplification, but if you keep this concept in your mind, you'll find making sure that marketing is doing the right things a whole lot easier.

## *Ensuring that marketing drives results*

Marketing can't just create leads out of nowhere. It needs to create a strategy for tackling the marketplace that's appropriate to your business. Smaller businesses don't usually have vast amounts of money to pour into marketing.

Therefore, you have to ensure that you choose the strategy and tactics carefully and that each has associated goals, metrics, feedback mechanisms and tangible results you can analyze to see whether your investment is paying off.

**Figure 9-1:**
The mini-lifecycle – marketing and sales (MQLs = marketing-qualified leads; SQLs = sales-qualified leads).

Having said that, don't expect immediate results from marketing. As I describe in Chapter 8, marketing has a much wider reach than sales and is dealing with significant complexity in designing its strategy. The department also takes care of a longer portion of the pre-contract phase (time-wise) than sales. For example, when your sales cycle (SQL to signed contract) is three months, your marketing cycle (contact/target customer to MQL) is probably 9–24 months.

So when it comes to lead generation, you need a hefty dose of patience and a willingness to invest despite being unsure about whether the investment is going to pay off.

Don't start a marketing effort and then pull out three months later. You have to give it at least 12 months before you start switching strategy. That doesn't mean that you can't tweak your tactics based on results, however – indeed, you should.

To discover the four essential areas that you need to consider before marketing can generate leads, check out the earlier 'Revving up the Marketing Engine' section.

## Tuning up the marketing engine

Marketing is like an engine that's designed to take an input and create an output. As Figure 9-2 shows, marketing needs fuel to drive the engine.

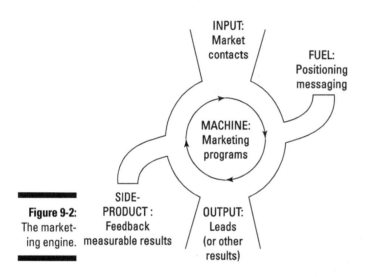

**Figure 9-2:** The marketing engine.

A side product from the marketing engine is the feedback from the marketplace and the measurability of the results. These outputs represent the all-important feedback loop.

Each time you design a marketing *program* (focused on specific business goals) and the *campaign* (the series of marketing activities designed to support the program), ensure that the engine has everything it needs to function well.

Imagine that you're an employment agency and that you offer services to help your customers be up-to-date with current employment legislation in your local area. Have a think about what sort of marketing program you'd construct to serve existing clients and attract new ones.

You have a lot of options – Figure 9-3 shows one possible program that uses a few channels to build up to a webinar and follow-up afterwards.

**Figure 9-3:**
A sample
marketing
program.

| Step # | Input | Campaign element | Fuel | Measurable result | Feedback |
|---|---|---|---|---|---|
| 1 | List of prospective customers | Email linking to a blog post | Information about the new legislation written as a blog (a) linking to a blog post and (b) providing an opportunity to contact us for more information. | - Email is opened<br>- User clicks through to the blog post | Unsubscribes<br>Direct replies |
| 2 | List of existing and past customers | Newsletter 'SPECIAL' with an excerpt from an article about the legislation (teaser). Links to the blog post. Lets customers know that there will be an upcoming webinar on the topic. | Information about the new legislation written as a blog (a) linking to a blog post and (b) providing an opportunity to contact us for more information. | - Email is opened<br>- User clicks through to the blog post | Unsubscribes<br>Direct replies |
| 3 | List of prospective, current and past customers | Email with details about an upcoming webinar 'How to implement the new legislation'. | Information about the webinar (who are the speakers, what will be covered, how to register) | - Email is opened<br>- User registers | Unsubscribes<br>Direct replies |
| 4 | Repeat step 3 two more times at weekly intervals. | | | | |
| 5 | Registered attendees | Webinar | Webinar content (slides etc.) | - Number of attendees | No shows<br>Survey results |
| 6 | Webinar attendees/no-shows | Email with link to a recording | Recorded webinar | - Email opens<br>- Click throughs/ views | Unsubscribes<br>Survey results |
| 7 | Webinar attendees/no-shows<br>Current or past customers | Call campaign | Script: anything further we can provide? | Number of calls where a connection was made | Requests for follow-up<br>Returned calls |

This simple program embodies a few key principles. To start, count up how many:

- ✔ Contacts you have in your original list.

- ✔ Emails that get opened.

- ✔ Click-throughs you get. In other words, if your email has a link to a web page (for example), your email marketing software is able to tell you who has 'clicked through' to that web page.

- ✔ People registered for the webinar.

- ✔ People who attended.

- ✔ People who viewed the webinar later.

- ✔ Follow-up calls that resulted in a conversation and how many of those wanted a further follow-up.

The intent of the program is to progress from awareness (creating a need for information/expert help) through to driving leads. If a call with a prospective customer resulted in that person asking for further help, this request is a clear opening to pass that lead to sales, which can bring in a subject-matter expert and see whether it can sell some services.

Sales and marketing should try to agree in advance what a qualified lead looks like. In some cases, sales only wants to talk to people who are some way into the buying cycle – other times, it wants to jump onto a vague interest, because it thinks it can convert that vague curiosity into a real opportunity. The key is to have marketing and sales collaborate over the design of programs. At the absolute minimum, make sure that you agree when lead handover is appropriate.

Marketing and sales use the term *BANT* to describe the perfect qualified lead – the person has *budget*, *authority*, *need* and *timing* that fit your criteria for an SQL.

Designing a program like the one in Figure 9-3 requires a lot more than creating hypothetical steps. If you have questions such as, 'Where's the list going to come from?', 'Who's going to write all those emails?', 'How do I put on a successful webinar?', you're no doubt aware of the large amount of work this kind of design can entail.

Right now, however, I just want you to get a sense of how a marketing engine works and what you need to be thinking about when you design programs.

Don't be overambitious when you start creating your own marketing strategy (see Chapter 10). Start small and learn from experience. You're trying to figure out what works for you.

## Carrying out the hard work of marketing

Before you can begin constructing a marketing program or its supporting campaigns, marketing needs to help you deepen your understanding of the market (check out Table 9-2).

| Table 9-2 | What Marketing Needs from You and What It Gives Back |
|---|---|
| **From You: Leadership, Sales, Delivery** | **From Marketing** |
| The profile(s) of the types of companies with which you want to do business. The roles in those companies that you typically interact with (see Chapter 5). | *Buyer Personas:* Description of people with specific roles, their interest and involvement in the buying cycle and their 'hot buttons' (what will compel them to move forward). Buyer personas may vary depending on the different services you're selling or the industry they come from. |
| How the sales cycle has played out historically. What does the buyer seem to need and at what stage in the process? (See Chapter 2.). | *Buyer Process Map:* The buyer's journey documented as a diagram or spreadsheet for each persona. It illustrates what triggers a buyer to move from one step to the next. |
| Any content you already have (for example, brochures, case studies, proposals, presentations, as well as customer reviews, emails with feedback – just about anything you can dig up). | *Content Marketing Plan:* To rationalize and extend content to serve all the needs shown in the Buyer Process Map. Over time to include all the content needed to support buyers in their processes and sales in selling to them. |
| What you're currently doing online or with your networks. | *Social Selling Strategy:* Contains data and insights from research. An approach to be used to support the buyers and sales. |
| How leads have been acquired up to now. Which are the strongest channels and what looks like a good bet to invest in? Plus, the history of wins and losses and why they've occurred. What criteria seem to result in a successful sale? What warning signs exist that a sale is unlikely? | *Programs and Campaigns:* For each stage in the buyer's journey; intended to drive lead generation. |

The engine can start running only when all this background work is done, programs are planned, content is written and systems are in place. Marketing is always looking to be several steps ahead of the buyers, and so it needs to create content that buyers value (and ideally wouldn't be able to find anywhere else). With so much information available online these days, writing engaging content is getting more and more difficult.

You know that you have the right team when you're proud of what you see coming out of marketing, even while you're asking, 'Where are my results?' If you're the one doing the marketing, keep extending and deepening your knowledge of it and the value it brings to your growing business. This way, when you do come to hire marketing people, you know what you're looking for.

# Setting Accountabilities between Sales and Marketing

Naturally you want your business to grow year after year. You probably already have a sense of where you're trying to end up in a year's time (read Chapter 6 for how to plan your numbers). Up to now, you may have operated on a wing and a prayer hoping that the coming year's results will be better than last year's, but without a plan for accomplishing that goal. If so, time to use some business development practices to strategize and then operate to fulfill your goals.

Say your goal is higher revenue, which translates into an accountability that salespeople call their *quota* – the net new sales they have to achieve this year. That number is on the shoulders of whoever is responsible for sales, or possibly split between sales and account/project managers who look after delivery to your clients. When things aren't on track, everyone scowls at the sales folks. I know what that feels like – I've been there. Fortunately, marketing is now able to take its share of the responsibility for generating leads, which the salespeople can convert into closed deals. As I describe in this section, marketing can be responsible for generating leads that drive a specific percentage of the number.

Driving leads isn't marketing's only goal. It also needs to research, inform and support sales and delivery to sell more.

# *What am I striving for? Establishing the goal*

In *Chapter 6*, I look at creating your goal(s) and some of the measures you can use to see whether you're staying on track. With marketing, you definitely want a few soft goals, but you also want the ultimate prize – qualified leads (I define the latter in the earlier section 'Appreciating the differences between sales and marketing').

Start with an overarching statement of your marketing priorities for the year, so that you, marketing and sales are aligned. I summarize here a couple of examples from two businesses (from the Hubspot research project '2014 Planning Insights from Marketers Like You'):

- ✔ If you can't measure a campaign or program, don't do it. You have to show ROI (return on investment) so that every marketing activity contributes to a business goal. Lead generation and conversion to a sale are the priority; providing relevant content throughout the customer journey is the tactic for driving leads and supporting conversions.

- ✔ Marketing efforts combine content with context consistently to deliver the right content to the right people at the right time. Increase your focus more on buyer personas, and deliver compelling content that motivates your audience to go from information to action.

Delivering the right content to the right people at the right time is something I touch on in Chapter 11. Notice also how marketing and sales need to be focused on business goals. Say that your goal is to add $2 million in revenue this year. Marketing says 'how will we do that?' Their strategy is to increase demand; the marketing plan will consist of programs and their associated campaigns with a goal to increase demand.

Having an overall priority for marketing helps you to choose the right goals, which need to include a mix of strategic and tactical goals, some that are softer and some that have hard metrics. Review your overall business goals, determine your marketing priority and tie marketing's goals to those business goals. A few suggestions are:

- ✔ **Locating net new customers:** Requires a flow of leads, so definitely set targets for how many leads you want marketing to generate. Consider how many sales you need and back that into how many leads you need to produce. For example, if you start with marketing leads (say 300 contacts) and convert 5 percent of them to MQLs (15 marketing-qualified leads, which convert at 66 percent to SQLs (10 sales-qualified leads), which convert at 50 percent to opportunities (5), which converts at a 20 percent close rate to *one sale.* These numbers are the average across a wide variety of types and sizes of firms. Know your numbers.

Be realistic: set a goal that's higher than prior performance, but don't expect marketing to generate all the leads – 25 per cent of leads coming from marketing is a good figure to try as a starting point.

✔ **Creating a new service or an expansion into new geographies:** Requires a whole new marketing strategy. Set a budget and timeline for getting through the strategy and into the execution stage.

✔ **Enhancing your web strategy and social presence:** Needs a timeline and budget. Separate the initial project (getting things set up) from the ongoing activity of maintenance (adding new content, posting new blogs and so on).

✔ **Keeping your content fresh and up-to-date:** Requires a content development calendar, ongoing research, review of feedback and writing/content development effort. Make sure that the content is directly relevant to your key goals (namely, it can be used in programs and campaigns to drive the engagement you're looking for from the marketplace).

Craft your own marketing goals and then figure out how you can measure them.

## 'How will I know that marketing is achieving its goals?' Measuring marketing

A natural tension exists between the 'do it once, do it right' mentality of marketing (which tends to take time and consume dollars) and the desire to get to the market ahead of the competition: this tension is the conflict between entrepreneurship and the careful crafting of the marketing strategy. Neither side is wrong; both positions are valid. In the end, the goal has to trump perfection though, and so marketing needs to deliver in a timely manner. Sometimes you just have to be willing to get out there. Try saying, 'this is a pilot' – it gives you freedom to not get it absolutely right first time.

Marketing is getting increasingly interested in and engaged in measuring results. Don't hire an old-school marketer (who gets uncomfortable when asked to be accountable for results). Make sure that your marketing people have that focus and eagerness to contribute to business goals and don't resist the concept of goals and metrics.

The key thing is to establish goals, communicate them, set up ways of measuring that they're happening and inspect them regularly. Table 9-3 contains some examples of marketing goals.

| Table 9-3 | Sample Goals for Marketing | |
|---|---|---|
| *Goal* | *Metric* | *How to Track the Metric* |
| **Quarterly intelligence report**: Includes trends in your space and competitor/partner activity. | Delivered on time with valuable insights that are actionable. | Look back to the previous quarter's report and see what has taken root in the firm's consciousness. |
| **Specific projects**: For example, redoing the website or establishing your social presence. | Timeframe and budget. | Track the progress of each project on a regular basis (probably weekly). Those weeks really fly by! |
| **New case studies**: Set a quota for new case studies per quarter. | How many depends on how big your customer base is and how frequently you complete an engagement. | Create a forward-looking plan for the case studies that can be done this quarter. Review each quarter to make sure that they were done. |
| **Volume of content getting to the marketplace**. | Target numbers for blogs, press releases, newsletters, emails, social posts, adverts. | Get a monthly report from marketing. Be careful, though: don't trade quality for quantity; inspect what's going out (or a reasonable sample).<br><br>Also, you should be able to get reports on the market's response (opens, click-throughs, downloads, direct responses). |
| **Leads generated by marketing**: No more than 25% of total leads to start with. | Lead conversion per cent = number of marketing-qualified leads converted to a sale/total number of leads converting to a sale (should also trend towards 25%). | Track how many marketing contacts convert to leads, how many leads convert to opportunities, how many opportunities convert to sales, as well as the total dollar value of those sales. |

'Lead' can mean something different to marketing than it does to sales. A contact filling in a form on your website asking for someone to call them may be a 'lead' from marketing's standpoint (an MQL) but probably isn't a lead from a sales perspective (an SQL). I cover these different ideas about what constitutes a lead in Chapter 12.

You need to give marketing time for the engine to warm up and start producing results. Far more subtle forms of influence go on in the early stages in the buying cycle than in a 'let's get to it' sales process. Fortitude and respect is needed all round.

# Ensuring that Marketing Generates Interest

As I state in Chapter 8, a natural division exists between buyers who're still thinking about *whether* to buy and ones that know they *will* buy; in simple terms, marketing deals with the former, sales with the latter (although note that marketing can be supportive of the sales process and in customer retention and upsell, too).

In traditional marketing speak, marketing drives *awareness*. It highlights, sometimes even creates, the need; it educates the customer about potential solutions and it makes her aware that your business exists and that you may have the right solution for her. Marketing also needs to collaborate closely with sales, choosing the right moment to hand over a lead.

## 'Hey, we're over here!' Getting attention

Conventionally, the purchase funnel, Figure 8-4, was just that, a funnel, and marketing and sales saw their jobs as pushing customers down the funnel to purchase, using well-designed marketing and sales techniques. Today, the view is rather different:

✔ Buyers speak to their friends and family and do a whole load of research online after they identify a need and determine that they have to do something about it. Marketing needs to insert your company into that buyer research phase.

✔ Focus for new sales has shifted from the initial purchase towards loyalty and repurchase considerations. In other words, you may get increased business from your existing customers more easily than from new ones (although you need those too!). Both marketing and sales are giving existing customers more attention. Not only might they buy more, they're also great advocates for your services.

Figure 9-4 compares the traditional way of thinking about buyers (just get them to the purchase) with a full-lifecycle model (you take care of them throughout the lifecycle). This doesn't just stop and sell, deliver and we're done. No, it includes the 'loyalty cycle', where a buyer can re-purchase over and over and recommend and refer you to others. Worth some attention, don't you think?

To create awareness of your solution (or brand), marketing needs to be messaging prospective customers so that when they're *triggered* – that is, they make the decision to buy to fulfill their need – your company is on the list as a possible solution.

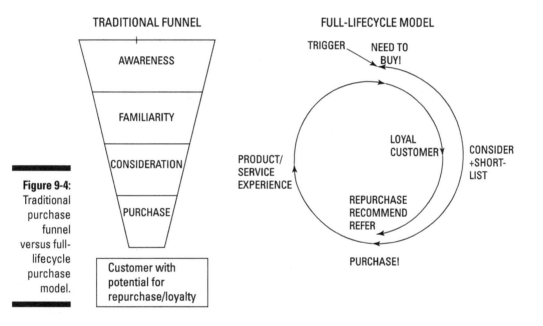

**Figure 9-4:**
Traditional purchase funnel versus full-lifecycle purchase model.

A marketing program or campaign is directed at different points in the awareness stage, from the point when the customer doesn't yet know that she has a need, to being ready to engage actively with someone in your organization so that she can evaluate and then choose you or eliminate you from the running. Naturally, not everyone is going to be interested in everything you put out into the marketplace, but you can start to examine *what* specific contacts pay attention to (from their behavior, such as clicking through on an email) and extrapolate *where* they are in the buying cycle (from the content you provide).

To use the example from the earlier Figure 9-3, if as a potential customer I open an email with information about the new legislation, I'm trying to educate myself to discover *whether* I have a need (do I have to do something about this?'). If I attend a webinar titled 'How to Implement the New Legislation', I probably *know* that I have to do something. These two communications are trying to capture people at different stages in the buying cycle.

In the most sophisticated marketing programs, the degree to which individual buyers respond to them – for example, whether they open an email and click-through, or attend a webinar, or fill in a web form asking someone to contact them – results in an ever-increasing 'score' associated with that individual. As you'd imagine, someone who responds to all the opportunities to communicate with you is a warmer lead than one who ignores you completely or whose engagement is minimal.

The skill of marketing is to create the kind of valuable content to which buyers respond, to get it in front of them when and where they need it, and to recognize when the time is right to hand the lead over to sales.

## 'Over to you!' Timing lead handover correctly

Marketing and sales need to agree when a lead gets transferred from marketing to sales to follow up on. Based on the programs you design in Chapter 10, you may well base the transition point on the buyer's actions. Table 9-4 contains a few simple examples.

**Table 9-4      To Hand Over or Not To Hand Over (a Lead)**

| Customer Action | Hand Over? |
| --- | --- |
| Opens an email that you sent linking to a case study, white paper or webinar registration. | Probably not. They looked at your email but didn't act on it. Keep messaging them. |
| Attended an online seminar/presentation (webinar). | Maybe/maybe not. Certainly worth calling attendees to see where they are in the buying cycle and qualify further. Sales doesn't necessarily have to take on this task. |
| Signed up on your website for someone to contact them. | Maybe. Sales usually wants access to proactive leads right away, but make sure that marketing is capturing enough data, such as name, title, company, phone, email and purchase timeframe, even budget. If you have several services, a checkbox for what the lead is interested in may be helpful too. |

| Customer Action | Hand Over? |
|---|---|
| Attended a trade show and spoke to a marketing person at your booth. Said they're buying your type of services within three months. | Yes and quickly. Sales should follow up, but be aware that prospects get excited at trade shows and they may not be quite so ready when sales calls them. You just have to decide whether sales or marketing is to nurture them. |

Use Table 9-4 to create agreement between marketing and sales on when a lead is ready to be handed over, based on your own marketing activities. Critically, when a lead is deemed to be ready for sales, it must promise to follow-up every time and treat the lead like a diamond in the rough. If the lead isn't ready for the sales process, sales can hand it back to marketing.

Contacts may jump into the buying lifecycle at any stage – they may not track with the process from start to finish.

I look further at the topic of leads and how marketing and sales need to handle them in Chapter 12 (after you outline your programs in Chapter 10).

# Chapter 10

# Creating Your Marketing Plan

. . . . . . . . . . . . . . . . . . . . . . . . . . . . . . . . . . . . . . . . . . . . .

### In This Chapter

▶ Deciding on your marketing priorities and tactics

▶ Developing and implementing your marketing plan

▶ Allocating the necessary funds

. . . . . . . . . . . . . . . . . . . . . . . . . . . . . . . . . . . . . . . . . . . . .

*T*his chapter follows on from Chapter 9 and helps you to create your own marketing plan. You need to align your marketing plan with your business goals, so that the tactics you choose as part of your plan directly impact your results and help you fulfill your overall goals.

I show you how to translate those business goals into a marketing priority and a plan, consisting of practical marketing tactics (programs and their associated campaigns), which you can activate with the right people and financial resources.

If engaging in marketing feels like reaching for the moon, think of it more like getting into orbit. Chapter 9 discusses how modern marketing works, so unless you're already familiar with this area I suggest that you read that chapter before this one.

# Preparing To Market Your Business

Often, marketing teams undertake activities because they seemed like a good idea at the time. Although nothing's wrong with being opportunistic (sometimes it even pays off), marketing shouldn't involve jumping from one activity to another without an underpinning priority and plan.

Here's what you need to start working on your marketing plan:

✔ Clear business goals with associated metrics (see Chapter 6)

✔ An internal SWOT (strengths, weaknesses, opportunities and threats) analysis on your own marketing as it is today

✔ An understanding of the competitive landscape and other market forces (see Chapter 5)

✔ A good understanding of the different buyers that participate from the customer side in the purchase process (see Chapter 5)

✔ An outline of the customer's lifecycle (see Figure 2-1)

As your marketing planning comes together, you may notice that your overall goals and marketing priorities are somewhat fixed (at least for a good while), but that the tactics (the channels you use or the specific campaigns you run) are entirely flexible and can be tweaked based on how well they perform.

Read on to discover the basics of a great marketing plan, including the importance of defining it accurately, researching marketing opportunities properly, and thinking seriously about channels and tactics.

## Defining your plan

Time to visit your business goals for the next year (Chapter 6 describes how to create them). These goals are the foundation for your marketing plan.

Here are a few things you may want to achieve:

✔ Grow revenue in your current market

✔ Retain current customers and expand your revenue from your existing customer base

✔ Expand into a new region or industry

✔ Add a new service (but tread carefully – see Chapter 5)

✔ Expand relationships with your partners, or add new ones

Choose one or two goals that are most important to your company for the year. If you're expanding what you already do, you may be able to tackle three goals. If you're breaking new ground, such as moving into a geographic patch where you're not known or launching a new service, that one goal may be all-consuming for marketing and anything else may be too much to tackle (alongside its day-to-day activities).

Your goals help marketing to define its priority for the year. Take a look at the examples in Table 10-1.

| Table 10-1 | Examples of Creating Marketing Priorities from Business Goals | |
|---|---|
| *Business Goal* | *Marketing Priority* |
| Increase revenue by 30% over the previous year using existing services and geographic reach. A good goal for a new marketing department. | Enhance marketing messaging around programs and enlarge your contact database with the right target companies and contacts. |
| Expand into the mid-West market with a goal to open a sales office by the end of the year. More appropriate for an established marketing department. | Develop mid-West marketing plan and programs for brand establishment and recognition, while sustaining existing markets. |
| Offer a new service in your current geography. Again, more appropriate for an established marketing department. | Develop new service marketing plan and programs for brand establishment and recognition, while sustaining existing services. |

At this point, start selling your marketing plan to your staff. One of the biggest failings of marketing is when it neglects the internal customers: people in your organization who are going to use the developed marketing tactics, who are direct recipients of leads that marketing generates or who can contribute valuable information to marketing.

## *Researching marketing opportunities*

Your customers are an important resource in your planning: after all, they've already bought from you. If you haven't yet done so, talk to a few customers about the steps they went through before signing a contract with you.

Be systematic about stepping through those early stages, because that's the part of the customer experience that marketing has the most power to influence. If you've more than one buyer in a customer organization, try to talk to everyone who was involved when that customer bought from you. You can use the customer interview questionnaire at www.dummies.com/go/businessdevelopment.

Here's what you're trying to discover:

- ✔ What caused customers to realize that they had a need? What pain can they no longer tolerate?

- ✔ Where did they look to find out what solutions existed, what others were doing and what may be a good fit for them?

✔ What actions did they take along the journey? Did they read particular publications, go to certain conferences or attend specific webinars?

✔ How did they select certain services firms to talk to (yours included)? How did they find out about you?

✔ When they contacted you, what did they appreciate about your interactions? What would they have wanted more of? What was missing?

✔ Why did they choose you?

Capture your notes on the interview form (you use them in Chapter 11).

When your marketing is just getting going, you want to capitalize on this information and create your plan to match the ways in which customers have historically looked for services like yours. Implementing or expanding already-proven channels is a great way to boost your pipeline of opportunities and hence your short-term growth. Don't forget to take your SWOT into account – your weaknesses may limit what you can do today or tomorrow, but your SWOT gives you some clues as to where to expand your marketing capabilities. Use your strengths first and start working on the weaknesses.

While you're about it, consider also what your competitors are doing. Do you see ads in the local newspaper or trade magazines? Do they belong to the Chamber of Commerce? Can you sign up for a newsletter online (a private email address, as opposed to your business email, is useful here) or attend a presentation they're giving?

Just following the model of what's been working up to now, for you or your competitors, may be more than enough for the first year. If you've the capacity to swing out a bit, you can add one or two new ideas, but don't overwhelm yourself. If you've never created and run a webinar series, for example, be aware that such an endeavor is a lot of work.

So, carry out a sanity check. Are you busy today? Tomorrow? Be realistic about what you can afford, what you can take on, what you can get help with and how well you're able to manage and monitor your results.

Don't do marketing without measuring (check out Chapter 9). If you do, you can get to the end of the year and have no idea what's working and what isn't. Measurement helps you save money on unproductive efforts.

Before you decide what marketing channels you're going to use, assess your readiness in terms of your *collateral,* namely foundational marketing pieces (basic collateral and broader content such as a brochure, services sheets, testimonials/customer stories, white papers, ebooks), and capture your first thoughts about channels you think may work for you (see Figure 8-6).

# *Choosing your channels*

At this point in planning your marketing plan, here's what you have: your value and offer, your business goals, your marketing priorities, a realistic view on where you are with your collateral as well as initial ideas for channels that you can use, such as local ads, your website, blogs or a speaking event. That's a great start.

So what's next? Well, today's marketing is all about:

- ✔ Valuable content that entices your contacts to continue paying attention to you and motivates them to go from information to action
- ✔ Marketing efforts that treat each relationship as unique, often called *1-to-1 marketing*

Traditional channels are still important, of course, but pushing content to larger audiences when your time and budget is limited takes a technical, online approach.

## *Content as your source of powerful communication*

You know your business, so you're the best judge of whether you have content of value to offer that you can turn into 'thought leadership' pieces (by that I mean ideas that are cutting edge that can be turned into white papers, blogs or ebooks). Sustaining a relationship with someone who's not yet in the buying cycle, or is being slow and steady in the early stages, is hard without some pretty compelling content. This area is where marketing people have great skill – they can tease out of your organization (you, your subject matter experts and your customers) the kind of content that provides unique insights into what your contacts (prospective customers) should be concerned about when they think about their needs/pains.

Compelling content comes from what Influence Ecology, an education company, calls *specialized knowledge,* as opposed to *general knowledge.* Specialized knowledge is the skills, training, credentials and know-how that your company has that others don't (and your customers definitely don't!). General knowledge is knowledge that's usually expected for people who are involved in business, such as a basic understanding of bookkeeping, or how to go about hiring staff.

Imagine that you run a bookkeeping business. It's likely (though not inevitable) that your knowledge is of a general nature and your customers can get your type of services from many places. Therefore, you can't charge much more than the going rate – in other words, you're a bit of a commodity. Your value may be that you service your clients so well that they save thousands in accounting/taxation service fees each year. If so, that's your content of value.

In contrast, now imagine that you run bookkeeping services only for the film and video production industry. You have specialized knowledge: you understand this area's cost accounting, how and when funding comes in, how it gets distributed to contractors, vendors and other costs, how royalties work, what distribution channels exist and how their fee structures operate. You probably know all the pitfalls of bookkeeping in this specific area. In this case, that's your content of value.

The marketing approach in these two cases needs to be quite different (the first uses direct positioning to a wide audience, the second uses narrow deep nurturing). These requirements call for different approaches, channels and tactics.

### Talking to customers 1-to-1

You may find that you have some great content and are ready to blast it out to the marketplace, and yet you're often disappointed with the results. Why is that?

Although you may feel that your company is the greatest thing since sliced bread (and I have no doubt it is), the marketplace is only interested if you've something that solves a widespread, current and pressing problem. Sometimes potential customers don't even know that they have a problem, such as, for example, how they can use the overwhelming desire to be connected in cyberspace 24 hours a day, which is rapidly becoming a must-have for the entire human population. Does an opportunity exist there?

More likely, though, your solution solves a specific issue that occurs at a point in time for a narrow and specific segment of the market. Even within the domain of companies that fit the profile for your services, only a certain percentage are anywhere near the buying cycle at any given moment.

So although traditional marketing channels, such as advertising, are still important and can be effective, given that in the services area the stake is so much about people, the marketing approach is becoming increasingly personal too.

The good news is that you can tell where individuals from a target company are (whether they're somewhere near or in the buying cycle, or completely uninterested) by their behavior. Being able to capture where they are and message them appropriately based on their interest at that time is the foundation of behavioral, or 1-to-1, marketing.

Although communicating with prospective customers one-on-one may seem like an impossible feat, the advance of marketing technologies is bringing that practice within the reach of even quite small companies. The technology brings one-on-one communication together with marketing automation, that is, the tools that manage communication with the marketplace in an automated fashion. If that sounds good to you, turn to Chapter 11.

By the way, Peppers and Rogers started the 1-to-1 movement back in 1993. The firm's website (`www.peppersandrogersgroup.com`) is a mine of useful information on whole lifecycle customer management.

### From theory to practice

Enough of the flights of fancy. Perhaps you're thinking: 'What am I realistically going to be able to do in the next year in terms of expanding our marketing?' One thing's for sure, you can make only so many phone calls and attend only so many networking events, and so my comments about automated marketing aren't entirely pie-in-the-sky.

Apart from meeting you directly, what sorts of channels and content are most compelling for buyers? A great infographic from Content Crossroads provides the following analysis: business-to-business buying decisions are influenced by white papers (70 percent), case studies (56 percent), blog posts (48 percent), webinars (40 percent) and videos (39 percent). Check out the whole infographic at: `www.contentcrossroads.com/2013/06/infographic-wealthiest-content-in-b2b-marketing`.

To expand beyond your personal reach, here's a list of the basic things you need to put in place to start devising your plan. They're also a good foundation to grow into sophisticated marketing in 2–3 years' time, when your revenue justifies such an investment.

- ✔ Get a solid website that can deliver your content on demand to your marketplace.

- ✔ Create and keep adding to your portfolio of case studies or testimonials.

- ✔ Hone your thought-leadership position. What do you want to say to the market that's useful for firms to know around your services? What's the underlying story that makes your offer compelling?

- ✔ Choose content vehicles that you think will work for your type of business. Consider white papers, ebooks, infographics, blogs and webinar presentations.

- ✔ Choose the channels that best distribute your content. Figure 8-6 has a few of the most common online channels used by services firms.

- ✔ Choose your sales management tool (see the sidebar in Chapter 13 for details) and email solution (for example, MailChimp, Constant Contact, iContact or, if you want an automated solution, see Chapter 11).

Later on in this chapter (in the 'Creating your marketing programs' section), I dig into more detailed preparation of your content and channels.

You may notice that some types of content (for example, blog or webinar) are also channels (technically, a *weblog* is the channel and a *blog* is the specific article that you 'post' onto the weblog). Every non-personal channel requires some sort of content, but the reason for distinguishing them is so that you carefully consider whether you have good content for that channel. No point putting on a webinar if you've nothing fascinating and compelling to talk about. Think about it like this – whatever you have to say that prospective customers value is the place you need to look to develop content.

## *Brainstorming your tactics*

You now need to go to a deeper level of detail with the channels and content that you selected in the preceding section. Some of your channels deliver content direct to the target customers, but don't forget that human intervention is necessary at key points in the buying cycle, especially as that customer progresses along the buyer journey. In practice, your content will be used in multiple channels and at multiple points in the journey – for example, when someone writes a compelling blog post, expect your sales people and account managers to share it individually with their critical contacts.

Before you start detailing your plan, here are a few things to bear in mind:

- ✔ Different channels work best at different stages of the buyer's journey. For example, blogs are great for early stages, because they're educational, webinars work well when the customer is really looking for solutions, but prior to them making any direct contact with vendors.

- ✔ You can repurpose contact across channels and sometimes across stages. For example, you can write up webinar content as a white paper, break it down into a number of blogs, share it on social networks and weave it into your website. Look for every such opportunity – it saves a huge amount of content development overload.

- ✔ Think about your content from the point of view of each persona (role) within the prospective customer, depending on how important those roles are in the decision-making process. Often, early stage of research is done by an individual who's not the ultimate decision-maker, so content at different stages has to address each persona's interests and concerns. Look at Chapter 5 where I talk about mapping your key buyer personas and getting inside their heads. Have those personas in your mind as you work on the plan. In the following try-this exercise, do it several times for each persona.

I discuss the planning of tactics in two stages. As I say, no point using a channel if you don't have something appropriate to say. Your business wouldn't benefit from that channel, anyway; or perhaps you can use it later, as you grow.

So, starting with content, use Figure 10-1 to work out what you have already or what you can develop relatively easily.

| Content (E=Essential, O=Optional) | What is this? | Needs short-term development | Can be longer-term development |
|---|---|---|---|
| Website (E) | The hub for your content and where you want your marketing to drive contacts to | ✓ | |
| Services sheets (E) | Brief descriptions of your various services: usually one page each | ✓ | |
| Case studies (E) | Customer stories of your successes: usually 1/2 pages. The customer may be named or it can be a blind case study. Testimonials are an alternative | ✓ | |
| About us (E) | A one-page piece that positions your company: usually provided on request or made available at events or as a leave behind | ✓ | |
| Checklist (O) | A short piece that presents some of the pitfalls or things to remember about your area of expertise: e.g., 'Ten Things to Do When. . ./Avoid When. . . | | ✓ |
| Quantitative infographic (O) | A highly visual piece that summarizes key facts and figures in an easy to consume way; can be used for a quick education of the customer | | ✓ |
| White paper or eBook (O) | An authoritative piece that shares some of your thought leadership or expertise: white papers are usually short (1 to 5 pages); eBooks are more extensive | | ✓ |
| Blog (weblog) post (O) | A short point-of-view piece, often as part of an overall theme of mini-articles; quick to read and get value from | | ✓ |
| Video (O) | An alternative to text-based content, video has become very popular as a marketing medium and drives good SEO and interest | | ✓ |
| Presentation (E) | Powerpoint or other format used to present your company to a prospective buyer or as part of a presentation at an event; uses material from all your other content | ✓ | |

**Figure 10-1:** Mapping your content.

## Distinguishing collateral and content

In terms of what you say in the public arena about yourself as a business, I want to distinguish between *collateral* and *content*:

✔ **Collateral:** Items that provide evidence of your capabilities and competence in the marketplace, because this evidence is especially important in the sales lifecycle. Examples include your website, LinkedIn Company Profile, services sheets, case studies, corporate presentations, sales kits, including customer questionnaires, pricing tools, ROI (return on investment) calculators and proposal templates.

✔ **Content:** Dynamic material of value at different stages of the customer lifecycle, but especially important in early positioning, that is, in marketing campaigns. Examples include landing pages, blogs, white papers, thought-leadership pieces, one-off speeches (at an event), email text, press releases.

The examples of collateral and content aren't hard and fast: salespeople use collateral routinely and predictably in the sales cycle; they're also really pleased to have a stream of fresh, valuable content to share with prospects and customers.

Naturally, you need to focus on the essential items: your collateral, marked with an (E). If you're light on those, focus on getting those done for the next three months and then revisit the content map. If you're unclear about the distinction between collateral and content, take a look at the sidebar 'Distinguishing collateral and content'.

Picking the channels to use depends on a number of factors:

✔ What content you have.

✔ What channels you believe your personas use. For example, in some industries, social media are hardly used – yet!

✔ The resources you have in your company that can actively feed those channels with content.

You may start in a spirit of optimism and ambition, which is perfect; that provides you with a future roadmap. However, see where I discuss what it takes to implement your plan in the next section.

Use Figure 10-2 to select your channels. I give you a jump start, but you need to adapt it to your business, so add and take away as you see fit.

Again, make sure that the essentials – the (E) items – are in your sights short term and that you pick sparingly from the others, unless you can quickly repurpose content from one channel to another.

| Channel (E=Essential, O=Optional) | What is this? | Create the need | Research / Plan | Reach out | Engage | Partner |
|---|---|---|---|---|---|---|
| Website (E) | The destination for your marketing efforts | ✓ | ✓ | ✓ | ✓ | ✓ |
| Email (E) | The invitation to look at your content, register for your event etc.: in other words, a call to action | ✓ | ✓ | ✓ | | |
| Landing pages (E) | The specific website pages that contacts first reach when they click a link (for example, from an email, advert or post on the social networks) | ✓ | ✓ | ✓ | | |
| Blog (weblog) post (O) | Apart from short, very consumable content, blogs can point to more extensive content such as white papers, video or other pages on your website | ✓ | ✓ | | | |
| Webinars (O) | Online presentations that help prospective customers learn about your service area or other relevant content | | ✓ | | | |
| Video (O) | Literally a channel, as in YouTube channel | | ✓ | ✓ | ✓ | |
| Search engines (E) | A way of positioning key words so that your website and other channels show up high in search engine results. Optimizing your website to support search is essential, but paying for keywords or other search engine positioning is optional | ✓ | ✓ | ✓ | | |
| Social networks (O) | Channels where you can reach audiences that may not come to your website, with short pieces of content and relevant updates. The intent is to build a following of people who read your content | ✓ | ✓ | ✓ | ✓ | |
| Surveys (O) | An opportunity to make contact with and gather market information from a wide number of people; also gathers useful data you can publish as content | ✓ | ✓ | | | |
| Adverts (online and offline) (O) | | ✓ | ✓ | ✓ | | |
| Local memberships (O) | | | ✓ | ✓ | | |
| Speaking opportunities (O) | | | ✓ | | | |

**Figure 10-2:** Mapping your channels.

Keep your staff informed as to what content is going out into the marketplace and who such content is being directed to. For one thing, it gives them the opportunity to use that content themselves to continue to woo prospects and customers by adding yet more value. Also, consult your sales and account managers about what communications need to go to prospects and customers that are 'in play'.

Nothing is more disconcerting to sales than an email going from marketing to a prospect that introduces your company and services when that prospect is about to buy. The prospects' response is often 'Doesn't your left hand know what your right is doing?' My policy is to disable marketing communications after a prospect is a Sales Qualified Lead (in the sales process). One type of communication is valuable for all your contacts, though, at whatever stage in the buying cycle, and that's a general newsletter. Just ensure that it makes compelling reading.

# Putting Marketing into Practice

Having content and channels is all very well (see the preceding section). But here I discuss how you move from there into specific marketing programs that create awareness of the problems you solve, the considerations that prospective customers should take into account, and consideration of your brand and services.

Your specific strategies and goals have a big influence on your marketing programs. Expanding your services in your current marketplace to a wider group of customers is one thing, but introducing a new service or breaking into a new geography or vertical (industry) is quite another.

## Creating your marketing programs

A marketing *program* is an assembly of specific tactics that drive towards a common business goal and marketing priority. Therefore you need a separate marketing program for each of your goals, which is why I suggest that you don't have too many goals on the go at once.

### Campaign basics

A program may use different campaigns to drive towards the same goals. A *campaign* is a series of activities that markets a service using specific channels and methods. Campaigns can be centered on specific topics of thought leadership, namely your unique perspective and cutting-edge ideas (such as the one I discuss for the HR company in Chapter 5 alerting the market to new legislation). You can think of the thought-leadership topic as a theme for your campaign.

Each campaign needs to include:

- ✔ A goal and objectives for the campaign
- ✔ The results you want to produce
- ✔ The focus of the campaign

✔ The campaign duration (how many weeks or months you're going to run it)

✔ Who the campaign is directed at (the companies and personas)

✔ The campaign assets you need (they're often called *anchor assets* – in other words the key types of content that are required)

✔ A campaign calendar (see the next section)

### *Your campaign grows*

In this section, I help you develop your program and specific campaigns designed to fulfill on that program down to an actionable level of detail. Note that your program may contain multiple campaigns.

A practical example is the best way to illustrate the development of a marketing program and its supporting campaigns. Read the following example and tailor it to suit the specific needs of your firm.

Imagine you recently joined the local Department of Education in Facilities Planning in Chicago and the city has a new school to build. The overall building stock is pretty aged, but you need to find out whether the new school can use the latest best practices. The County Planning Department wants the new premises certified as a LEED (Leadership in Energy and Environmental Design) building, but you don't know anything about that, other than it's connected to environmental friendliness. You'll be on the decision committee for choosing an architect.

All around you in the area are some highly competent architects who probably want to bid on the project. You want to be prepared and so you check out the LEED website. You need less than two minutes to figure out just how much is involved and so you start looking for architects who are certified as LEED consultants.

Now switch roles and imagine that you're one of those architect firms. You have a goal to secure $1million ($630,000) of LEED design projects (hopefully leading to construction projects). Therefore, your marketing priority is to increase leads and your marketing program needs to consist of a number of campaigns to drive those leads.

So, dealing with an early-stage buyer, such as the new guy at the Department of Education in Facilities Planning, what would cause him to take an interest in your company? Here are my ideas:

✔ **LEED certification (clearly):** Shows your competence to design such a project.

✔ **Experience in building schools:** In other words, case studies.

✔ **Helpful content:** To educate a novice about the important things to know about LEED, especially for education departments.

What sort of a campaign would the architect's firm create to reach its goal of winning more school construction projects? In Table 10-2, I provide an outline campaign plan, which you can use as a model for creating your own.

| Table 10-2 | A Marketing Campaign Plan |
|---|---|
| *Strategic Aspects* | *Description of the Example Campaign* |
| A goal and objectives for the campaign | To drive three design project sales in the mid-West in the next 12 months |
| The results you want to produce | Engagement by 20 education departments in at least two content items |
| The focus of the campaign | Creating awareness of LEED and understanding why you need to engage an experienced firm with certified LEED consultants and local presence in the target states |
| The campaign duration (how many weeks or months you run the campaign) | Six months |
| Who you're directing the campaign at (the companies and personas) | Planning officers and other decision-makers in the seven target mid-West states |
| The campaign assets you need | Assets to demonstrate:<br><br>✔ Knowledge and trustworthiness (willing to share domain knowledge)<br><br>✔ Impartiality (willing to provide useful resources with no expectation of a return)<br><br>✔ Relevant experience (able to tell a convincing story based on prior work) |

So far, so good. Now I speculate on what your campaign assets may be. No right answer here, of course, so if you come to a different conclusion that just proves the diversity of the marketing options:

✔ A set of video recordings (or a webinar series) covering:

 – What is LEED and what aspects are relevant to school construction projects?

 – What does constructing a LEED-rated building mean in practice?

> – How does the rating system work for LEED buildings, with examples of some rated schools?
>
> – How would an education department partner for LEED construction? What would we need to understand about LEED accreditation?
>
> ✔ Content for the customer's Request for Proposal (RFP) for a LEED-rated construction project.
>
> ✔ 'Ten Things to Ask your Architects about Their LEED Work.'
>
> ✔ Video of a prior client talking about its building project and LEED rating.

If you review this list carefully, you can see that the different items are aimed at different stages in the buyer's journey:

> ✔ **Set of video recordings:** Directed to the research/planning stage.
>
> ✔ **Content for your RFP and 'Ten Things to Ask your Architects . . .':** Related to reaching out/engaging.
>
> ✔ **Video of a prior client:** Most relevant to engage/partner.

That's not to say that certain assets aren't valuable across the buying cycle, or even into the delivery stage. For example, perhaps the video series can be a good education piece for the architect firm to share with a new customer.

You may notice that I use video for two of the asset categories. If you can gain some economy of scale with a particular tactic, that's a good thing. You can just as easily create infographics for one and a video for the other. If you have internal people who are a dab hand at some of this stuff, even better. You always have a multitude of options.

Also, aim to create *progressive assets,* in other words ones that you can use to nurture prospective customers through the buyer journey. Although you may not be quite ready for fully automated marketing, get into the useful habit of thinking in sequential steps, because your marketing makes more sense to the target audiences that way. You can't guarantee where and when a specific target is going to engage with your content, but you certainly find out something about them when they do.

### Campaign channels

Your mind may be racing ahead to which channels to use for this campaign and all this content. Well, it depends on the nature of your company, your previous experience and your resources. Table 10-3 shows a few options that the architectural firm can choose.

| Table 10-3 | Translating Content into Channels | |
|---|---|---|
| *Content* | *Channel* | *Advantage/Disadvantage* |
| Video (research/ plan stage) | YouTube | Easy to upload new content. You can rely on YouTube to deliver (stream) your content on demand. You can boost your traffic based on search. |
| | | You do, however, need to set up a secure YouTube channel for your company and manage it. |
| | Website | Takes the prospective customer to your website. |
| | | May require the creation of landing pages. |
| | DVD integrated with a presentation on LEED | Can be mailed out with an information packet or left with a prospect. |
| | | Burning and printing onto DVDs can be a bit fiddly but outsourcing isn't that expensive. |
| Content related to LEED for an RFP | PDF | Easy to produce and distribute. |
| | | Easy for competitors to download and use, unless you take steps to secure the content, which is troublesome. See also landing page below. |
| | Website | If you've a 'resources for customers' area, you can publish your PDF, but require certain details from users before they can download it. |
| | | Unauthorized users can gain access unless you're particularly strict about protecting your content. |
| | Landing page | You can create a specific *landing page,* which sits in front of your content. Users have to identify themselves before they can use your content. |
| | | Your website or marketing automation tool has to be capable of quickly creating landing pages without the need for a web developer. |

| Content | Channel | Advantage/Disadvantage |
|---------|---------|------------------------|
| Ten things to ask your architect about LEED | As above | As above. |
| Video of customer story | As video asset above | As video asset above. |

These are some primary channels for your content. You can of course also promote that content through emails, blogs, news items, articles and the like. All these channels can repurpose content, but it may, and probably will, take additional work to adapt the message to the channel.

### Campaign plan

Bringing all this material together, what does the campaign now look like? Figure 10-3 shows one format for capturing your campaign detail. Marketing folks can detail their campaigns in many ways – spreadsheets are popular, as are flow diagrams and even Word documents.

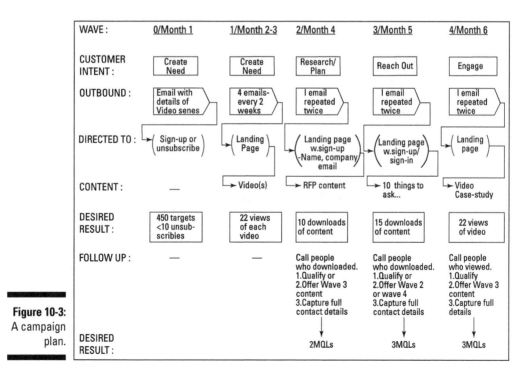

**Figure 10-3:** A campaign plan.

For smaller companies, I recommend a separate plan for each campaign (or possibly a group of campaigns relating to a single program).

### Campaign tips and tricks

Here are a few things to remember when you put your campaigns into action:

- ✔ If you're using emails, you have to give contacts an opportunity to opt out of your communications. It's the law.

- ✔ Focus any calling effort on the most active contacts. Although it takes work, keep track of who opens what emails and whether they click through to your content. Most emails systems give you this sort of reporting. Someone who opens two emails and watches two of your videos and then downloads 'Ten Things to Ask Architects. . .' is more valuable than someone who opens your emails but never clicks through. Note exactly which campaign elements your contacts acted on and, from Figure 10-3, what stage that means they're at. Your conversation with them needs to be different for each wave of the campaign.

- ✔ Emailing your messages several times is okay (you can make small changes each time). People often intend to look at your content but then don't get round to it. For regular content, two emails are probably enough; for events, you can email three, even four times (a week apart) to remind people to register.

Your campaigns don't have to consist of emails drawing your prospective customers to your content. They can include a lot of other elements too, such as a press release, article in a periodical or blog posts. Ideally, though, you want to let people know about your content, wherever you're publishing it, and so email marketing is a core skill to master.

## Creating your marketing calendar

With some planned campaigns, you want to pull them all together into a marketing calendar. Not only does this calendar show you the schedule for all the campaigns you're running, but also you can add other marketing work into the calendar, such as a revision to your website, or writing new collateral.

A calendar also allows you to spot any peaks of activity that may exceed what the team can deliver. For instance, if you have a webinar going on, content being put together for your new website, a press release to be written and a couple of case studies that are due, plus two new email campaigns launching, you may well be over-reaching. Use your calendar to move things around to balance out the workload.

Don't forget that certain times of year can be slow in terms of getting the attention of your target market. If most of the industry you're targeting goes off to a major annual conference the second week in March, avoid that time for pushing out content (unless you're going to be exhibiting at the conference, in which case you need a whole campaign around that). Different industries have different financial cycles (for example, the public sector compared with the commercial sector). Take major national holidays, summer and late December/early January into account. Use December to plan your marketing campaigns and calendar for the following year.

Your calendar typically spans a 12-month period. You can be as granular as you like – just ensure that you've enough detail to avoid major tasks getting overlooked. If a marketing individual is managing the calendar and marketing effort full-time, you can leave the detail to that person. If this job is a part-time effort for someone, or a weekend activity for you, the more detailed the calendar, the better.

Figure 10-4 shows part of a simple spreadsheet marketing calendar for the architect example in the preceding section.

| LEED Campaign | Jan | Feb | Mar | Apr | May | Jun | Jul | Aug | Se |
|---|---|---|---|---|---|---|---|---|---|
| **Wave 0** | | | | | | | | | |
| Acquire/clean database | | | | | | | | | |
| Write email copy | | | | | | | | | |
| Run Wave 0 | | | | | | | | | |
| **Wave 1** | | | | | | | | | |
| Video Scripts | | | | | | | | | |
| Video Shoot | | | | | | | | | |
| Write email copy | | | | | | | | | |
| Run Wave 1 | | | | | | | | | |
| **Wave 2** | | | | | | | | | |
| etc... | | | | | | | | | |
| etc... | | | | | | | | | |
| **CAMPAIGN #2** | Jan | Feb | Mar | Apr | May | | | | |
| (enter details) | | | | | | | | | |
| **OTHER MARKETING INITIATIVES** | Jan | Feb | Mar | Apr | | | | | |
| (enter details) | | | | | | | | | |

**Figure 10-4:** A campaign calendar for the mid-West architect example.

The calendar starts to reveal just how much work is involved in even the simplest campaigns. The one for the architect firm probably takes hundreds of hours of planning, not including video shoots. When the calendar's all set up, the time then goes into running the separate *waves* (stages of the campaign, usually distinct and separate activities), monitoring results, managing the database (for example, *opt-outs* – people who don't want your emails – and *bounces* – emails that haven't been delivered) and producing reports for others who have to act on the results of the campaign.

During the planning stage, check whether you're being over-ambitious. Running one campaign really well is better than doing three badly. I go even deeper into campaign development in Chapter 11.

## *Creating and managing collateral and content*

Your company has a clear focus for its services and specific value that it brings to its customers. You may also have a mission and vision defining who you are. You don't want to have to alter this bedrock of your company for a long period of time. Even so, the world is changing and the market creates more and more sophisticated and automated ways of getting your message, maybe even your services, to the marketplace.

You absolutely *must* have some collateral to sell effectively, otherwise you look unprofessional. You *should* have content to influence a prospective buyer to consider you and to keep your messaging new and interesting. For a further clarification on collateral and content, read the earlier sidebar 'Distinguishing collateral and content' and see Chapter 11 for more on the importance of content.

As a result of this distinction, you find that collateral includes pieces that you update from time to time, but where the basic messaging is pretty static. It needs to be, because it represents your brand and services and provides evidence that you're good at what you do. Content is much more dynamic. You're constantly creating new pieces to fuel your marketing campaigns. Some pieces will be usable again and again, whereas others are one-time efforts.

Start with your collateral and give it a really good look over, beginning with your website. I provide a few ideas in the sidebar 'How bad is your website?'. Work on collateral first, so that your sales effort isn't hobbled by poor collateral. Then move onto your content development to support your marketing.

# How bad is your website?

Prospective clients first experience your firm in a number of ways: for example, through a personal meeting at an event or through a well-crafted email. If they have any interest in you, they're on your website in a hop, skip and a jump. Unfortunately, many services websites are truly dreadful: they look aged and unprofessional, no one is keeping them fresh and interesting, and they're probably at least five years old.

This situation shows up as follows:

- The home page doesn't make clear immediately what the firm does.

- The focus of the website is for the firm to talk *at* website visitors about what it does, instead of talking *to* visitors about the sorts of needs they may have that the firm can help with (and how).

- The content is typically written in expert language (not everyday English), so is not accessible to the target audience.

- The site has way too much text (hint: no one reads anything anymore – they don't have the time!).

- The home page has typos, creating an instant impression of carelessness.

- The content is generic – it doesn't seek to address the specific audiences.

- The content is static and rarely updated.

- The tone and style of the written material changes across the website (different people wrote it and it lacks a consistent 'voice').

- The website doesn't have areas for dynamic content (okay, sometimes it has a news area, but the last entry is two years old).

- The navigation is poorly constructed so the user can get lost and not know how to get back.

- The site doesn't display well on tablets or smartphones.

- The site has no 'calls to action', things that the visitor can click on to drill deeper into valuable content or to make contact with you.

To evaluate a website well, you really have to be in the shoes of the website visitor. Imagine that you've no idea who your firm is and take a look at your site through those eyes.

Start by listing who you think visits your website and what their goals are – these are your target audiences. For example, you have prospective customers, actual customers, partners and potential employees visiting your site. What are they trying to accomplish and how easy is it for them to do that?

Take a look at your competitors' websites too, especially firms you admire and want to emulate. Apply the same process – are they doing better than you?

Use the list above to rate how you're doing in each of the areas for each audience. Don't think that you have to have a hugely sophisticated website – you just have to be clear, engaging, talking to the audience in ways they understand and so can get at what they want.

Modern marketing techniques are going to drive your audience to your website, wherever they came from in the first place. Make sure that that your website is ready for them.

If you have any experts on websites among your friends and family network, share your findings with them and ask them to give you objective feedback.

# Making the Most of Your Resources

In the final analysis, of course, reality has to set in (darn it): the amount of marketing you can do is dependent on your resources – the staff and their skill sets, the help you can get from outside and your budgets.

## Breaking the plan down to decide on resources

Some of the issues you face are questions such as: What resourcing needs (such as people, systems, outsourcing, budgets) have to be considered? How do I provide those resources? Who should take care of what?

A lot of marketing falls down because the plan for resourcing ends up with one person, say the marketing manager, taking on all the marketing work. Meanwhile, everyone else ceases to pay attention, unless the results are sub-par – and boy do they then notice!

Marketing is an investment, so don't just hand it off, or let it decline into tactical work. To grow your business, you need the following:

- **Marketing strategies and tactics for how you're going to support the growth goals:** Precisely what this chapter is all about!

- **Specific results that you want marketing to drive:** Typically a number of leads (for which marketing can be directly responsible) and opportunities and wins (the responsibility of sales).

- **A way to check that marketing effort is paying off:** You have to be able to measure against the pre-defined metric of number of leads. If your team members are fairly experienced, they may have an idea of what's typical for your space.

- **Flexibility to change tactics if things appear not to be working:** Run pilots, for example with a smaller subset of the market, to see how the campaign goes. You can also try *split* tactics (doing a campaign two different ways to see what works best – see Chapter 11).

Even if you're not the one doing the grunt work, don't move on to your next priority, thinking that you're done. Management, sales leadership and account managers also need to contribute to marketing, not just the marketing staff. You also need to give them the resources (tools and budget) they need to get the job done.

# Satisfying marketing's appetite: Who does the marketing?

Marketing is a needy discipline – as it should be – reliant on input from the market, the company, the competition, external partners (such as channel partners or subcontractors) and customers.

For a small company, Table 10-4 shows what a typical marketing team looks like and the support the members need from the rest of the company. I break the roles down to help you plan for future growth, but realistically you may have just one person (maybe even part-time).

| Table 10-4 | Marketing and Support Teams |
| --- | --- |
| **Marketing Role** | **Support Needed** |
| **Marketing manager:** Responsible for marketing plan, campaign design, tools, reporting and results. | Management input on plan, approval of campaigns and oversight on results. *Sales* collaboration on campaign design. |
| **Marketing co-ordinator:** Responsible for content creation, graphic design, campaign execution, database management. | Mostly help with content – getting raw information from *management* about the firm's services, customer case studies from account/project managers, collateral or other marketing support from partners. |
| **Lead developer:** Responsible for nurturing contacts until they're qualified (Marketing Qualified Leads – MQLs) and ready to be handed to sales. | Agreement from *sales* as to what constitutes a qualified lead. |

In Chapter 11, I provide more detail on who does what in marketing.

As well as hiring marketing staff, you can also consider contractors or even marketing firms. Just be ready for the cost! If you hire a marketing person or a firm, they come in asking where their budget is.

You may well need to make the investment when:

- ✔ Sales can no longer keep up with your growth goals.
- ✔ You need to expand your geography or range of services and the current team doesn't have the capacity to deal with that.

✔ You're poised to grow from a company that hardly anyone has heard of to one where people call you.

✔ Certain revenue goals are met and the investment is feasible.

Each type of services firm is different, so take a look at your competition – companies of different sizes – and find out who's investing in marketing. Look at the quality of their websites and brochures; have someone sign up for their newsletters (using a personal email address) and check their job postings.

How much budget do you need? For a small services firm, think somewhere around 5 per cent of gross revenue: 60–70 per cent of this budget needs to go on payroll or professional fees, 30–40 per cent on marketing costs. Truthfully, it matters less *what you budget* than the fact that you *have a budget*. A budget tells the organization that marketing is important, worthy of investment. If you don't set a budget, you're not really serious about marketing.

## *Making marketing accountable*

Clearly, marketing needs to measure its generation of leads. To do so, you need to track the number of MQLs passing from marketing to sales. Some email automation systems (see Chapter 11) can report metrics automatically, but if not you have to track your results manually.

To design the reporting, sit down with marketing and sales and work out what the process is for capturing the numbers – of MQLs, and then of Sales Qualified Leads (SQLs) that convert to opportunities and then to sales. You need to know which closed deals were sourced by marketing, as opposed to a salesperson attending a local event, for example. I discuss MQLs and SQLs more in Chapter 9.

Marketing may well do a lot of good work to influence other sources, such as leads coming from partners. Make sure that it gets recognition for its work: creating collateral from partner resources, running campaigns funded or supported by partners and the like. The leads may go direct to sales, but marketing helped.

Make marketing accountable for the budget spend. Ask for a projected budget spend based on the marketing calendar (check out the earlier section 'Creating your marketing calendar' for details). Set authorization limits on what it can spend without approval. Keep an eye on that budget!

# Chapter 11

# Automating Marketing – More Leads with Less Effort

*Y*our business needs a flow of new customers on a regular basis, otherwise, bang goes your revenue goal. All marketing is an effort to increase attention from prospective customers looking for services such as yours. As a result, the department can be tempted to busy itself adding value to existing opportunities and customers and neglect generating brand new prospects.

The purpose of *demand generation,* by contrast, is to reach out to firms that aren't yet active buyers but are in an early stage of identifying that they have a need and have to do something about it. That's a tall order. Getting the attention of people you know is one thing, but reaching out to thousands of strangers to stimulate interest is quite another.

In this chapter, I focus on *automated* demand generation as a subcategory of marketing activity. I look at some automated demand generation techniques, helping you to plan for the use of demand generation tools and technologies and to create and deploy effective programs. In the process, I give you the chance to evaluate whether the time is right for you to be looking at marketing automation.

# Introducing the Automated Demand Generation Game

If you're a car manufacturer, you don't wait for buyers to show up at the dealership and hope that they buy your latest model. If you've ever had one of those postcards with a promotional offer: 'No money down, first month's lease payment waived', you probably noticed that it arrives about three months before your current lease is about to expire. Better still, if you use the promotion code to visit the website and look at some models, the phone rings from the dealership. Co-incidence? Absolutely not. These highly sophisticated marketing programs trigger when the time is right – for you! The good news is that, these days, you can do this sort of automated marketing too.

Waiting for the phone to ring with a hot prospect ready to talk to you right now is a singularly unproductive activity. Instead, you want to generate demand. When your phone rings without you exerting any manual effort to make that happen, you know that you've nailed demand generation *and* that your brand is getting recognition in the marketplace as a result of your automated marketing efforts.

How do you get to this desired state? Technology to the rescue! Automated tools are within the reach of marketers today that allow sophisticated approaches to nurturing relationships with your contacts.

*Marketing automation* refers to the tools, processes and programs that remove the drudgery from marketing's day-to-day job of generating interest. Marketing automation directs your contacts to your valuable content in order to begin and then nurture a relationship with your company, while tracking how those contacts behave during the buying cycle and providing analysis of what's producing the desired results.

Marketing automation takes you from the world of *mass marketing* (pushing out mass communications to a large audience all at once) to 1-to-1 marketing (see Chapter 10 for details); the latter triggers the next step in the campaign after a contact takes a certain action, such as clicking through to your website and viewing or downloading some content. Enough of the right actions by the contact tells you that a lead is probably ready to talk to sales.

Leads that are qualified by marketing – marketing-qualified leads (MQLs), see Chapter 9 for more – and that sales welcomes, have some basic characteristics:

- ✔ They fit the profile of the kind of company you want to work with (Chapter 5 has more on finding your customer).
- ✔ They have an identified need that fits what you offer (in other words, you can solve a firm's problem/fulfill its need).

✔ They have budget, a timeline for purchase and the right people ready to get involved in a sales process.

However, continually asking contacts 'Are we there yet?' is hard. Why would they want to talk to you anyway: they don't know you, they just know you want to sell them something. Instead, if you can offer value to their deliberations, wherever they are in the buyer's journey (the first half of the customer experience in Figure 2-1), they may engage with *that* content. Marketing automation is the secret sauce that pushes out content and monitors responses, waiting for the evidence that the contact just became a MQL.

If you're wondering what a buyer's journey looks like, I expand the customer experience into a detailed buyer's journey in the section on 'Designing demand generation programs' later in this chapter.

## Understanding the buyer's journey

Buyers are a lot less interested in talking to salespeople than they used to be. These days they look online, to the social networks and search engines, to get content delivered through a wide range of channels, to inform themselves fully before they take the dreaded step of picking up the phone to call your company (or your competitors).

When prospective customers are talking to sales, they're in the later stages of the buyer's journey – and that's your opportunity to influence the outcome through your detailed attention to the sales process (see more in Chapter 14). But what are they doing during the 60–75 percent of the buyer's journey when they're not talking to you?

Right now, your evidence of that probably comes from existing customers and recent wins or losses (if you bother to ask them the right questions). This data set is necessarily small, so it can be misleading.

Automated demand generation gives you insight into what buyers of your type of service actually *do* during the early stages of the buyer's journey, but with much larger volumes of data than you can possibly get from personal interviews, or even from online research. When you build an automated program, you start to gather behavioral data that's useful at three levels:

✔ It tells you what to do next for that contact (and I'm talking about an individual person within a target company here).

✔ It can provide you with *analytics* (reports that tell you about overall performance and trends) on what your target customers respond to most favorably, what drives them from looking at your communications to picking up the phone and calling (or any other action that indicates to you that they're getting close to qualification as a lead).

✔ You can start ranking behavior that's most indicative of a target customer converting to a sales lead and then into a customer.

✔ You can assess which campaign elements (specific emails, ads, webinars) are working well and which are less effective.

## Providing insights for your prospective customers

In the early stages of the buyer's journey, potential prospects aren't interested in your company, your brochures or what services you have to offer. They're looking for insight into market trends, what solutions others are using to solve the same need that they have and what the advantages and pitfalls are of solving the problem at all.

If prospects are in the early stages of their process, anything that looks like 'trying to sell them something' is really annoying. They may be researching so as to make a case for implementing a solution to the 'real' buyer – that is, the one who's going to sign the contract. They may be trying to work out whether doing nothing is still better than doing something. You don't know what they're thinking, but wouldn't finding out be great?

At each stage of the buyer's journey, the types of insight you can provide change. That's why understanding the buyer's journey and how they respond to your content is so important.

## Attracting an audience

Even if you have great content, you still have to get it out in front of your target audience. Who that is varies according to which service you're trying to position and to whom within the target company you're sending the message. This situation isn't 'one size fits all'.

You already have some contacts who consume content – your customers, prospects in the pipeline, partners, and your friends and family. Not only do they probably look at your content, they may be willing to share your content with their network if you make doing so easy for them.

If you want growth, you can't just speak to people you know. You have to expand your reach. Ultimately, you need the majority of your audience to be people in the target companies you're trying to convert into customers. To get at the really valuable contacts, you need to put content where your targets flock together – such as within specific LinkedIn groups, conferences or highly authoritative websites to which a significant number of your buyers subscribe. You can also research or purchase lists that fit your criteria. Obtaining, growing and maintaining your database of contacts is an important aspect of demand generation. I go into more detail on building your database in the later, appropriately named 'Building your database' section.

The reality is that the more you try to have people *opt in* to your communications – that is, follow or sign up for your emails or other content – the more likely you are to have random people reading your content even though they're not a prospect at all (or at least they lack the authority to purchase much more than a box of teabags). As you get sophisticated with demand generation, you become able to rank your incoming leads based on the specific campaigns they respond to or actions they take. See Table 9-4 for more information.

# Asking whether Demand Generation Is Right for You

Young services companies don't usually jump right into the complexities of automated demand generation. More commonly, a time comes when the sales force is running at a hundred miles an hour and marketing just can't keep up with the volume of manual work it has to do to create and manage the marketing programs.

Without doubt, that's the tipping point when you realize that you need to find a better way of working. Read on to see whether automated demand generation is that better approach.

## Deciding when to consider automated demand generation

When your marketing team is tapped out, it starts to become a bottleneck to growth. At this time you need to take a good hard look at automation, because it gives you the opportunity to expand your efforts without a big investment in more resources – in other words, you can do a lot more with a modest expansion in staffing and expenditure on technology systems.

Automated demand generation is a relatively new discipline, less than five years old, so if you're not doing it yet that's no surprise. However, market pressure is building fast to jump on the bandwagon – Oracle, owner of the marketing automation tool Eloqua, predicts that 50 per cent of business-to-business companies will be using demand generation tools and practices by 2015. (Take that prediction with a pinch of salt, though – the early adopters were companies with the resources to invest big time in building complex programs targeting millions of contacts; smaller firms like yours may take a little more time.) The good news is that the tools are getting more affordable and easier to use; the bad news is that experts in demand generation are currently commanding high prices in the job market.

I say earlier that the investment in demand generation can be relatively modest. For a small firm, say under $5 million ($3.15 million), it may seem like quite a big investment – you face an upfront cost in acquiring tools, designing programs and growing your database. But once you get started, the automated nature of the programs requires less manual intervention and allows you to expand the volume and reach of your communications. As soon as you can afford it, do it. Demand generation is the most cost effective way to expand your reach and get from $5 million to $10 million and beyond.

So, do you need demand generation? In Table 11-1, you can see some factors to consider.

### Table 11-1    Do You Need Automated Demand Generation?

| Factor to Consider | Should You Go for It? |
| --- | --- |
| You start to see a plateau in your growth caused by a stream of leads that just balances your customer attrition (that is, new customers are just about replacing customers that have completed). | Yes. You've been in growth mode and things were looking promising, but now revenue growth is slowing. Make sure that the market you're addressing has the potential for your revenue ambitions – otherwise you may have to expand your operations to new markets. However, it looks like a good time to make the investment. |
| Your database of contacts has grown to several thousand and you've every intention of building it further. Typically, you've been doing email marketing by creating lists, which are getting fragmented and are a headache to manage. | Yes. As your database grows, you get more sophisticated about expanding to different roles (personas), industries and geographies. You already have good content, but to direct communications that are even more targeted, you need to be able to select the right contacts from your database (called *segmentation*). Therefore, you require tools that can manage a unified database of contacts and allow queries to be created that select from that database for a specific campaign. The reporting also needs to be automated. |

| Factor to Consider | Should You Go for It? |
|---|---|
| How big are you? How many customers a year do you need to acquire? How competitive is your space? Companies at around $5 million (£3.15 million) in revenue, needing to add several new customers a month, where competition on any given deal can be from four or five other companies, tend to start eyeing demand generation. | Maybe. If your growth goals are ambitious and the market is fairly competitive, companies use automated demand generation to gain advantage: the discipline is relatively new, so you can be an early adopter in your space. Review Chapter 10 and design some basic marketing programs before you make a decision. |
| Your content attracts unexpected (good) attention. | Maybe. You've pushed content out there, your speaking engagements have become increasingly popular and people are signing up for your newsletter in droves. Things are getting too much to handle. You're clearly onto something, and so automating is going to expand on your results without a big increase in staff. |

## Gathering the required resources

Here are the resources you're likely to need to implement automated demand generation:

- ✔ Consulting advice to help you map your personas and your buyer's journey, evaluate your current content and assess your readiness to start marketing automation.

- ✔ One additional hire in marketing, or cutting back on other programs and retraining staff on the new approach. You benefit from upgrading your existing staff – they come with the significant advantage of knowing your company really well. Everyone in the marketing space is starting to learn demand generation, so they deserve the chance to discover these new techniques too.

- ✔ A solid customer relationship management tool (such as Salesforce), a flexible website that can support campaigns with *landing pages* (special web pages that act as a gate to the content) and a marketing automation (MA) tool. I discuss websites briefly in Chapter 10 and talk more about tools later on in this chapter (see 'Choosing your infrastructure tools').

So what investment may you need to get started? I base the following numbers on an assumption that your current campaign planning has some elements you can repurpose for an automated demand generation pilot. In other words, when your systems are set up and talking to each other, you can get a pilot program going in two to three months.

Roughly, here's where your money goes:

| | |
|---|---|
| Demand generation consultant for two months | $10,000 |
| One additional marketing person – annual cost | $40,000–80,000 |
| MA tool (software service) – annual cost | $10,000 |
| Data purchases per year | $10,000 |
| Content creation per year | $20,000 |
| TOTAL PER YEAR | $90,000–$130,000 |

You can probably absorb some of these costs internally, but as you can see, this investment is one better suited to companies with around $5 million ($3.15 million) in revenue or more.

If you're thinking that you can use less expensive ways to do marketing (such as using social marketing tactics, press releases, pushing your content to multiple places (content syndication), hosting network events, offering free workshops, cross-promotion with other businesses, supporting community events, focused SEO across all content and website, using less expensive email marketing tools and using interns), bear in mind that all these activities require expenditure and take human effort, which people often pretend is 'free'. It's not. Some of these approaches can be low cost, and some may be just perfect for you – build a marketing program that works for you and consider automation when you're ready.

Be realistic. Don't expect instant results and don't think that marketing can drive more than 20–25 percent of total leads in years 1 or 2. The best marketing organizations get to 30 percent or so in the services field. Even so, that's quite a contribution, bearing in mind the cost of a good salesperson.

# Adding Automation to Your Marketing Armory

The value of marketing automation is the automation (duh!) and the ability to pick out contacts that are targeted prospects likely to be ready to talk to you. When you combine an already effective marketing program with marketing automation, you can expand your reach, your frequency of campaigns and your ability to laser target specific groups within your target market. Your existing marketing strategy, programs and campaigns, designed to support your business goals (see Chapters 9 and 10), are the cornerstone of your future marketing automation. Don't throw all that out – you're not starting again, you're enhancing your capabilities with some new tools, techniques and ways of designing your programs and campaigns.

Before you can get there, you need to go through some considerations.

In order to adopt marketing automation in your company, you need to consider the following three things:

- ✔ **Infrastructure and staffing for marketing automation:** In everyday English, tools and people (internal and external).

- ✔ **Demand generation programs that use automation techniques:** In other words, the contacts, campaign design and content ready for the first wave of the campaign to launch.

- ✔ **Procedures and best practices for running and reporting on automated programs:** What your reporting can tell you and what to do if the pilot doesn't seem to be getting traction.

In this section I describe who in your company is needed at every stage as you look at tools, build your database, design your automated programs and test and evaluate your campaigns. I provide sections on each of those stages.

You're going to need different people as you work through the stages: maybe an external marketing automation consultant or firm, an additional marketing team member, a specialist who writes content and creates graphics, or a videographer who captures your content in compelling high definition. Consider getting creative with your staffing: for example, full-time, part-time, contract, interns. Get help as and when you need it to manage your investment.

## *Choosing your infrastructure tools*

Regarding infrastructure, marketing automation depends on three interconnected systems, as Figure 11-1 shows.

As you can see, connections exist between all the systems: data passing to and fro, or users of specific parts of the system taking advantage of the capabilities of other components.

The key thing to take away is that these three systems communicate with each other to progress your relationship with contacts that choose to act on your invitations. Their actions tell you where they are in the sales process, so that you waste less time on pointless cold calls to people who have no interest in your service right now – allowing you to focus on contacts that show signs of life.

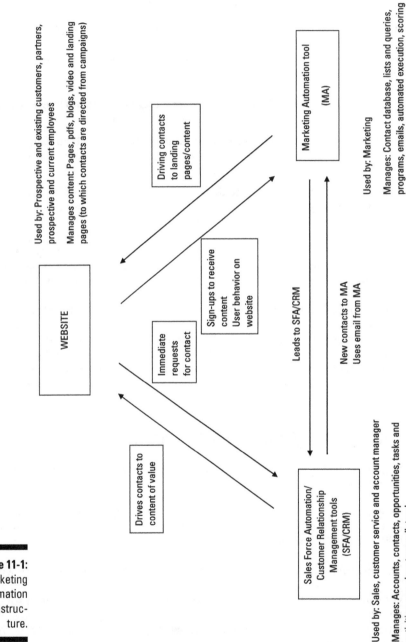

**Figure 11-1:**
Marketing
automation
infrastruc-
ture.

## Marketing automation infrastructure in action

Imagine that your company just created a new white paper and an email has just gone out from the marketing automation tool to 3,000 contacts with a link. When recipients click on the link, they're taken to a landing page. This page may have some content that positions the white paper, or even asks for additional information from the contacts, before they can download the white paper.

Between the marketing automation system, which can capture email click-throughs, and the website, which can track user actions on the website and gather more information about the contact, your knowledge about the contact increases based on data and behavior. This information can be pushed through to the sales automation system, so that a salesperson who chooses to contact that person knows who she is, what she's been doing on your website and what type of content she's already been looking at.

Now imagine that the same contact fills in a form on the website to download a piece of content called '10 things to ask your new _____ services firm'. This action is recorded in the marketing automation system, which determines that this contact has 'scored' enough points to be classified as an MQL. This lead gets posted immediately into the sales force automation system and sends a message to a salesperson. She calls, finds out that the lead is a real opportunity and then disables any further emails going from the MA tool, because she's now going to manage the communications in person. The salesperson can direct the prospect to specific content on the website, or use emails that have been created as part of campaigns in the MA system, to edit and send individually to the prospect.

If your head is spinning right now, welcome to the world of marketing automation.

As with most other aspects of business development, you have to make choices about how these three systems interact. Some companies manage their landing pages with their MA tool, leaving the website as the place where content is accessed or downloaded. Some treat their sales force automation/customer relationship management (SFA/CRM) tool as the master contact database; others use the MA tool for this task. All three systems also offer reporting and analytics. Setting all this up takes some depth of knowledge, so if you're not particularly technical, get help! I discuss SFA/CRM tools in more detail in Chapter 13. Note that most firms where sales is a complex process use an SFA/CRM tool and then add an MA tool when they're ready. If your sales process is really simple, you may be managing sales with a spreadsheet and you're more likely to use a simple email marketing tool, not a full-blown MA tool.

The choice of tools and how they get set up is an important decision that you need to take collaboratively. Get your marketing and sales leaders, head of account management and head of customer service, if you have one, all involved. Ideally, you want to pick systems that are easy to integrate (get to talk to each other) and require the minimum of customization. Using the solutions 'out-of-the-box' is ideal.

Your head of marketing needs to drive the choice of MA tool. Make sure that it can:

✔ Handle a database of contacts and allow you to determine what data you want to store.

✔ Provide a way of querying the database so you can select contacts for a specific campaign.

✔ Create and store email templates and allow you to create specific email from those templates.

✔ Create automated campaigns, including the different stages of the campaign and the rules that determine when the next stage of the campaign should be implemented (typically for an individual).

✔ Track behavior by allowing you to assign points to each action that the contact takes. The sum of the points tells you when the threshold for designating the contact as a MQL has been reached. Time to call them!

✔ Integrate with your SFA/CRM so that contact data and new leads can flow between the two systems. Ideally, your MA tool also integrates with your website, especially if you require site visitors to log in before you provide them with valuable content.

✔ Provide detailed reports on specific campaigns, as well as summary reports, dashboards and the like, on campaigns overall.

For your website, you typically need a content management system (CMS) if you're going to keep adding fresh content to your website. The next time you go in for a website redesign, make sure that you implement a CMS, even a free one like WordPress. It may cost marginally more at the time, but you don't have to pay a web designer ongoing fees to add new content for you – your folks can do that themselves.

Prepare yourself for at least three months of setting up. It may go quicker, but you're one of the lucky ones if it does.

If this all seems like overkill, consider lower-cost options, such as a simple online email marketing tool, SFA and CMS tools. They won't be integrated (passing data to and fro to each other), but if your volume of activity is fairly low, they're a good choice, until you're ready for the big time.

## Building your database

Small firms often pull together contact lists and shoot out emails using simple tools (which are well designed and easy to use). Then they go through the same process again the next time they want to send out a mass email.

The problem with lists is that they go out-of-date quickly and multiple lists may have the same people in them – so that telling who's received what is difficult. As your volume of contacts grows, managing your communications and keeping your data up-to-date becomes increasingly difficult.

Initially, your contacts are probably existing relationships and you add to them from business cards you collect, from people who call in to the office, or fill in a form on your website, or from research you do on LinkedIn or other tools such as Hoovers, Dun & Bradstreet, InsideView, Data.com, Netpropex or the like. The list of sources is endless and it takes a lot of effort to collect and capture all this contact data. You can even buy lists from a list broker.

When you move to marketing automation, you need a database of contacts that you're going to reach out to with your marketing efforts. You may have the beginnings of such a database in your SFA tool, but it's typically rather stagnant, because sales can do only so much to keep in touch with hundreds or thousands of contacts. The database (think contact record) usually stores *firmographics,* namely data such as the company size, number of employees, industry, contact name, title, department, email, phone number and website.

Marketing automation (MA) becomes really powerful when it starts to add behavioral data to the contact record. Where firmographics allow you to segment the database by geography, company size, industry, job role or any other criterion for which you have the data, behavioral data allows you to understand the contact's position in the buyer's journey. You can allocate points to specific behavior and then select an aggregated score that's the threshold for defining a MQL.

Your MA tool can also help you identify which contacts are out-of-date from emails that bounce back as undelivered. This identification gives you the opportunity to eliminate inaccurate contacts or to find out where they've gone.

You can grow your database from list purchases, research, sign-ups, personal contacts – just remember that you can't blast out unsolicited emails. When you use MA, you start to build a reputation as a sender of email – you get your own score for how trustworthy you are. If you misbehave, you can get shut down as an email sender. So make sure that you understand the CAN-SPAM Act or other legislation that applies in your country, or hire a firm to manage your emails and reputation for you. Also consider emailing your existing contacts and asking for them to share your email with their network. Include something that may excite or interest the new contacts. This approach helps you get additional 'opted-in' contacts (people who have agreed to accept your communications).

Email marketing is a complex legal area – get help and keep within the law.

When you first acquire a list to add to your database, you get excited at the possibility of all those new contacts. Be aware that bought lists are up to 30 per cent inaccurate, and so send your list to a data-cleansing service to test the email for deliverability and to send the first email, which gives contacts a chance to subscribe or unsubscribe from your communications. The first email should be a 'teaser', letting contacts know what your upcoming series of communications is going to be all about. If they're interested, they stick with you.

Now you have a clean list based on a data-cleansing company that has a solid email *reputation* (namely, its emails haven't been blacklisted by the major email providers, such as Gmail). Because this type of company sends millions of emails a day, your database of, say, 10,000 emails isn't going to impact its overall reputation for having high levels of email delivery and low levels of complaints. This area is complex, which is why you need a marketing automation or email marketing specialist in your network of support.

Database management is a time-consuming activity, but not rocket science. Your marketing co-ordinator should be able to manage your database as well and create content for your marketing programs, with help from others in your organization.

## Designing demand generation programs

Before you build your first automated campaign, you need to take a stab at mapping the buyer's journey in a bit more detail. Doing so is important because the prize is better qualified leads based on scoring that's driven by behavior; therefore, you need to understand that behavior in finer detail, so that you can design programs that fit the buyer's journey. What might that look like?

### Mapping your buyer's journey

Figure 11-2 shows a sample early-stage buyer's journey based on the section on creating your marketing campaign in Chapter 10. It concerns an education department that's looking to build an environmentally friendly (LEED certified) school. I use that example to show how to use the buyer's journey to automate that particular campaign. Your own buyer's journey will have its nuances.

This journey is independent of your intervention, and so it gives you an objective view that allows you to design a program that aligns with the buyer's desires at each step, providing exactly the right information at the right time.

| The buyer's journey | | | | | | | |
|---|---|---|---|---|---|---|---|
| **Step** | **Step 1** | **Step 2** | **Step 3** | **Step 4** | **Step 5** | **Step 6** | **Step 7** |
| **Stage** | Need/ problem awareness | Commitment to further action | Research information/ understand challenges | Define requirements | Identify solutions | Build business case | Identify vendors/ start assessment |
| Internal influence | Complaints and issues with current situation/ solution. Business imperative. | Stakeholders agree with the need. Budget considerations. Bandwidth considerations. Act now/ act later. | Information from Planning Department. | Internal requirements and expectations. | Procurement parameters. | Timeframes for approval. Influencers and their 'weight' in the process. | Internal solution (we can handle it). Favored/ existing vendors. Procurement process. |
| External influence | Competitor action. Market trends. Market imperatives. End of life issues. | Public opinion. Parent action groups. Local and national media coverage. | Other cities, counties and their projects. | Tools to identify requirements. | Firms and consultants. What others have done. | Reports on LEED and why it is important. Quantitative data. Estimates of costs to implement LEED. | Network. Social sites, vendor websites, case studies and other content. Information from professional associations. |

**Figure 11-2:**
The buyer's
journey.

A company has multiple 'buyers'; a lot of B2B purchases are made by committee, so when you design a program for a CFO, for example, map the buyer's journey separately from the one for a CEO or CIO or head of HR. These people's involvement and concerns are different.

### Designing your program

Figure 11-3 shows the program that maps to Figure 11-2. This program is just one of many options, but the underlying principle is sound: give the contacts what they want, when they want it. This campaign is based on the architect example in Chapter 10 and is an automated version of the one in Figure 10-3.

From the buyer's journey, you can probably see that this buyer can respond to any one of dozens of possible campaigns elements. You have to be selective about what you can get done because you can't do everything that's possible.

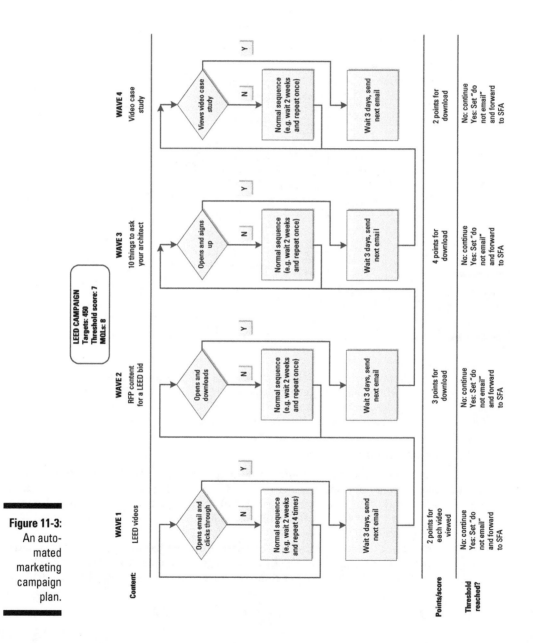

**Figure 11-3:**
An automated marketing campaign plan.

Imagine that a contact doesn't respond to wave 0 or 1, but clicks on a LinkedIn post pointing to the content for wave 2. That tells you that the contact is somewhere between steps 4 and 6 of the buyer's journey (Figure 11-2). Then:

1. **The MA tool waits 3 days and then emails wave 3 *to that contact* and to others who responded to wave 2 with the same action.**

2. **If the contact picks up wave 3, the MA tool waits 3 days and then emails wave 4.**

3. **If at any stage, the score exceeds the threshold for an MQL (see the key on Figure 11-3), a lead gets posted to the SFA tool for a qualifier/salesperson to call the contact, checks that she received the materials and offers her a chance to talk to someone who can help (in this case, a partner in the firm).**

4. **An appointment is set; the partner's responsibility is to convert the conversation into an opportunity.**

Notice that when the program's elements are all in place, the first wave kicks off and the whole program runs itself, with each contact being handled at the pace that's appropriate to it. Bingo – 1-to-1 marketing. Note how personal this process feels to the contact – instead of just getting an email every month, she now gets the next piece of information *when she needs it.*

Whatever the campaign element, whether blog, email, LinkedIn ad or search engine pay-per-click, you want to measure the response rate, so even if it's not an email, you drive clicks to your website, so that you can start to capture contact data. When you have contact data (minimum is an email address) you can start tracking behavior from your email campaigns.

Campaigns that have extremely low response rates probably don't generate a customer down the line, so response rates tell you something about the effectiveness of your campaigns. However, as your automated campaigns start to get traction, you can add other measures, such as customer acquisition cost (CAC). To add them, you track MQLs and calculate the cost of acquiring the MQL as an absolute dollar value at the end of the campaign. For example, if marketing spends $5,000 ($3,150) on a campaign and the result is ten MQLs, each one effectively costs $500 ($315) to acquire in marketing terms. Marketing's goal is to drive this number down.

Automated programs take some experience to design. This work belongs in the hands of your head of marketing, unless you hire a specialist to do the design. Your best writers and designers can put together the details, such as the content for ads, emails or white papers, but the marketing leader should be on the hook for approving the design of the program and for its success.

When MQLs pop up, someone needs to make calls: a salesperson or a *lead qualifier* – someone who can follow up on an MQL and qualify the lead into a sales opportunity.

Although I'm focusing on prospective customer campaigns, don't neglect partners and existing customers. Work out good programs for them. However, because the contact numbers are typically small, you can run these campaigns through your MA tool, but they don't usually need a lot of steps or to be automated. Note that you can run a non-automated campaign (such as a single email blast, or several email blasts that you initiate manually). In other words, MA tools have all the capabilities of a simple email marketing tool and a lot more.

Email seems simple, but good email campaigns take some finesse. You may well appreciate the glossary of email marketing terms at `http://blog.anchorcomputer.com/index.php/about-us/email-marketing-glossary-and-common-terms`.

## Testing and evaluating your programs

You need to test your new MA tool with a pilot, so develop a program that's relatively simple, even one without any automation, such as a single email shot. After you gain confidence that the system is working, you can start getting fancy, as the rest of this section describes.

### Headlines that work

How many unsolicited emails do you get a day? How many that you signed up for? Do you read them all? Fifty per cent of them? Ten per cent? When you're swamped, an email requires a compelling subject line to grab your attention.

Think about your audience, what bothers them in your specialty area and what would have them open that email, click through and read all your content. I have an email today in my inbox that says 'Hiring Advice: Selecting Your Interview Questions Wisely' (yawn). Here are a few of my own subject lines, just for fun:

- ✔ Is your business development a third-grader's lemonade stand?
- ✔ Why marketing is like your washing machine.
- ✔ You know the score on the football game – so how's your business doing?
- ✔ Sales. Business development. The same thing, right?

If contacts receiving your emails don't get past the subject line, you're in the 'deleted' folder in the wink of an eye. You get less than three seconds before that delete key is pressed, so make it compelling.

Like everyone, I get a lot of emails from people trying to sell me services. Here's the third in a series of emails from a prospecting company. The subject line was 'Should I stay or should I go?':

> Hi Anna,
>
> I've tried reaching out several times to go over your lead generation strategies at RainMakers and have not heard back from you. This tells me a few things:
>
> 1) You're all set with your current prospecting strategies, if this is the case please let me know so I will stop bothering you.
>
> 2) You're interested but have not had the time to respond.
>
> 3) You're being chased by a hippo and need me to call Animal Control!

His other emails were equally imaginative and funny, even if not perfectly written! They're all still in my inbox. When I need prospecting help, I'll call him.

Make your subject lines and emails compelling. Come to think of it, make all your content compelling – it has to stand out.

### A/B split testing

If you're going to start with a pilot email campaign, you may want to test your headlines, body text or other aspects of the email (such as send dates and times). Your MA tool should have the function to allow you to test different emails automatically. If not, you can do it manually on a pilot group, though you may find it a bit laborious.

Here's how *A/B split testing* works:

1. **Create two versions of the content, for example two different subject lines (hence the A/B idea).**

2. **Split your pilot list into two.**

3. **Send your two emails and see which gets the better open rate.**

4. **Use that version for your final email.**

For step 2, the pilot list doesn't have to be exactly in half, but do try to make it random (for example, split by last name, A–L, M–Z, rather than, say, by state, which would introduce regional biases). You can, of course, segment your database, say select all CIOs and then do an A/B split test on them by last name.

You need enough emails to make the results reliable, so this technique is for a larger database. You should also be able to do this type of testing on your website, with different headlines, images or other content. Ask your web expert if you're interested in finding out more.

### Channels additional to the core campaign

Your campaigns managed inside your MA tool are centered on email, but the general idea is to provide great content and then direct contacts to where to find it. You can use a lot of other ways to drive people to your content, just be aware that you're no longer in control of who the message gets to, whereas your database at least contains a core of good targets.

Here are a few examples of other options:

- ✔ LinkedIn (adverts on group pages or sponsored updates).
- ✔ Banner Ads on sites that your contacts are likely to go to (usually under a pay-per-click model).
- ✔ Tweets and retweets (if you've enough followers, or followers that have large numbers of followers).

If you're not an expert in the three techniques above, get help, because they all require some expertise. You don't want to waste your money getting it wrong.

### Points per action and threshold scoring

When you design your campaigns, the first waves are typically directed to the early stages in the buyer's journey and later ones kick in if the contact starts reacting (check out the earlier Figure 11-3). You normally allocate lower points to action in earlier stages, more to later ones. This rule isn't hard and fast, but is a good general one to start with. Your threshold score is also a bit of a guess to begin.

Track your leads and see whether they develop into solid opportunities that the salespeople can propose on (and this process can take months, of course). If you've enough data, trace back to the points and scores and see whether your setup is a good predictor of real opportunities (ultimately closed deals too, but salespeople should be delighted to have a real opportunity from marketing – it's up to them to win it).

## Making the phone ring

The first time someone calls as a result of a campaign you're running is a special day – even if it turns out not to be any kind of lead! Ultimately, you want prospective customers to be calling you and that typically happens only when they're referred by someone they trust (and these leads are really precious), or when your name is 'out there' sufficiently that people know you by reputation (for example, your partners are talking about how great you are, you've won awards or your people get invited to present at speaking engagements).

To get to that point is a journey. Marketing automation is a great place to start, because you need to position yourself in a credible way with large numbers of people.

One place to start elevating your results is to get your lead qualification caller and salespeople to pay close attention to what marketing is doing. Ensure that you:

- ✓ **Make sure that marketing callers and salespeople knows what campaigns are happening:** Your MA or email marketing tool can send 'seed' emails to a list of internal people. Put your callers and salespeople on that list. Also send them your campaign plan before you start the campaign.

- ✓ **Route leads automatically:** The quicker someone calls a lead when they pass the score threshold, the better. You hear people talk about 3 minutes, or within 15 minutes, but those practices are normally B2C or product sales, not services. You can set policy dependent on how urgent people think your services are. If it's reputation management, get on it right away. If it's HR services, that day is usually fine. The point is that a lot of people signal their interest to a company and never hear back. And then companies complain that prospects don't call them! Your MA tool can route leads to your SFA tool, if they're integrated.

- ✓ **Enable sales with new, fresh content:** Make your campaigns and content available to sales so that it can use them to send to its own contacts. If your MA and SFA tools are integrated, this process may even be automatic. For example, I can send emails from Salesforce (my SFA tool) that were originally created as mass campaigns in Silverpop (my MA tool).

- ✓ **Share campaign results:** Your tool can create reports to show how campaigns are doing. Get feedback from sales on leads that you passed to them too and review the campaign metrics with the team at the end to see what's working and what isn't.

- ✓ **Consider content quality:** If you're getting a poor response to your campaigns, but you think that your database is a good one, the problem may be down to poor content. Get feedback internally and ask a couple of trusted advisors what they think about your content. An awful lot of good content is out there – maybe yours just doesn't stand out enough.

May the force of marketing automation take you to the phone ringing off the hook.

# Chapter 12

# Forming a Winning Team: Marketing and Sales Cohesion

*In This Chapter*

▶ Aligning sales and marketing to increase revenue

▶ Helping marketing and sales get along

*A* growing services business has to expand its strategies for reaching more and more prospective customers as well as retaining and growing existing ones. Doing the same old thing year after year just doesn't hack it.

When acquiring new customers, the burden of effort falls on marketing and sales, but unfortunately these functions often don't see eye to eye. In the most extreme cases, they're severely at odds, with finger-pointing if the results are lower than management wants. Yet one of the keys to successful business development is having marketing and sales operating in concert. Research from the Aberdeen Group (in 2010) reveals that companies grow faster when marketing and sales co-operate effectively.

This chapter explains why collaboration is necessary and explores how to achieve that aim and produce maximum results. I look at where the divide between sales and marketing arises and suggest ways to make sure that the two parties play nicely in the sandbox, avoid problems (watch out for any submerged cat-mess mines!) and build one whopping big sandcastle.

# 'We Can Work It Out': Sales and Marketing Join Forces

The Beatles had the right idea (even if they couldn't carry it out in practice and stay together as a band): sales and marketing can work out their differences.

Although they're separate disciplines, marketing and sales are trying to talk to the same audience: your target customers. Plus, both ultimately want to secure the same goal: the growth of your business. When internal stresses build up between marketing and sales (and also delivery), the customer's experience around the lifecycle ceases to be seamless. Check out Figure 12-1, which is a simplified version of Figure 2-1, with marketing, sales and delivery providing care and feeding the customer from appetizer through to dessert.

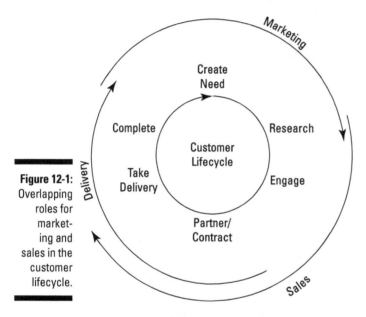

**Figure 12-1:** Overlapping roles for marketing and sales in the customer lifecycle.

The figure shows the significant overlaps between the three disciplines. Services is a team game and when your people work in compartmentalized groups, all sorts of issues occur.

In this section I discuss the importance of sales and marketing alignment as your business develops, identifying clear responsibilities and roles, as well as shared goals.

## Reassessing roles as your business grows

When your business started up, perhaps one person, or maybe two or three people, did everything. The advantage in those early days is that everyone knows everything what's happening all the time.

Confusion doesn't arise all that much about who does what in small organizations, because people undertake several functions and everyone knows everyone. Perhaps one owner takes on marketing and sales and another heads up delivery, and that's about it. You may still encounter the occasional issue, of course:

- ✔ If you love selling, you may get impatient with the complaints from delivery about how you overpromised and now it can't deliver.

- ✔ If you're an operations leader, you may think that sales is sloppy and should do a better job defining the scope and getting more money for the work.

Even so, organizations with, say, less than ten people rarely hear someone remark 'I thought you were going to do that!' The problem is that in small organizations the original people aren't going to be good at every aspect. They can't be: people aren't wired to excel at everything.

As your business grows, job roles inevitably need to become more specialized. Adding new people to the organization can cause fractures in the previously smooth, if imperfect, management of the customer lifecycle. That's the point when you need to work hard at getting alignment between your department leaders (like marketing, sales and delivery) and with the customer experience cycle.

## *Laying out the connections between marketing and sales*

Although sales, marketing and delivery have different skills and focuses, they're pulling towards the same end. Inevitably, therefore, their roles are linked and indeed interdependent – as I show in Figure 12-2.

Delivery always is, or should be, really busy, so marketing and sales need to reach out to delivery for what they need – such as feedback and case studies from customers or support for the sales process to help scope, price and sell a deal. (I include delivery in this section, because delivery is critical to new sales and to feedback to marketing and sales. The discipline gets more attention in Part V.)

Say that you have three leaders heading up marketing, sales and delivery. In an ideal world, who takes care of what around the customer experience is clear. Table 12-1 is a more detailed version of Figure 12-1, as a working model. Organizations vary in whether and where sales and marketing are involved around the cycle, and so adapt this table to your own situation and needs.

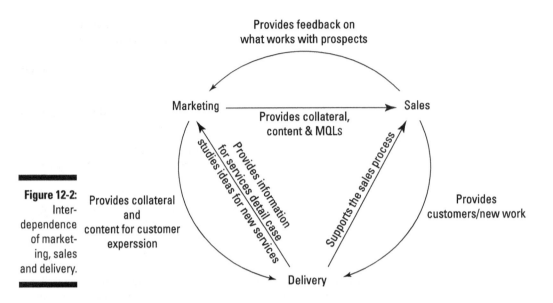

| Table 12-1 | Customer Lifecycle and Who Does What | | |
|---|---|---|---|
| **Customer Lifecycle Stage: The Customer** | **Marketing** | **Sales** | **Delivery** |
| Creates the need. | Positions content that interests target customers. Positions the brand. | *Provides insight to marketing as to what's important to customers.* | *Provides insight to marketing as to what's important to customers.* |
| Researches/ plans. | Provides content to educate and inform. Prepares for actual touches (human intervention). | *Provides insight to marketing as to what's important to customers.* | *Provides insight to marketing as to what's important to customers.* |
| Engages with vendors. | **Qualifies as an MQL.** | **Qualifies as an SQL.** | **Supports sales in meetings with the prospect.** |

| Customer Lifecycle Stage: The Customer | Marketing | Sales | Delivery |
|---|---|---|---|
| Partners with a specific vendor/signs a contract. | *Provides additional collateral as needed for specific sales.* | **Creates specific scope and proposes services. Wins the deal. Gets contracts signed. Gathers feedback whether win or loss.** | **Assists in scoping/ proposing solutions/ pricing.** |
| Takes delivery | | *Supports handover to delivery.* | Takes point on the management of delivery. |
| Completes with the vendor by signing off and providing feedback | **Gathers customer feedback and information for a case study.** | **Receives feedback from delivery concerning the customer.** | **Manages customer sign-off on the work. Takes the lead on customer feedback processes.** |

Note that the items in italics are the support that one function provides to another – this sometimes makes them points of weakness (that is, they don't get done or handed over effectively). Another area of concern is where the departments are collaborating (the text in bold) – these are prime opportunities for misunderstandings as to who's doing what and who's responsible for the outcomes.

Organizations that take a customer-centric viewpoint and even start to break down traditional departmental barriers tend to do much better in acquiring, retaining and growing customers.

Discuss Table 12-1 as a team and thrash out any issues or friction. (Check out Chapter 13, where I supply loads of suggestions for structuring this discussion.) The key is do it fast, within a month, and revisit frequently.

## Setting common goals and targets

Being clear about marketing and sales' responsibilities is essential (see the preceding section), but actions have no bite unless you tie them to specific goals. When you create strategic goals for the organization, you need to break them down into specific targets for marketing and sales. Chapter 6 shows you how to choose those strategic initiatives and make them quantifiable.

Imagine that one of your goals is to drive $4 million ($2.52 million) in net new sales in the next year. Typically you obtain your leads from referrals, from customers or from your network, plus your partners have been good at sending you great leads too. Over the last 12 months, you closed $3 million ($1.89 million) in net new business, and so you're looking for $1 million ($630,000 more). You started investing in marketing three months ago and the department is ready to start programs to drive leads. You want your pipeline for the next year to look like Figure 12-3.

**Figure 12-3:**
Expanding the pipeline: shaded area indicates when a handover occurs.

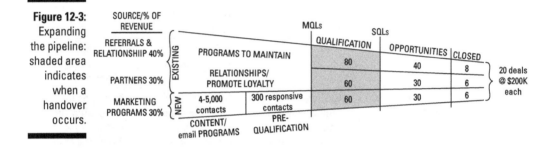

Not only does marketing need to drive leads, it must also support sales with materials, organize and drive campaign activities that engage partners, customers and other relationships, and simultaneously maintain ongoing marketing of your brand and company. Marketing is a direct and indirect contributor to lead generation, and because expanding channels and adding new ones *is* the strategy for growth of net new sales, marketing has to play a major part.

Sales needs to understand that marketing-produced leads are neither better nor worse than ones from other channels. Here are a couple of examples of leads that don't originate from marketing:

- ✔ **Leads from partners:** These may or may not progress to be prospects. Although the leads usually want what you have to offer, they often don't have enough budget or they already have a preferred vendor (not you) or they're looking at next year anyway.

- ✔ **Referrals from your network:** These leads can be rather varied in quality – your contacts are so eager to help that they refer anyone they can, with no reference as to whether they're a fit or even need the precise service you have to offer.

In both of these cases, sales spends time qualifying, some of which is 'wasted'. Sales may moan about this, but it knows it comes with the territory.

TRUE STORY

## Investing in marketing to drive revenue

Chapman's business was entirely driven by speaking engagements. Every time he spoke at a conference, people wanted to work with his company. Problem was, he had little time to focus on sales, so although he closed business from his speaking engagements, he could've been driving a lot more business than he did.

He hired a marketing intern, Rajesh, to manage which conferences he should go to, make all the arrangements and do a bit of pre-event marketing. Rajesh went with him to conferences and took responsibility for following up with everyone, creating a pipeline of leads as well as supporting Chapman with sales materials, scheduling and follow up. Chapman increased his business by 75 percent in one year and was able to hire a salesperson to work alongside Rajesh.

When sales staff complain that marketing leads aren't 'ready to buy' (that is, when a handover occurs – see the shaded area in Figure 12-3), my answer is, talk to them about it. Tell them what you want in a lead, *but* remember that some leads seem ready, but aren't. Give marketing feedback and then cut the staff some slack. After all, you may find a diamond in the dross tomorrow. You don't find out unless you talk to them, and skillful qualification can turn up a business problem that a customer didn't know it had.

# 'Come On, Come On, Let's Stick Together!' Marketing and Sales Can Collaborate

Imagine a 100-meter relay race, in which teams of four athletes compete against each other to run 400 meters in total as quickly as possible. A swift, smooth, on-the-move handover of the baton is often the crucial moment in winning. Now imagine that one runner refuses to take the baton because it's not perfectly positioned, or perhaps the preceding runner insists on throwing the baton to him before he's ready. Without doubt, this un-co-operative team is going to come in last (if the members finish at all and don't resort to brawling part way around the track!). Clearly the team in which all four members understand the strengths, limits and roles of the others is more likely to win.

In this section, I cover some of the contentious issues that arise between sales and marketing. I also provide responses and actions you can take to help the two departments work for the common goal of increased business for your company.

## Clearing up misunderstandings that threaten unified business development

Sales should welcome any support it can get, whether leads or great *collateral* (brochures, case studies, presentations). Selling is hard enough, but if sales doesn't have the right infrastructure, the staff spend time compensating for that, instead of working with prospects.

Similarly, marketing needs to be responsive to the needs of salespeople, provide what they want and listen carefully to feedback about what they hear when they have conversations with prospects.

Here's the good news for the salespeople. If they try to qualify a lead and it doesn't work out at that time, they can throw it back over the fence for marketing to nurture, while gaining themselves precious sales time with their active opportunities.

Sales is always going to need to generate leads of its own, but nothing's sweeter than an incoming lead or a contact that has matured to the point of being ready to buy.

Even so, a few areas of tension occur frequently between marketing and sales. When you understand the following issues, you're well placed to combat them:

✔ Sales likes to go straight for the jugular and qualify any contact by digging into whether he's ready to buy. That's understandable – the staff are on the hook for results. I know that the best salespeople don't do this, but a lot of others still do.

Marketing doesn't agree with this approach – it opts for understanding where the contact is in the lifecycle and providing the *right* communication. Heads butt regularly over this topic. But now that you know, you can foresee it and smooth the relationship.

✔ When a lead contacts your business, sales is entitled to qualify the lead if they can. If the lead comes from a marketing program, however, it isn't the same as a sales-generated one. A gap always exists between marketing-qualified leads (MQLs) and sales-qualified leads (SQLs) (the shaded area in Figure 12-3), because some MQLs have to be recycled to marketing.

The gap isn't the result of marketing producing 'bad' leads. Sales can be vocal about this topic and causes unjustified offence to marketing in the process. Make sure that both sides appreciate the other's requirements.

✔ Sales doesn't like *tire-kickers*, that is, people who have vague interest in what your firm does, but no buying intent *right now.* Some of these tire-kickers may want to buy some day, some won't. Marketing and sales have a joint responsibility to convert prospective customers into qualified leads and into actual customers. They play different roles at different times and they need to come together and appreciate and respect each other's capabilities and contribution.

Contacts aren't trying to waste anyone's time; they're trying to get what they need right now (even time-wasters with their own agenda are entitled to pursue it).

✔ Sales has to respond quickly to provide information that keeps the sale moving forward. Marketing should work closely with sales to understand what it needs to do to support the sales process and provide flexible, well-written and well-presented materials that sales can quickly adapt.

Don't have sales staff spending time writing collateral – this activity is not usually their strength and is a waste of their time. Marketing gets pretty aerated when sales staff create 'ad-hoc' materials, because they so often go off-brand: in other words, they wreck the careful, patient work of marketing in creating and working within the specific positioning and messaging that presents the company in the best light.

Now, I'm painting a dire picture here and some sales and marketing people can justifiably say that they never behave this way, but I've seen this adversarial situation over and over. An alternative scenario is that the owners want growth but are in denial that marketing is needed. They're holding on to an old-world view that all they need is more salespeople.

The market isn't interested in sales approaches that are 10–20 years out of date. They're voting with their fingers and going online for a bit of self-service. That's what marketing can provide.

Have you ever found yourself thinking, 'My business is plateauing – I'll just hire another salesperson'? No, don't – unless you have particularly strong leads coming into sales but just too many of them (great problem, right?).

If your salespeople are expected to *produce* all the leads, hiring new salespeople or replacing existing ones rarely works. You just end up burning your way through perfectly good people who tap out their own network within a year and then dry up – unless they're that one-in-a-hundred salesperson who really can self-generate. And boy, are they expensive to hire!

## *Acting to support unified business development*

The situation that I describe in the preceding section isn't the be-all-and-end-all, fortunately. But in a complex customer experience cycle, lots of information is flying around and plenty of opportunities exist for the ball to get dropped.

One of the biggest complaints by target contacts is that when they do call or fill in a web form, they don't hear back, or they have to wait 24–72 hours for a call. If your organization can honestly say that this never happens, you are *so* the exception.

To expand your marketing channels, you're likely to need new employees and some different tactics, processes and systems to ensure that you don't ignore opportunities to make another sale.

In the earlier Table 12-1, I look at who does what when. Here I discuss a few key tactics that bring marketing and sales closer together:

- ✔ **Provide multiple ways for prospective customers to connect with you.** Advertise, push content out there, be active in online groups, have a web form on your website, send out newsletters and attend events. Measure what each channel produces and use the productive ones. Everyone in your business will be happy.

- ✔ **Don't lose data.** When you get contact information, have a place to put it and a way of letting the right person know what needs to happen next. Start by thinking this process through in advance – how do incoming calls get handled, where do you enter that stack of business cards you picked up at a networking event, what do you do with a referral? Your systems need to cope with the complexity of handling relationships at all stages of the lifecycle. See Chapters 10 and 11 for marketing systems and Chapter 13 for sales/customer management systems.

- ✔ **Be consistent in your approach to capturing data, nurturing leads and qualifying them, and then selling to them and delivering.** You need to define the criteria for passing a contact from one stage in the lifecycle to the next, for example from marketing to sales, or from sales to delivery. Some are obvious – if a customer signs a contract, sales obviously has to hand over to delivery, but defining *what* information needs to be handed over is essential. This applies equally to all stages of the customer lifecycle. Miss something and everyone's life becomes a misery. Your systems need to capture data all along the lifecycle, so make sure that they're flexible enough.

✔ **Reduce the MQL/SQL gap.** The key here is qualification. A marketing lead has passed certain tests, but they're not the same tests as sales applies to a lead. If you can agree what an MQL looks like so that a salesperson is willing to talk to the lead, you're off to a good start. Over time, if you keep the conversation going, the gap narrows as each party gets better aligned with the other. Review qualification criteria and questions, data needs and rules around transitioning a contact from one stage to another regularly, and make sure that all this information is available and up to date.

✔ **Provide rich collateral and content for the whole team to use.** Find a central storage place and encourage people to use it for materials they need, instead of using collateral or content they've had on their own laptop or tablet for a while.

You don't want so much process that it drives people crazy, but most folks quickly forget what they said to a contact last week. Therefore, define the minimum information that you need to capture and have some simple checklists to make sure that the right data gets captured at the right time. It removes one reason for marketing and sales to fight.

## Helping marketing and sales to get on

The culture of an organization starts at the top. When the ownership of a company values marketing and sales equally, this belief permeates the organization. In contrast, you're wasting investment if you hire people and then expect them to overcome existing internal prejudices: you're simply setting up those new people for failure.

Assuming that you're committed to a balanced organization, how on earth are you going to get marketing and sales to get on? After all, sales is from Mars, marketing is from Venus. (I wish I'd coined that, but the observation is from Emily Coleman from Competitive Advantage Marketing.)

Here are a few things to think about as you start to tackle your sales and marketing alignment project:

✔ **Choose how to handle the leadership of marketing and sales.** Best models are: (a) for both to report to the owner/CEO, or (b) marketing to report to sales, assuming that your sales leader is knowledgeable about and supportive of marketing.

✔ **Break the corporate strategy down to make the work of marketing and sales a joint strategy.** Carry out this process collaboratively. Agree on metrics that can be measured and contribute to the strategic goal. See Chapter 6 for examples of metrics that make a difference.

The most important metric is deal closure (for both parties). But for marketing, I also like to measure how many proposals came from marketing leads, as a secondary measure, at least until the two sides trust each other enough to be jointly accountable for the sales result.

✔ **Create a customer-centric model for the lifecycle and map marketing, sales and delivery to that lifecycle.** Build your processes around that lifecycle. For example, consider what constitutes a move from one stage in the lifecycle to another from the customer's viewpoint. Some organizations go as far as renaming the standard funnel stages (Figure 8-3) from internally focused terms, such as 'lead', 'qualification' and so on, to more customer-centric terms, such as 'need acknowledged' and 'need defined'. (In fairness, this strategy is probably for a well-established team: the faint-hearted don't want to try changing how marketing and sales has talked about the funnel for 50 years or more.)

The point is to drag your team back to the customer's viewpoint whenever it seems to be getting inwardly focused.

✔ **Add a *lead qualification representative* to manage all incoming leads and collect data/qualify them before handing over to sales.** This role is typically for marketing, but definitely forms a bridge between marketing and sales.

✔ **Use best practices from sales (such as interacting one-on-one with prospects).** Make sure that sales gets what's valuable to it at that time and build that into the marketing programs.

✔ **Choose what data points are really valuable to know as you progress your relationship with a target customer.** Marketing is particularly good at gathering data that's highly beneficial to sales. Some of this data can be accumulated automatically; from data sources, customers providing information about themselves and data gathered about their behavior. Some data has to be researched manually. More and more, though, systems for collecting data are becoming more automated (such as capturing contact data from your website and feeding it into your SFA or MA systems – see Chapter 11). The better you know prospects, the better you get at recognizing which ones are really primed to buy. Data can also tell whether you need to adjust your services, or even create new ones.

✔ **Define how quickly leads need to be responded to and by whom.** List all your lead sources and agree a timeframe for responding and whether a lead qualification rep or a salesperson will call.

✔ **Set regular pre-brief/debrief meetings between sales and marketing.** Review what's working and what's not, what sales is hearing in the market what marketing is seeing in market, upcoming campaigns, goals and results, and so on.

✔ **Think about compensation.** Sales has typically been 'base salary + commission', whereas marketing is used to a base, maybe with an annual bonus. The time may be right to consider a more commission-based approach to marketing compensation too. Just make sure that this approach is tied to metrics that marketing can actually impact (which is why I suggest that you write proposals as a good measure).

Aligning marketing and sales is a long-term proposition, no matter how agile you are in creating the strategy. Results take time to manifest on the ground and ongoing refinement to improve them. Stay committed and keep at it.

# Part IV
# Seeing What Sales Can Do for You

| 1. The Marketplace | 2. Customer Profile | 3. Service Offerings |
|---|---|---|
| What are the choices that a prospect could make? | Who are we targeting? | What solutions are available to sell? |
| 4. Competitors | 5. Customer Needs/Pains | 6. Things to Remember |
| Who might we lose to? | What problems can we solve (and not solve)? | Checklist of things to be sure to do (eg next steps). |
| 7. Key Questions | 8. Benefits, ROI and Evidence | 9. Pricing, Timelines and other Info |
| What to ask them & what they might ask you. | What they'll get from working with you, plus case studies to prove it. | Contractual things you need to discuss. |

Find out about building successful sales teams at www.dummies.com/extras/businessdevelopment.

## In this part . . .

- ✔ Develop your sales-leadership skills, whatever your background.

- ✔ Discover solid sales practices that work.

- ✔ Dig into how to get a 'yes' from a prospective customer.

- ✔ Negotiate great contracts with authority and confidence.

- ✔ Hand over a project from sales to the delivery team effectively.

# Chapter 13

# Becoming the Leader of the (Sales) Pack

## In This Chapter

▶ Leading your business to sales success

▶ Assembling and leading a team

▶ Driving forward your sales process

*L*ike armies, sports teams and husbands, business departments need leaders with vision, insight, energy and commitment (good personal hygiene doesn't go amiss either, because you're unlikely to follow a leader you can't get within three feet of!).

Sales is no different. Sales is the lifeblood, the driver, of business growth and success, so it has to be a central part of business development. If you don't know who's on your prospective customer list, who your next three customers are likely to be or whether to hire or layoff staff, you require good sales leadership. Without it, your plan for the growth of your business is going to be hobbled right out of the starting gate.

But business development is about more than sales and simply winning new business, so this chapter helps you move beyond the typical sales cycle and into genuine business growth. I help you prepare for sales leadership and discuss its day-to-day concerns: put simply, that's plan and then do. I cover the things you need to think about and aim to help you enable salespeople to succeed (whether that's you or a team of others). I guide you in identifying key areas on which you need to focus your leadership to drive good business practice for all involved.

# Appreciating the Importance of Sales Leadership

Sales without leadership is like a rudderless ship – you may go somewhere, but it probably won't be where you want to. Whether you're experienced in sales or not, this section shows you how to enhance sales success through your leadership. No surprise that you create a direct impact on your company's revenue, customer list and projects when you become a great head of sales. Even if you're the solitary salesperson, this section helps you to think like a leader and enhance your sales results.

As the leader, you need to do the groundwork upfront to make sure that you give sales (or marketing or customer management) a new lease of life. Then you need to nurture sales as a discipline. In this section I take a look at knowing your product or service inside out, building an effective and clear sales process, using sales tools to best effect, and setting goals and using metrics.

As leaders, everyone comes with in-built strengths and weaknesses. As you grow, one of the most important moves you make is to get help in the area of your weaknesses. Check out the chapters in Parts I and II as necessary and revisit them as your business expands.

Don't try to get leadership perfectly right and don't go it alone. As you plan for sales and then execute on your plan, use other people as a resource to help you, in the planning and in the execution. Value implementing your plan quickly over seeking perfection. No matter how solid your plan looks, you need to tweak and change it frequently. The world isn't unchanging so your sales plan can't afford to be either.

Perhaps you're wondering how to identify your strengths and weaknesses. Well, if you jump out of bed in the morning because you can't wait to do something, that's a strength. If you're procrastinating about something on a regular basis, that's a weakness. When you encounter a topic in this chapter that doesn't sound like fun, take that as a sign to pay more attention to it, give it extra effort and monitor it carefully. Until you can afford to hire someone else to do it, that is.

## Getting clear what your business sells

Salespeople often talk about knowing their sales *bag* – in other words, the products or services that they're supposed to sell. The same is true for you in your leadership role. Clarity and unity are crucial so that you can ensure that all your company's employees are pulling in the same direction.

## Keeping the balance right

Jim has a thriving software-as-a-service business (offering an online accounting system for small businesses) but he needed to increase the size of his contracts – too many small clients requiring a lot of handholding were reducing his profitability. He started monitoring contract size in his pipeline. Immediately, he was spending more time with larger prospective customers and closing bigger deals.

As a leader, your responsibility is to make sure that your organization is clear about what it's selling. If you think that's obvious, have a go at the following experiment.

Ask everyone in your organization (management too) to write down what your company sells. If possible, do this anonymously and request that people don't consult with each other. Perhaps use a suggestion box in the office or an online survey using a tool such as Survey Monkey if your people are remote. Do this exercise yourself too and compare what you write with the responses from others. Afterwards, ask yourself how well aligned your business is.

Some organizations have a large sales bag – lots of things that the salesperson can offer the customer. This is typical for bigger companies selling to larger organizations who need many complex products and services. More likely you have a limited number of things to sell and that's a good thing for a small company.

If you're not sure what belongs in your bag, take a look at Chapter 5 where you can create your *offer* (the foundation of your sales bag). Make sure that the whole organization is clear on what you're selling.

Salespeople can be tempted to sell what's easiest. You, as a leader concerned with business development, may have other priorities, for example:

- ✔ Selling a balanced mix from the bag
- ✔ Selling what's most profitable
- ✔ Selling the deal that results in a retained customer, one who pays monthly fees or buys regularly

## Sorting the mess into a process

Jenny's online marketing business is always busy – with never an end to what she can do for her customers and their marketing. She describes her service as feeling like 'how long is a piece of string?'. Her desk is littered with client work and lots of colored sticky notes. When I ask to see her sales pipeline (of prospective clients), she points to her desk and says 'in there, somewhere'.

So we created a simple process to manage the mess into planned and purposeful activity. In other words, we instituted a sales process that was a good fit for her business.

Monitor *net new customers* (customers that you've never done business with before) to make sure that you're getting the business mix you want. How often depends on how many new customers you acquire over what period. If you close several a month, do it monthly; if only one or two a quarter, do it quarterly. As a benchmark of where you are today, take a look at your current customer roster to see what the mix looks like. Are you happy with where it is? If this roster is unbalanced, you can identify where you can work with the team to fix that.

## Establishing a sales process

When the bag's packed and everyone knows what you're selling (as I discuss in the preceding section), you need to define a sales process that the team can follow to ensure clarity on what to do, when and how. A sales process also gives you, as leader, a foundation for monitoring and measuring how sales is performing.

### Investigating whether you need a sales process

Your customers take a journey when they consider a service like yours. Seek to understand your customer's buying journey as closely as you can (Chapter 3 helps you map it).

A *sales process* is your view of the customer's buying journey, with the steps, tasks, recording, procedures and resources that allow your sales team to manage the buyer's journey effectively.

Don't become a slave to your process. Sales is a mix of art and science – the sales process is part of the science. Be ready and willing to break the rules when doing so is called for (see Chapter 14 for ideas on being creative in the sales process).

As you map your sales process with your team, you create the steps, tasks and other parameters to allow your team to operate with consistency. If you don't have a sales process, Table 13-1 shows why you probably need one.

| Table 13-1 | Do You Need a Sales Process? |
|---|---|
| *Without a Sales Process* | *With a Sales Process* |
| Sales management and tool use is weak. | Robust tools are driving the sales process: robust data capture, good reporting, predictability. |
| The sale is more luck than judgment. Salespeople do what their guts tell them for any specific prospect. | You can see what needs attention and what can wait. You can also respond to changing circumstances quickly. |
| Key questions don't get asked. Success is based on luck, not on rigor. | You have a focus for your leadership – with information you have the power to ask the right questions and drive the right results. |
| Key steps get missed, which can result in misunderstandings, backtracking, lost opportunities or, worse still, a nightmare contract. | The process and its supporting management tools provide a framework for consistent sale behavior and catch issues before they become a problem. |
| Team members vary in how they report their progress. | Everyone on the team is reporting on progress in the same way. |

Sales becomes a robust discipline in your company with a sales process.

### Mapping your sales process

Review the following list and identify the items that are relevant to your business and can support your sales team:

- ✔ **Stages in the sales process:** See whether you can clearly identify distinct stages (for example, qualification, proposal, negotiation), and if so break your sales process into logical and sequential steps. Design each stage to have a distinct purpose. Ensure that you have pre-requisites for moving a deal from one stage to another.

- ✔ **Tasks at each stage:** Unless this is obvious, note the typical tasks or activities at each stage.

- ✔ **Who does what:** If selling is collaborative (for example, the salesperson needs to bring in a subject matter expert or an owner at a specific point in the sale), document the roles and responsibilities in your sales process (for more details, see the later section 'Engaging in collaborative selling').

✔ **Resources:** Beyond the people on your team, if you have resources (for example, sales collateral, qualification questionnaires, proposal formats, quotation forms or services agreements), note where and how they need to be used.

Some sales process maps include marketing and customer management (that is, they map the entire customer lifecycle I cover in Chapter 3). Your choice, of course, but here I focus on creating just the sales process map. You can extend the map if you need to later.

The simpler you can make your sales process, the better, but don't make it so simple that it lacks value for the sales team. If you have inexperienced salespeople, the sales process map becomes an educational tool as well as a process to follow. If you can, use your team to help you build the sales process – after all, they're the ones out in the field doing the selling.

Choose a format for your sales process map that's most effective for your business and team. Flowcharts, spreadsheets, tables, diagrams and presentations are all good formats. You can also choose between maps that are stage-, role-, resource- or task-based – many are a blend of all these types. Just make sure that you provide a quick guide (something that can be pinned above a desk for day-to-day reference).

Figure 13-1 shows a sample sales process.

You can find the template at www.dummies.com/go/businessdevelopment or, if that's not a perfect fit for you, search for *sales process maps* online and especially look at some of the images. You're sure to find one that works for your company and team.

### Allocating responsibility

A sales process needs to highlight who's responsible for doing all the tasks, recording all the information, progressing the sales, writing contracts and managing the whole complex process. In a complicated services sale, quite a number of people can be involved in getting to a win.

Table 13-2 shows examples of roles that are typical in the sales process – adapt it to your own situation. Don't think that you have to go out and hire a bunch of people to be successful in sales. In a small company, typically one or two people do marketing and selling, supported by people from the delivery team, who may be the same two people! The reason for breaking down the roles (as you see them) is to help you plan for growth. As things get busy, you soon realize who you need to hire first.

**Sales Process with Resources, Collateral and Gating**

| | Prospect | Qualify | Present | Propose | Negotiate | Contract |
|---|---|---|---|---|---|---|
| **PURPOSE** | Schedule an appointment to Qualify | Ensure Prospect is a fit, has budget, and is ready to buy | Pitch offer to all Prospect's stakeholders | Prepare and present formal proposal | Handle final amendments to scope/proposal. Negotiate fees | Receive verbal agreement and formalize with signed contract |
| **WHO** | **Marketing or Sales** | **Sales** | **Sales and Subject Matter Expert (SME) with CEO/Owner** | **Sales with SME** | **Sales with others as necessary** | **Sales with others as necessary** |
| **GATING (prerequisite to enter this stage)** | Prospect profile meets 80% of criteria (see Chapter 5- Presenting Your Offer) | Meeting has been set to qualify opportunity | Prospect passes Qualification questions. Budget is confirmed | Prospect (all stakeholders) have had a presentation and are willing to take a proposal | Proposal is submitted to Prospect and presented | Prospect has given a verbal yes to the proposal |
| **SALES RESOURCES** | Emails/Scripts/NDA | Questionnaire | Presentation (custom) | Proposal references | References | MSA /SOW |
| **MARKETING RESOURCES** | About us | Case studies | Corporate presentation Case studies | Case studies | Case studies | |

**Figure 13-1:** Sales process with resources, collateral and gating.

| Table 13-2 | Roles in the Sales Process |
|---|---|
| **Role** | **Responsibility** |
| Salesperson (see Chapter 1 if you don't have a salesperson) | Being the lead person on the sale. Executing the sales process for specific opportunities. Co-ordinating communication with the prospect/customer and co-ordinating the rest of the team. |
| Marketing co-ordination | Providing company messaging, collateral and other resources. These resources may be general, but can also be specific to this sale, for example, when the salesperson needs a vertical (industry) twist to the story. Also demand generation for email and other ways of generating leads. |
| Subject matter expert (usually someone who delivers the service to the customer) | Providing in-depth knowledge of your services and/or the products that you implement and how they're delivered into the sales process. This person can be someone from another company (as in an alliance or partnership; see Chapter 20). |
| Project manager (usually someone who delivers the service to the customer) | Creating the project timeline, resources needed and costs (or co-ordinating those elements of your proposal with others on the delivery team). |
| Proposal writing | Assembling the proposal or response to a more formal Request For Information/Request For Quote/Request For Proposal from the prospect. Managing the quality of the proposal. |
| Contract co-ordination | Drafting the contract, statement of work, services agreement. |
| Sales leadership | Coaching the team. Providing expert advice where needed and suggesting approaches that increase the likelihood of a sale. |

As a leader, you need to ensure the following:

✔ You're gradually building towards a robust sales function that's well supported.

 ✔ Clarity exists as to who's responsible for what (several roles can be allocated to one person).

 ✔ People know what they can rely on others for.

 ✔ People are clear what they need to do themselves, namely, what you hold them accountable for.

Sounds elementary, doesn't it? Just check, though – do you have some of the basics in place, such as job descriptions, including accountabilities? Or an organization chart?

Even if you're a small business (say less than ten people), it needs to cover certain functions. Your organization chart may have your name or your business partner's name in many of the leadership boxes right now, but if you create the role descriptions for each business function, you know what you're looking for when you hire the next employee.

Job descriptions are a great starting point for sales process accountabilities. Say that your project manager has a general accountability in her job description for 'supporting net new sales by providing budgets and time estimates to sales staff'. You can translate that into a sales role document as shown in Table 13-3. Basically, take the responsibility from Table 13-2 and extend it to tasks, and if appropriate, to expected results.

| Table 13-3 | Sample Role Description | |
|---|---|---|
| **Role** | **Responsibility** | **Tasks** |
| Project manager | Creating the project timeline, resources needed and costs (or co-ordinating those elements of your proposal with others on the delivery team). | Based on project scope:<br><br>• Creates resource requirements for the project<br><br>• Provides current biographies of team members to the salesperson<br><br>• Creates project budget for approval by Sales Leadership<br><br>• Provides a high-level project plan for the project |

Don't overlook compensation. Each business sector is different, but as a general principle, all people involved in the sales process need some level of results-based compensation.

You need to define your own role for your day-to-day involvement in sales. Although the salespeople are in charge of specific opportunities, you're present to drive success and that takes oversight, for example, asking the team probing questions about progress with the sale, making suggestions (things the team may try to push along a slow sale), getting a decision or negotiating powerfully.

Try not to jump in and sell for them. Doing so may be tempting if you're the best *closer* in the company, but you don't encourage growth by undermining your sales team's confidence. Being in the process is okay – just make sure that your team knows that you're there to help but that they must lead the sale.

If you're a one- or two-person business, all the above may seem like overkill. Just think of it as planning for your larger business and what better time to do that than now. To my mind, if you act like a larger business, you become one.

## Tooling up for sales

With a sales bag and a sale process in hand, you need two additional types of resource for the sales team:

- ✔ **Marketing resources** (see Chapter 10): Company positioning, website and case studies (broadly, all types of 'collateral' information). Ideally, marketing is also driving leads for the sales team.

- ✔ **Sales resources:** A sales management tool, usually called a Sales Force Automation or a Customer Relationship Management (SFA/CRM tool), to manage the work (see the sidebar 'Giving your sales process a kick-start'). Also, sales-specific assets such as qualification questionnaires, presentations, quote/proposal formats and contracts. These items are unique to your business. Also helpful can be 'battlecards' or 'playbooks' (which I cover in Chapter 14).

If you're already using a sales management tool (such as ACT! or Salesforce), that's great. Skip to the next section.

Here are a few things to consider as you look at the options for your sales management tool:

- ✔ How many people are going to use it (some services have a minimum number of 'seats', though some don't)?

- ✔ Do you want a solution that can serve marketing as well as sales?

✔ Do you want your solution to be a one-stop shop for sales (resource, lead, opportunity, task and reporting management system) or are you willing to have additional solutions for managing other resources such as collateral, proposals, contracts and sales notes?

✔ Are you willing to accept the solution 'as is' or do you want to be able to customize it to your process, capture the data you want and produce the reports you require?

Find out what others in your type of business are using and do a bit of online research. You can even do a free trial for 30-days on certain solutions. Just make sure that you can get your data in easily and out again at the end of the trial if you change your mind.

If really necessary, you can manage your sales, contacts, opportunities and pipeline in a spreadsheet – doing so is better than nothing. Ideally, use a shared one on Google Docs or Microsoft OneDrive. With a spreadsheet you miss out on the value of the data that a sales tool collects over time, however, and that becomes a valuable resource for your business development.

If you've hired a salesperson who's worth her salt, that person expects a 'proper' sales management tool. If she doesn't, you may be dealing with some-one who operates in a lone-wolf style and trades in 'fluff' rather than in results (for more on fluff, read the later section 'Supporting sales').

## Giving your sales process a kick-start

If you don't have a sales management tool (SFA/CRM), you need one to provide the framework and resources within which your sales process comes alive. Think about it like this: if you have more than a couple of people involved, or if your sales process has quite a few steps and is complex or fairly lengthy, you need a sophisticated tool to support that sales process. If you're a one-man or one-woman band, you still need a tool but it can be a little simpler.

Having a tool doesn't drive results. You have to use it effectively too. Here are some of the benefits of a sophisticated sales tool:

✔ You have a single place for management contacts, tasks, activities, notes, completed proposals and opportunity pipeline.

✔ You can store all your marketing and sales resources together and be confident that you're using the most up-to-date versions.

✔ You have a reporting function that helps you examine your performance.

Fortunately, a whole host of sales tools are offered as services. I recommend that small businesses use online software as a service (SaaS) such as Capsule, Zoho or Salesforce. You have lots of options and fairly low monthly fees.

## Setting goals and metrics

When you have a sales process and sales tools (check out the two preceding sections), you're able to set goals and *metrics* (quantitative measures that you check periodically) specific to the sorts of results you want to see – which is a crucial part of business development. For example, you should have your revenue goals for the year already established. Break that down into revenue from repeat or ongoing customers and revenue from net new customers.

 Be cautious forecasting net revenue. In services businesses, payment is often hourly or milestone-based (payment made when certain work is completed) or at the end of the contract. When your typical sales cycle is three months from the point when a real opportunity emerges, you don't see revenue from deals being closed in the first quarter of your financial year until the end of the fourth month. You can have stretch goals and dream big, but forecast conservatively.

Table 13-4 shows some things that you can measure. The table isn't exhaustive, just suggestions, so adjust it to suit your own business. If you've never really measured things much, choose just two or three to start with – suggested ones are in bold in the table.

| Table 13-4 | Goals and Metrics | | |
|---|---|---|---|
| *Goal* | *Metric* | *What Tool?* | *How Often* |
| Forecast revenue | Actual versus original goal (by month) | Typically a spreadsheet with backlog combined with forecasted revenue from new sales | Monthly |
| **Size of pipeline (drive up)** | Total size ($/£). Number of opportunities at proposal/quote or better | Sales tool or spreadsheet | Weekly or monthly |
| Number of leads (drive up, but watch carefully – you want leads that convert) | Number of leads that are active | Sales tool (spreadsheets don't work well here) | Weekly or monthly |

| Goal | Metric | What Tool? | How Often |
|------|--------|-----------|-----------|
| Number of leads converted | Number of leads that get converted to pipeline opportunities | Sales tool | Monthly |
| **Average deal size (usually drive up)** | Average of your deals where a budget is forecasted | Sales tool or spreadsheet | Monthly |
| **Win/Loss ratio (drive up)** | Percentage of wins to losses | Sales tool or spreadsheet | Quarterly |
| Length of sales cycle (shorten) | Average length of sales cycle in months | Sales tool | Quarterly |

Choose what matters to your business, but don't overdo it. You don't want to be digging up the plant every few days to see how it's doing. Trust your process and people, but inspect based on your metrics. You can do so at a company-wide level or by individual.

# Building and Leading Your Sales Dream Team

Whatever kind of leader you see yourself as – Marlon Brando in *The Wild One*, Yul Brynner in *The Magnificent Seven* or Woody Allen in *Antz!* – one thing's for sure: sales isn't a 'lone-wolf' activity, especially in the services sector. To be honest, the lone-wolf scenario only works for tenacious investigators in detective movies (and of course for anti-social wolves). As the term 'sales team' implies, sales is a group game, so you need a pack of like-minded animals all pulling on the same direction.

The right sales pack is essential to successful business development, because sales people do better when they learn from and support each other, and you need other team players, people from marketing and delivery, to sell successfully and hence to grow your business. In this section, I cover identifying your core team needs, contacting other people who can help and signing up team members.

Unless you're a one-person business with big ambitions, you need to involve the people responsible for delivering your service in the sales process (see the earlier section 'Establishing a sales process') at key points.

## Creating your pack of sales maestros

Select or confirm your team from your employees or trusted contractors, but bear in mind that the sales process involves a lot of skill sets and someone who's great at selling isn't necessarily going to be great at writing contracts. Some shifting around of responsibility may be necessary, so rolling out a sales process requires sensitivity.

The other big decision is whether you want sales to be continuous with delivery: for example, an account manager can be a salesperson *and* the project manager, or you can have a salesperson handover to an account or project manager for delivery. When planning your team, you need to be clear about whether a handover is involved and when.

I like salespeople to be motivated for *net new sales,* namely sales that bring in brand new customers. Otherwise, they can be tempted to *upsell* existing clients (persuade them to buy additional services) because doing so is easier (this practice is termed *going after low-hanging fruit*). If your delivery cycle is short and highly focused on a single offer, the continuous model can be preferable. You choose.

Figure 13-2 shows a typical team structure and who does what. Adapt the organization chart to your company situation and put names in the boxes – often the same name in many boxes for a smaller business.

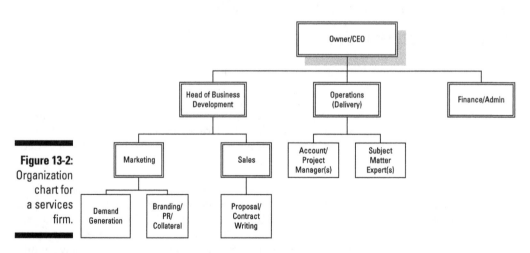

**Figure 13-2:** Organization chart for a services firm.

As your business grows, the organization chart is sure to grow too, usually by splitting the functions you've already identified. Make sure that your original organization chart shows the major functions that you need to 'grow into'.

## Using people outside the pack

Beyond a core sales term, small businesses need a network of what I call 'friends and family': the business connections, long-standing clients, partners and advocates interested in your success.

Think about your network and choose a small number of individuals you know well, who can support your efforts and who'll be straight with you. For example:

✔ Sales leaders that you admire

✔ Your business coach or mentor

✔ Contacts in companies who are a perfect fit for your services

✔ Leaders from your key business partners

✔ Executives who've run a business like yours

You can use these people in a variety of ways:

✔ To refer leads

✔ To be a sounding board for new ideas

✔ To provide advice when business development isn't going as you planned

Enroll your business friends and family in your sales process and create scheduled opportunities to interact with one or two of them.

Don't expect them to be thinking about you all the time – you need to be pro-active to benefit from the relationship. Your internal sales team won't always tell you how things really are, but your business friends and family will.

My Vistage coach (www.vistage.com) has had a huge impact on my business life and growth, and as a bonus he previously led a successful sales team. He helped me with my organization planning and growth strategies, especially when I started to expand geographically.

## Enrolling people to execute your sales strategy

When your sales pack is identified, at least in your head, you can start to think about leading them. You may not have every last detail solidified yet, but as long as you have a reasonable sales process (check out the ear-lier 'Establishing a sales process' section), goals for the forthcoming year, ideas on how to measure things and brief roles, responsibilities and results expected from each person, you're in good shape to start enrolling your team.

I sign up team members with a one-on-one meeting. Make sure that you remember that they all have their own career goals, strengths, weaknesses and concerns. In the meetings, consider the following aspects:

- ✔ Highlight your business goals – revenue goals, percentage growth, number of new customers.
- ✔ Explain that you're establishing a new sales process to help drive those results.
- ✔ Tell members that you need their expertise/want to provide a new career opportunity/expand their roles and responsibilities.
- ✔ Outline detailed roles and responsibilities (as in Table 13-3).
- ✔ Discuss workloads and compensation.

When the team's done, what about you? Having conversations with yourself in the office isn't a good idea (men in white coats and all that), but you do need to review your own role(s) and responsibilities and ask yourself whether you can do them all effectively. Specifically, can you delegate anything?

Give people a chance to meet with you a second time to share their feedback. They may have questions, concerns or ideas and you want to hear those before you do a whole team meeting. Also, ask them to think about how they're going to deliver on their role and their results and to bring those ideas to the sales kick-off meeting, because they'll be presenting them.

In the first whole-team meeting, cover the big picture and pull the team together:

- ✔ Reiterate the goals.
- ✔ Review the sales process – walk through it in detail.
- ✔ Clarify roles and responsibilities and have the team members outline their ideas.
- ✔ Acknowledge everyone's contribution to future success.
- ✔ Ask for ideas and concerns.
- ✔ Discuss metrics (as I describe in the earlier section 'Setting goals and metrics') and lay ground rules.

Keep your sales process fluid in the detail – team ideas can be particularly insightful and anything they add increases ownership and commitment.

# Delving Deeper into Leading the Sales Process

Have you noticed how business operates more smoothly when everyone knows who's doing what and in what order? That's what a process brings – order, consistency, thoroughness. Thinking through what your sales process should be (always with your prospects in mind, of course) helps your people sell more efficiently and avoid pitfalls, such as forgetting to ask the customer certain critical questions, or doing a poor job of presenting your solution. Owning the process, making it solid, yet flexible, gives sales leaders the results to hang their hat on – new sales.

In this section I discuss some areas of sales leadership to review further, before you move onto a step-by-step analysis of the sales process (for details, see the earlier section 'Establishing a sales process') and how to work it on the ground with your team. I describe handling your sales pipeline and leading the sale process, collaborating successfully, addressing issues effectively and acting appropriately in a timely manner.

If you're in doubt where to spend your sales time, use 75 percent of it coaching and co-selling (supporting a team member in an actual sale) and 25 percent in administration, including sales meetings. I describe *what* to do in coaching/ co-selling versus administration in this section and Chapters 14 and 15.

## 'Put that it your pipe and smoke it!' Managing a sales pipeline

The heart of your sales process is the *pipeline* (that is, a list of prospective customers who are actively engaged in discussions with your firm). You use it to maintain a clear picture of the health of your sales activity. If you don't have a handle on this aspect, you're managing by guesswork. Plenty of models exist for pipelines, but most have the features shown in Figure 13-3.

You can't have a dependable pipeline without good data, so you need to enforce the following:

- ✔ Weekly updating of the opportunity *stage* (where the prospect is in the process), *probability of closure percentage* (an estimate of the likelihood of getting a sale) and *next steps* (what action you'll take to push the sale forward)

- ✔ Supporting notes and everything sent to the prospect, posted to your sales tool or on some other shared resource (such as SharePoint, Google Docs or a shared hard drive)

- ✔ Keeping all emails between team members and the customer

**Figure 13-3:**
A sample pipeline report.

**PIPELINE REPORT - WEEKLY**

| Report date: | 2/25/2015 |
|---|---|

**Weekly pipeline**

| Pipeline target: | $ | 500,000 |
|---|---|---|
| Current pipeline: | $ | 411,000 |

| Stage | Account Name | Opportunity Name | Amount | Probability (%) | Close Date | Next Step |
|---|---|---|---|---|---|---|
| Negotiation | ABC Company | Support Contract | $36,000.00 | 90% | 3/1/2015 | Review with customer CFO |
| Proposal/Price Quote | BCD Inc | Discovery/Scoping | $25,000.00 | 75% | 3/31/2015 | Demo on March 6th |
| Proposal/Price Quote | CDE LLC | Implementation project | $100,000.00 | 75% | 3/31/2015 | Presentation 3/10 |
| Presentation | DEF Company | Discovery/Scoping | $25,000.00 | 50% | 4/30/2015 | Presentation 3/25 |
| Qualification | EFG Inc | Implementation project | $150,000.00 | 30% | 4/18/2015 | Review scope with Jennifer |
| Qualification | FGH Inc | Discovery/Scoping | $25,000.00 | 10% | 6/30/2015 | Reconnect in late April for presentation opportunity |
| Prospecting | GHICompany | Discovery/Scoping | $25,000.00 | 10% | 7/30/2015 | First call to gather requirements |
| Prospecting | HIJ LLC | Discovery/Scoping | $25,000.00 | 10% | 7/30/2015 | Set up time for first call |
| **Grand Totals (17 records)** | | | **$411,000.00** | | | |

Update your pipeline weekly and make it available for the whole team. This pipeline can be a focus for your weekly team meetings (see the later section 'Excelling at team meetings').

If your sales tool allows (or on a spreadsheet if not), start forecasting the revenues from each deal in the pipeline and in which month that revenue will hit. Figure 13-4 contains a typical snapshot of such a spreadsheet, using the pipeline from Figure 13-3.

Use a *weighted number* for the revenue that you forecast monthly (split the overall contract value into months and multiply by the probability of closure of the opportunity). Notice, how, when all these are added up and combined with your *backlog numbers* (revenue predictions from signed contracts), it forecasts your future revenue. This spreadsheet tool helps you predict revenue, think about resources need and even plan recruiting.

Knowing where your pipeline stands is the key to business predictability and success.

## Working your sales process

Here are the key leadership tasks for working the sales process:

- ✓ Team meetings
- ✓ Supporting sales efforts for specific prospects/coaching individual team members
- ✓ Thinking inside and outside the process, that is, use your process but be prepared to be creative when needed
- ✓ Periodic reviews

Even if you're working alone on sales, review the progress regularly from a leadership perspective or, better still, with one of your trusted advisors – and do so monthly.

Put in place and provide leadership for scheduled meetings and a culture of being on time and being prepared. It starts with you.

### Excelling at team meetings

Table 13-5 shows a structure for team meetings with a few hints and tips.

As if that's not enough, try setting aside time for each team member monthly. Alongside your co-selling efforts, use that monthly time to:

- ✓ Review how team members are doing with their goals.
- ✓ Acknowledge achievements.
- ✓ Identify barriers and how to overcome them.

Drive your team's performance and you drive sales growth.

**Figure 13-4:**
Pipeline
revenue
forecast
(weighted).

| Account Name | Opportunity Name | Amount | Close Date | Probability | Jan | Feb | Mar | Apr | May | Jun | Jul | Aug | Sep | Oct | Nov | Dec | TOTAL |
|---|---|---|---|---|---|---|---|---|---|---|---|---|---|---|---|---|---|
| ABC Company | Support Contract | $ 36,000.00 | 3/1/2015 | 90% | $0 | $0 | $2,700 | $2,700 | $2,700 | $2,700 | $2,700 | $2,700 | $2,700 | $2,700 | $2,700 | $2,700 | $27,000 |
| BCD Inc | Discovery/Scoping | $ 25,000.00 | 3/31/2015 | 75% | $0 | $0 | $0 | $9,375 | $9,375 | $0 | $0 | $0 | $0 | $0 | $0 | $0 | $18,750 |
| CDE LLC | Implementation project | $ 100,000.00 | 3/31/2015 | 75% | $0 | $0 | $0 | $18,750 | $18,750 | $18,750 | $15,000 | $3,750 | $0 | $0 | $0 | $0 | $75,000 |
| DEF Company | Discovery/Scoping | $ 25,000.00 | 4/30/2015 | 50% | $0 | $0 | $0 | $0 | $6,250 | $6,250 | $0 | $0 | $0 | $0 | $0 | $0 | $12,500 |
| EFG Inc | Implementation project | $ 150,000.00 | 4/18/2015 | 30% | $0 | $0 | $0 | $0 | $7,500 | $7,500 | $7,500 | $7,500 | $7,500 | $7,500 | $0 | $0 | $45,000 |
| FGH Inc | Discovery/Scoping | $ 25,000.00 | 6/30/2015 | 10% | $0 | $0 | $0 | $0 | $0 | $1,250 | $1,250 | $0 | $0 | $0 | $0 | $0 | $2,500 |
| GHI Company | Discovery/Scoping | $ 25,000.00 | 7/30/2015 | 10% | $0 | $0 | $0 | $0 | $0 | $0 | $1,250 | $1,250 | $0 | $0 | $0 | $0 | $2,500 |
| HIJ LLC | Discovery/Scoping | $ 25,000.00 | 7/30/2015 | 10% | $0 | $0 | $0 | $0 | $0 | $0 | $0 | $1,250 | $1,250 | $0 | $0 | $0 | $2,500 |
| | | 0 | $ - | | 0% | $0 | $0 | $0 | $0 | $0 | $0 | $0 | $0 | $0 | $0 | $0 | $0 |
| | | 0 | $ - | | 0% | $0 | $0 | $0 | $0 | $0 | $0 | $0 | $0 | $0 | $0 | $0 | $0 |
| **Total Pipeline** | | | | | $0 | $0 | $2,700 | $30,825 | $44,575 | $36,450 | $27,700 | $16,450 | $11,450 | $10,200 | $2,700 | $2,700 | $185,750 |
| | | | | | | | | | | | | | | | | | |
| **Total Backlog** | | | | | $55,000 | $62,500 | $57,500 | $27,500 | $27,500 | $27,500 | $15,000 | $15,000 | $15,000 | $ 6,000 | $ 6,000 | $ 6,000 | $ 325,750 |
| | | | | | | | | | | | | | | | | | |
| **TOTAL** | | | | | $55,000 | $62,500 | $60,200 | $58,325 | $72,075 | $63,950 | $42,700 | $31,450 | $26,450 | $16,200 | $ 8,700 | $ 8,700 | $ 511,500 |

2015

| Table 13-5 | Team Meetings and What They're For |
|---|---|
| *Meeting Type* | *Meeting Purpose* |
| **Weekly** | Agenda: |
| No more than one hour.<br><br>A good time is Friday morning. It resets for the following weeks, but also enthuses the team to use Friday afternoon fully, which is a key selling time. | • Review results (wins and losses).<br><br>• Examine each opportunity and determine next actions.<br><br>• Hold interventions with coaching/decisions to co-sell.<br><br>• Ask for team members' individual reports on progress with initiatives.<br><br>• Plan specific actions for the next one or two weeks.<br><br>*Don't* use weekly meetings to get into deep discussions about marketing plans, sales strategies or new partner initiatives. Reserve those for the monthly or quarterly meetings. |
| **Monthly** | Agenda: |
| Up to two hours.<br><br>Friday morning. | • Review prior month's results, for sales and for revenue<br><br>• Cover progress with initiatives: marketing, sales and partners<br><br>• Float ideas for new initiatives to be considered at the next Quarterly meeting (but limit initiatives to 1 or 2 in each functional area)<br><br>• Review the sales process for minor adjustments, unless significant change is absolutely necessary<br><br>• Do a Weekly sales meeting at the end of the Monthly meeting |
| **Quarterly** | Agenda: |
| Up to 4 hours.<br><br>Have lunch with the team as well if you can. | • Quarterly results.<br><br>• Sales process review and implementation of more significant changes.<br><br>• Strategic initiatives – in-depth review on progress and goal-setting/responsibility allocation for the next quarter.<br><br>• New initiatives – review of new initiatives that you or the team are proposing. Decide whether to initiate, delay or scrap. If initiating, create goals (for example, case studies for top ten customers), timeline (within the next six months) and goal for the quarter (five new case studies this quarter and which customers). Also determine who's leading and who's contributing. |

**Table 13-5 *(continued)***

| Meeting Type | Meeting Purpose |
| --- | --- |
| **Annual**<br><br>One day or two half days – offsite is a great idea. | The annual meeting is an opportunity to roll-out a whole new game plan. You can split the meeting into two days: one for working on the plan, one for coming back and reviewing the final plan. At minimum, your meeting needs to include an annual plan, a review of annual initiatives (strategies) and an opportunity for a training session (sales refresh). |

If your team is remote, your interactions are going to be a mix of online, on-the-phone and face-to-face. Make sure that your later interactions include being together in the field, as well as at key meetings.

### Supporting sales

Almost always, the best person to have involved at the later stage of a sales cycle with a prospect is . . . (drum roll) *you!* You may or may not be a trained salesperson, but you're credible, knowledgeable, sometimes inspirational and you carry the natural authority of your title. Plus, if you've been trained in sales and are stepping up to leadership, you have some years of experience, are confident in your skin and skillful in negotiation. As you bring new team members into the sales process, you want to support them, not suffocate them.

Avoid jumping in and doing the work *for* new members, even if you can do it better than they can. Instead do it *with* them, or better still coach them. To get expansion and growth, you need more people than just you able to make a sale.

Using the weekly sales meeting with the pipeline as a focus, you need to inspect the deals one by one to understand where they are in the sales process. You can uncover essential detail, such as:

- ✔ **Top deals:** You can support these deals by co-selling with the person who's taking the lead on selling to the prospect. Let that person lead the sale but start attending the meetings with the client and support your team member in getting to close. This situation is a win-win.

- ✔ **Whether the deal is proceeding at a good pace or stalling:** Examine stalled deals and determine whether they're really stalled or just dead (such as when the customer is non-responsive to calls or weeks or months have passed since any activity).

- ✔ **How each team member tackles or contributes to a sale:** Match team members to the right opportunities based on their style. Co-sell with every team member at least two or three times a year.

✔ **Whether the sales process is stifling creativity:** Let the team know that breaking the rules sometimes is okay. Being disruptive in a sales process can win you a deal you were bound to lose on paper. Have the team brainstorm ideas for stuck deals, an opportunity that has a unique twist or a deal from a customer in a vertical (industry) where you've never worked before.

✔ **Whether you have 'fluff' in the pipeline:** Like the stuff your tumble dryer produces – it blocks things up and if not cleared out can be dangerous. *Fluff* includes deals with customers that don't fit the profile (see Chapter 5) but the salesperson wants to hold on to. Be rigorous downgrading or removing deals if you're not satisfied that they're 'real' or what your company should be pursuing.

## Engaging in collaborative selling

Good teamwork in the sales meeting, as I discuss in the preceding section, pays off when you're in the field, in the form of collaborative selling.

As well as co-selling with your salespeople, other team members may be involved in the sales, for example, subject matter experts or account/project managers. Selling complex services is a team game and each team member should have a specific role, not just be a warm body in the room.

When you roll-out your sales process, determine when and why other team members need to be brought in. Make sure that the person leading the sales is keeping others in the loop: the simplest way to do so is to invite the key subject matter experts and project managers to the weekly meeting. It alerts them to what they may have to get involved in and how they can support the sale, as well as prepares them for the sort of contacts they may have to deliver on.

A team may need a few practice runs to get comfortable with working together; having clear roles and responsibilities helps. Encourage debate, ideas and even mixing it up in terms of who works on what. If your project manager wants a shot at writing a proposal, that's fine. Building a team with cross-functional skills is beneficial to business development and growth because you don't want individuals being a bottleneck in the sales process, just because no one else can do what they do.

## Avoiding knee-jerk reactions to problems

Mike Tyson said 'Everyone has a plan until they get punched in the face' (and I'm not about to argue with him). When you feel the punch, though, you don't abandon the plan wholesale. You get right back on it.

Imagine that your 'punch' is that your sales pipeline is as sick as a sickly parrot. This reality happens to every business at some point – sales activity peaks and troughs based on factors outside your control, like the season or the economy, as well as on the strength of your team.

Keep historical copies of your pipelines and use them to compare periods, especially periods in prior years. You get a lot of insight into buying patterns and how to flex to shifting situations.

When you hit a troubled patch, don't knee-jerk, abandon the process or start new, ill-considered initiatives. Hold steady.

Although you may be tempted to beat up the team when things are slow, ask yourself, 'Do I need to panic now or later?' I usually kick off my sales meetings with exactly that question. If things aren't great, the team yell 'Now!' and then we proceed to work on what to do in the face of that situation. In Table 13-6, you can see a (somewhat over-simplified) analysis of when to *panic now* and when you can *panic later*.

I use the term 'panic now' tongue in cheek, of course. Having everybody running around yelling 'Don't panic! don't panic!' like a panicking sitcom character isn't going to solve a thin pipeline. Instead, I use the term to help people refocus the team's efforts. You need to manage that shift and decide when to shift again, based on the impact of those changes.

| Table 13-6 | Panic Now/Panic Later |
|---|---|
| ***Panic Now*** | ***Panic Later*** |
| **Status:** | **Status:** |
| • Few deals at proposal or better | • Many deals at proposal or better |
| • Some or few qualified prospects | • Many or some qualified prospects |
| • Some or many unqualified leads | • Some or many unqualified leads |
| • Revenue is threatened | • Revenue is secure and may be exceeded |
| • Layoffs may be needed | • Resourcing is a challenge |
| **Focus:** Leadership and team's attention should be on deals most likely to close. Team to focus on qualified prospects to push them down the pipeline (to proposal or better). Some effort at qualifying leads efficiently. Also look for upsells to existing clients. | **Focus:** Good attention on deal closure, with leadership attention on those least likely to close (why not push the envelope?) Mix this action with effort to grow the volume of new leads (longer-term benefit), because the pipeline will look like the panic now situation soon enough. An opportunity to catch up on strategic initiatives. |

A useful tool when you decide to shift attention in order to address a pipeline concern is a time management tool. You can download one at www.salesbenchmarkindex.com/time-management-tool-sbi, although you need to modify it to the different roles in your team. Have your people fill it in for a month (and do so yourself, too). Don't necessarily ask them to share it; rather, have them look at where they've spent their time and report back at the next monthly meeting. Did they feel they were shifting their focus in line with the 'panic now' plan? We're they surprised how much or little time they spend in actual sales activities?

Above all, create a safe sales environment where team members can get advice, help and coaching and are willing to receive feedback and direction from those more experienced. If your offer is sound (in the sense I define it in the earlier 'Getting clear what your business sells' section) and the team's clear that you're committed to their success, your efforts should flourish.

A bad economy can tank a business and at such time cutting to the bare bones of business development is tempting. If at all possible, though, *increase* your investment in tough times, for two reasons: first, you need to try even harder in a tough economy; second, your competition is probably pulling back so take your chance to stand out. Good sales teams don't let a bad economy stop them.

When the dot-com crash happened in 2002, Adam's business went from nearly 200 people to 18 – almost overnight. Talk about hanging on by your fingernails! So many firms were going under, but Adam was determined to hang on in there, whatever. He was fortunate to have some investment money stashed away, so he chose to invest in – business development. He brought in two highly experienced business developers, strong in sales and marketing, both of whom were about to get laid off from a firm similar to his. Within two years, he'd doubled his revenue while everyone was stagnating and his firm is still around today and has over 100 employees again.

## *Taking the right action at the right time*

Your team knows what to do and when, guided by yourself as its leader and the sales process as its roadmap. Sales process aside, though, how do you, as a leader, know what to do when non-standard situations arise? Coping with such events is essential to successful business development and ensuring business growth because otherwise the team can get in the rut of 'this is how we do it'. An occasional rogue response or process shake up is good for your sales team and your sales. Table 13-7 provides some leadership actions and shows when you can use them.

| Table 13-7 | Leadership Actions and When To Use Them |
|---|---|
| *Action* | *When To Use It* |
| Tweak the process | The sales process needs a refresh from time to time:<br><br>• Review quarterly for general updates.<br><br>• Respond to new ideas and new channels as they become appropriate (for example, social media or new concepts about prospect nurturing).<br><br>• Update when new tools are added (for example, you can add an email marketing/marketing automation tool).<br><br>• Review after team changes. Use them as an opportunity to see whether shifting certain responsibilities can help productivity. |
| Intervene | When a specific sales pursuit seems not to be going well:<br><br>• Get feedback from the team.<br><br>• Add additional resources.<br><br>• Provide coaching (see later in this table).<br><br>• Co-sell with the team (assuming that the opportunity is worth your time).<br><br>• Suggest some outrageous tactic. |
| Redirect the team | When the pipeline is unbalanced, sales are low, revenue is at risk or you have a drop-dead date for a particular deliverable (see also earlier in this table):<br><br>• Shift the allocation of time to key stages in the sales process that need attention.<br><br>• Ask people to assist their team members if they're overstretched. |
| Rebalance the investment | If your business goals change:<br><br>• Support new service offerings.<br><br>• Support new territories (geographic areas).<br><br>• Direct resources to marketing or the sales team as required by your strategy. |

| *Action* | *When To Use It* |
|---|---|
| Coach | When team members need support: |
| | • With a specific deal |
| | • With less than satisfactory results |
| | • When they don't communicate sufficiently |
| | • When a specific skill is missing (also consider training courses). |
| Redeploy | When team members are unable to fulfill on their role, but have been trying hard to do so: |
| | • Consider them for an alternative position (for example, salesperson becomes account manager). |
| | • Retrain them for another role (consider a sales co-ordinator, proposal writer or contract writer). |
| | • Encourage them to seek another position, keeping them on until they do. |
| Discipline | When a team member has been coached but continues to underperform, lacks diligence or doesn't behave in a professional manner: |
| | • Document issues. |
| | • Follow a rigorous disciplinary procedure (get HR advice). |
| Terminate | Replace the team member: |
| | • Terminate for non-performance or other disciplinary issue. |
| | • Eliminate the position (get HR advice). |

Leadership can be a joy, a sorrow, a challenge and a tribulation – and never more so than when leading a sales team.

Of all the roles in an organization, salespeople who're born to sell need positive strokes – reminders that they're really great combined with something tangible as a bonus. Reward such people beyond commission – anything from a $50 (£31.50) gas card to a cruise. And if you sold the largest deal this quarter, reward yourself too.

# Chapter 14

# Taking the Lead: Selling Under Control

. . . . . . . . . . . . . . . . . . . . . . . . . . . . . . . . . . . . . . . . . . . . . .

### In This Chapter

▶ Putting customers to the test

▶ Presenting your firm's services

. . . . . . . . . . . . . . . . . . . . . . . . . . . . . . . . . . . . . . . . . . . . . .

*H*ave you ever faced customers who, no matter how hard you try, keep disrupting the conversation, veering off into dead ends or being generally squirrely with you? The truth is that customers have the right to behave any way they want with you (at least until I ascend to power!), although if you're highly skilled you'll be able to handle the more slippery ones. In the end, however, customers are what they are, with all their concerns, fears and dreams. Just don't live in la-la land and think that you're going to change them. (Oh, to be president of la-la land – the people are so easy to please!)

Although I talk in this book about business development from the customer's viewpoint and encourage you to get inside your customer's head (see Chapter 3), I don't mean to imply that you have to be under the heel of customers and that anything they say goes. No, you have to coach customers through the process, preferably on your timeline and not theirs. Plus, you can start training customers to be the way you want them to be. I know that sounds far-fetched – but it really is possible.

One of the myths around selling is that the customer is in control. Nonsense! *You* choose whether to do business with customers. They certainly have an opinion on the matter, but if you're waiting for them to jilt you, you're not in control.

In this chapter I describe how selling impacts the growth and health of your company; in other words, how you need to sell to get the right results in the short and longer term. I put you in the driver's seat as I discuss two vitally important aspects of selling: *qualifying* leads (by which I mean how you determine that this *is* a prospect – a good fit for you *and* ready to buy) and how to pitch and present your services to that prospect.

This chapter isn't a primer for salespeople. If you're looking for that, pick up Tom Hopkins's excellent *Selling For Dummies* (Wiley).

# Okay, You're In! Qualifying Leads into Prospects

A lead needs to be qualified to become a prospect, who in turn needs to buy to become a customer. So what do I mean by qualification?

The ancient Egyptians believed that when you died, you had to take a river journey across the Nile and meet Osiris. He had some nasty tests to see whether you were worthy to pass into the green and pleasant land of the underworld – such as weighing your heart against a feather to make sure that it was lighter.

You don't have to cut out your customers' hearts to see whether you want to work with them (darned health and safety rules!), but the idea's the same. You're the gatekeeper and prospective customers have to qualify to pass through to the part of the sales process (presenting and proposing) where you're going to invest significant time with them. Gatekeeping has got to be worth your effort.

To be more precise, you're in charge of several gates, not just one. Take a look at the sales process in Figure 13-1, or appraise your own process if you have one: you need to have criteria for every stage in the process, from prospecting right through to contracting. Check out the section on 'Gating your sales pipeline' later in this chapter.

Ultimately, your ability to bring in the right customers with velocity drives your business growth. No wonder people confuse business development with sales! Selling well – not just anything to anyone, but to the customers who are the best fit, the most co-operative and the best payers – takes skill and assurance. Put your power suit on – this is selling. In the next section I cover how to qualify leads effectively.

## Getting your interactions right with customers

You get the clients you want only if you adhere to certain principles during qualification. Here are a few things to stick to like glue:

✔ **Know what you're going after:** Use your customer definition/profile(s) to determine whether a company is even a target for you. I cover developing customer profiles in Chapter 5.

✔ **Be in control of every interaction:** When you take control, you can guide the process to go your way and get the information you need in order to decide whether to proceed. You discover how to do that throughout this chapter.

✔ **Be prepared:** Have qualifying tools and processes that keep you single-minded about what your company needs.

✔ **Be authoritative:** Handle prospects so that they trust, respect and like you.

✔ **Be mindful:** During interactions with customers, you find out what they're like. Some behave like jerks – they don't respect your time, act as if they're entitled, don't give you what they promise and, at worst, are disrespectful. They aren't going to change. Don't work with them.

Technically, qualification begins when you first meet the customer. Your marketing team should be bringing you marketing-qualified leads (MQLs – whizz to Chapter 9 for details). Marketing targets specific people in specific organizations that, at first blush, are a good fit for your offer; they weed out the ones that aren't.

Well, that's the theory. In practice, you may not have a marketing department and you may even be the only one prospecting, desperately trying to generate leads. Either way, use the gates from Figure 13-1 to decide whether a prospect gets through to the next stage so that you get the customers you want.

Being in control doesn't mean that you don't care about customers and aren't willing to see things from their viewpoints. But if they're not good customers for you, better for them if you tell them quickly. Don't waste time hoping that they're going miraculously to become great customers.

## Handling leads, whatever the source

Say that you have a new lead. Great! It can originate from a number of places and *where* it comes from is important, because this fact affects how valuable the lead is and the rules for how you handle it. You want to qualify the lead before you spend a whole bunch of time on it. You're in the Qualify stage of the sales process (Figure 13-1) and the pre-requisite to enter the next stage (Present) is 'Prospect passes qualification questions'. So that's what qualification is all about – asking questions (which you design) to determine whether the lead is Qualified for further discussion.

How much time you're willing to spend on a lead depends somewhat on where it came from. Some are better than others. Here are some thoughts about how to handle the different sources of leads. Note that you need to adjust the HOT/WARM/COOL based on your own experience, so my comments are somewhat personal, based on the many firms I've worked with:

- ✔ **The 'call out of nowhere':** Someone you've never spoken to before calls and wants to talk to the owner or to sales about your services. Call back right away! Not only do you find out how the person found you, but also the call's a huge signal that this prospect is in the buying cycle. Status is HOT (like Studio 54 in the mid-1970s).

- ✔ **MQL:** You get a lead from marketing: someone just downloaded your white paper after attending your webinar last month. This lead is one for your next cold-calling session. MQLs are conversation openers and not sales-qualified leads. Best-case scenario: you find that the firm is a hot lead (it happens). More typically, after asking a few questions, you find that they're still early stage and you should hand them back to marketing. You probably don't have the time to nurture them for a few months. Status is COOL (but not the good, Humphrey Bogart kind – more like the IRS's response to your request for more time to pay).

- ✔ **Appointment:** Someone has set up an appointment for you, perhaps the lead qualifier from marketing or a service you employ to get leads. Assuming the lead-generation people are working to specific criteria, make sure that you have all the information and put in a call to confirm the meeting. Status is WARM, (great for bread, less so for soup), but may turn out to be HOT or COLD.

- ✔ **Met you already:** For example, if someone had a good conversation with you at an event, make a speedy call before he forgets all about it. Like playing roulette, this act is hit or miss and no way of knowing what the outcome is going to be. Status is WARM/COOL (as in 'the weather's really too mild, but damn I look great in this suede jacket!').

- ✔ **Website contact-me form:** A huge proportion of these responses aren't going to be a fit, regardless of whether they're ready to buy or not. Chances are they're not, because unlike your proactive outbound activities (such as sending emails and attending carefully chosen events) they haven't been vetted by your gating criteria and so can be anybody. Stick them in your next calling session. Status is that over 90 percent are probably VERY COOL/ALMOST COLD (the IRS's response when you miss the second deadline too). You have to call them, though, because one in a hundred will be HOT.

- ✔ **Referral:** If it comes from a partner, the referral may well be a great fit: call right away. If it comes from a customer, it may be promising or some way off. You have to call referrals within a day, because you owe it to your customer/partner to respect their willingness to help. Status is HOT/WARM (like the options on your tumble dryer – just don't shrink that jacket).

Whatever the source, at a minimum enter the people who fit your profile, but aren't yet ready to buy, into your database so that your marketing campaigns can message them. If you find out that they *are* in the buying cycle, kick their tires then.

## Determining who to sell to

You need to be selfish when deciding who to sell to. After all, if you're active in sales, you have a *quota,* a goal for how much you have to sell this year. Whether you have a salesperson's title or are fulfilling the role in a small business, you're on the hook to get sales. You also want to acquire really good customers for your company, not just any old customer.

Mostly, salespeople chase anything that moves in the hope that it turns into business. Given that you have only so many hours in the day, you want to use your time more wisely. The key to successful sales is to say 'no' as early as you can and focus your energy and attention on the customers you really want to close. You're much more likely to win if you do.

When you start qualifying a lead, you need the profile you develop in Chapter 5 and some qualification questions, plus a good questionnaire to make sure that you can define the extent (scope) of the work (see the next section).

Don't ever talk to a lead/prospect without researching the company and the person first. You should already have the basic information from your lead source. Use LinkedIn, the prospect's website and any other tools to find out more and assess whether the lead/prospect fits your profile.

## Gathering the tools to help qualifying

You have two basic types of tools when qualifying: checklists and questionnaires for getting answers; and how you conduct the process. Together, these tools keep you in control and get what you need to move forward with the sale.

Here are a few things to have to hand:

✔ **Agenda:** Set the agenda for the call/meeting, so that it goes the way you want and to manage the time. I usually start with introductions and then suggest the agenda and get the customer representatives to agree that it'll work. If they have any other items to add, make sure that you fit those in. I include a quick introduction to the company, qualification questions, a discussion on pricing (broad, but just to make sure that you're not both wasting your time), scoping questions, action items for both parties and then next steps. Get customers to commit to a time by which they'll send you any information you need.

✔ **Pitch script:** Aim to position your company's services and value in less than three minutes. The customer is probably not listening anyway, so make it punchy and fun, and put some personality into it – but get it done fast. Customers want to talk about themselves.

✔ **Battlecard:** On the off chance that the customer is listening, have your battlecard to hand so that you're ready for any questions.

A *battlecard* is typically a single sheet or poster with useful information you can refer to during a customer conversation. Figure 14-1 shows an example. Think of a battlecard as a salesperson's 'cheat sheet'. If you have more than one service, you may need additional battlecards.

✔ **Qualification and scoping questions:** The questions you ask are more important than what you say about yourself. Through your questions, you demonstrate that you know what you're doing – the result is immediate trust, at least as far your competence goes.

| 1. The Marketplace | 2. Customer Profile | 3. Service Offerings |
|---|---|---|
| What are the choices that a prospect could make? | Who are we targeting? | What solutions are available to sell? |
| 4. Competitors | 5. Customer Needs/Pains | 6. Things to Remember |
| Who might we lose to? | What problems can we solve (and not solve)? | Checklist of things to be sure to do (for example, next steps). |
| 7. Key Questions | 8. Benefits, ROI and Evidence | 9. Pricing, Timelines and other Info |
| What to ask them & what they might ask you. | What they'll get from working with you, plus case studies to prove it. | Contractual things you need to discuss. |

**Figure 14-1:** A sales battlecard.

# Taking the meeting

When you have all your tools and have done all your research, the time's right for a call or visit.

While you're judging the customer, they're of course judging you. If you show up as organized, more interested in them than in talking about your company, with lots of great questions and a clear finish to the meeting, you're better than nine out of ten salespeople.

As a minimum, make sure that you cover the first four questions in Table 14-1 during the first call.

| Table 14-1 | Qualification Questions |
|---|---|
| *What You Ask the Customer* | *Your Hidden Question* |
| What's the business issue you're experiencing that has us talking today? | Need: What's their need and can we fulfill it? |
| Who in your company is driving this project? Whose problems would get solved? Who's involved in making a decision? | Authority: Is this the decision-maker? Who's going to influence the purchase? |
| Are you actively looking right now? What's your timeframe to start working on the solution? | Timing: Is this an opportunity, or future potential? |
| Has budget been allocated? Who'll sign off on the go-ahead? | Budget: Who holds the budget? |
| What staff do you have on your side to manage the work? | Is this project going to go smoothly? |
| What's your endgame? What's the final result you want to produce? | What are their conditions for satisfaction at the end of the project and can we meet them? |

Ideally, you want to have enough time to ask your scoping questions so that you have all or most of what you need to create a quote or proposal. That's why you need a structured questionnaire, so that you don't forget anything. You don't want to work in a straightjacket, but you do want to be efficient.

In sales processes, most time is wasted when the question of budget or pricing isn't discussed early on. If you put a lot of effort into the proposal and you're wildly out, you cost yourself time that you need for better-suited prospects.

During qualification, let customers know what your services cost, or give a range. Ask for their budget and if they don't have one (they're fishing for proposals so that they know what to budget), give them your pricing. I ask whether they're still on their chair. (Yes, I really do.) They laugh and then they tell me what they were actually thinking: from 'That's roughly what we thought' to 'We definitely can't afford that.' If the gap is small, you have the potential to show value that justifies your cost. The point is that you can back out gracefully early on if you need to.

In some situations you can't share costs or budgets early on, such as formal requests for proposals (RFPs). In those highly regulated selling situations, for example in the public sector, you just have to follow the rules.

Some obvious qualifiers apply, such as the customer needing what you offer and having the money, but don't make the mistake of thinking that the sales process is all about getting as many customers as you can. Look back at prior sales and identify ones that seemed like a reasonable fit but turned out to be a nightmare. This mismatch can happen for lots of reasons, but you should try to avoid it, or at least have your eyes wide open.

Assuming that you've scoped the work accurately and the budget is fair, while talking with a customer keep in mind a list of warning signs that the project may go south. I think of it as the waste eliminator. If you're going to work with customers who aren't quite a fit for your profile or show early signs of being unco-operative, that's your choice, but the consequences can be destructive – delayed timeline, loss of profit, late payments or challenges to your invoices, unhappy employees, cancelled contracts.

The precise list depends on you, but I include a few suggestions in Table 14-2.

| Table 14-2 | Should You Sell or Should You Not? |
| --- | :---: |
| **If Customers . . .** | **Yes/No** |
| Keep their appointments and send you the material they promised | ✔ |
| Don't let you get a word in edgewise, and want to dominate the conversation | ✗ |
| Don't do what they said they would | ✗ |
| Are disrespectful to any of your team | ✗ |
| Take your guidance, are appreciative of your expertise and keep to their planned buying schedule (or pretty close) | ✔ |

How customers behave in the buying process is how they'll be when you work with them. Leopards don't change their spots. However, you can train customers to conform to your requirements – for example, during the sales process, if they promise something by Friday (say a decision), remind them Thursday that you're expecting to hear from them. If by Monday, nothing has happened, let them know that unless you hear from them by the end of the day, you're assuming that they're not interested and you'll be moving on. If you don't hear from them, you can guarantee that you wouldn't have won the deal anyway. Get going with the next lead.

# Gating prospects through your sales pipeline

When you're working with a prospect and progressing using your own version of the sales process (in other words, qualifying), you need some rules for moving prospects from one stage to the next, what I call *gating*. Here I discuss why gating is important and what rules you need to set. Figure 13-1's illustration of an outline sales process includes the concept of gating.

Young companies tend to be pretty informal about managing their sales efforts. I've seen sticky notes around owner's desks, no tool for capturing information about the prospect and no reporting to help prioritize what to do next.

When your company starts growing, you need more and more sales to achieve revenue growth from one year to the next. The time for informality is over. Here's why:

- ✔ You need to provide status on the pipeline to others in the organization: you need to see whether you're on track with the goals and they need to be planning for the projects that are likely to come in.

- ✔ Tracking where each prospect is in the process and noting next steps helps you manage your workload and prioritize the right actions.

- ✔ Adding new information about the prospect and the opportunity is highly valuable to you in the sales process and helpful to delivery. During the sales process and when you're handing over to delivery, you need solid information to make the transition flawless.

- ✔ You need a consistent approach if you add more salespeople, because you have to aggregate data for good reporting. Make that process easy by using a good tool (sales force automation or customer relationship management tools – SFA/CRM). Chapter 13 covers choosing such tools.

So how do you create and use the gating criteria for your pipeline?

- ✔ The criteria, which should be a version of Figure 13-1, tell you what test a prospect has to pass before it can enter the next stage in the pipeline. Think of it as a sanity check against excessive optimism!

- ✔ As well as basic qualification criteria, which tell you *when* a prospect is ready to move to the next stage, you also need to consider *whether* you should proceed with it at every stage. You want to spend your time with promising companies that you're likely to convert to customers. The preceding section gives you some ideas, and you can also mandate some actions by the customer that have the sales process moving like a hare, not like a tortoise.

For example, you may want to ensure that the decision-maker is going to be at the meeting where you present your proposal, as a condition for putting the effort into the proposal. What you choose to enforce is your choice and is going to be based on the nature of your business.

✔ Agree the probability percentage (likelihood that you'll close this deal) to assign to each stage. Most SFA tools let you adjust the percentage to fit what works for you. The percentage probability allows you to weight the potential revenue so you can get a rough estimate of actual revenue going forward. (See Chapter 6 for a model spreadsheet.)

The ultimate test of whether your gating is well-designed is whether you reach the sales goals you want. If your gates and probabilities are constructed well, your forecast of revenue holds up in practice. If it doesn't, gating is an area you need to take another look at.

In some cases, you may need to break your own rules. Say the job is smaller than you'd usually take, but the company is well-known and you want to add it to your customer list. Bigger projects may follow. You may well choose to move ahead – I would!

If your gut tells you, at the end of the qualification call, to move ahead, follow through and schedule the presentation. Find out who else will be in that meeting and get their names and roles – you're going to need them.

# *Pitching Your Services to Customers*

From a simple meeting with one person in the prospect company, to a full-on team presentation to a large roomful of people (yelp!), pitching takes many forms. It may involve just one meeting or several. The prospect may predetermine the format or you may be able to mold it to your preference.

For salespeople, pitching is like herding cats into an orchestrated show where the audience are potentially feral. You need a script, rehearsals and then – the actual performance. And you need and want the audience to chip in, but you can't necessarily predict how the people are going to behave. Or can you?

Here I delve into the customer's mindset, help you prepare effectively and guide you through performing on the day and analysing afterwards. I hope this section sells you on the value of aiming for pitching perfection.

## *What prospects want: Understanding customer mentality*

In this section I present some pointers to bear in mind that help you understand your customers' concerns, even though you haven't met some of the people you're pitching to and don't yet know them.

### *Selling to different roles*

The members of a group you encounter in a presentation meeting represent specific departments and have responsibilities relating to a specific business function (unless the firm's small, in which case several functions can be rolled into one person).

Imagine that someone's coming to sell your company something – say a new accounting system to replace that free or cheap bookkeeping software you're using today. Think about what *you'd* care about. Would you be committed, interested, sceptical, indifferent, hostile? What about your colleagues? You can probably see that you're not all in the same place. Translate that to your prospects, because *that's* what you're selling into.

In a pitch situation, you typically meet all sorts of people: organization leaders, finance folks, HR, operations, legal, marketing or sales, admin. You're dealing with several people at once, so while you're trying to wow the CEO with your vision, you're also trying to reassure the CFO that the risk is low and that costs will be reduced (or whatever your value is). Phew, that's some juggling act.

The concerns of all these people are quite different and you need to be able to handle them and to answer all their questions. Table 14-3 helps you cover your bases.

| Table 14-3 | **Managing Prospect Roles and Concerns** | | |
|---|---|---|---|
| *Role/Type* | *Perspective* | *Concern* | *How to Handle Them* |
| Owner/CEO | Future looking | Striving for a vision that's 3–5 years ahead and short-term results | Show how your service can support their vision (improve or provide something/get an obstacle out of the way and help them succeed). |

*(continued)*

**Table 14-3** *(continued)*

| Role/Type | Perspective | Concern | How to Handle Them |
|-----------|-------------|---------|--------------------|
| Finance/CFO | Looking for evidence from the past | Avoiding risk, reducing costs, increasing profit, not spending money | Show return on investment (ROI) or cost reduction. Increase revenue at lower cost. Reduce overhead or risk of future expense. |
| Operations/COO | Now | Doing what's most critical today/efficiency/keeping up-to-date to reduce costs | Show immediate efficiency and/or a vision for how to get there. Demonstrate competitive advantage/cost savings. |
| Marketing/sales/CMO/CSO | Future/now | Growth/establishing the brand/acquiring lifelong customers/making the numbers | Show the contribution of your solution to its goals (quota and the like) or other strategic initiatives, such as automation or cost savings. |
| IT/CIO | Future/now | Keeping systems up and running/controlling change/keeping up to date/justifying expense | Show how your solution makes the firm's life easier — maintenance, user satisfaction, security, cost and time reduction. |
| Admin/CAO | Looking for evidence from the past | Efficiency, containing costs, developing and following procedures | Show that your service saves time, reduces cost, speeds up processes. |
| Legal/chief counsel | Looking for evidence from the past | Avoiding litigation/securing the best legal deal/pointing out dangers | Show how your service reduces risk, keeps things up to date and reduces concerns. |
| Purchasing/CPO | Looking for evidence from the past | Running a tight process/dotting the 'i's and crossing the 't's | Demonstrate your sales efficiency, follow the prospect's process, and be patient and co-operative. |

Bear in mind that your target customers may not look quite like those in the table – simply apply the concept to your own situation. Each person is dealing with the now (surviving today), looking to the future (sometimes ignoring the practicalities) or looking at the past (for reasons why this arrangement won't work). All concerns are valuable to an organization: you just need to figure out how to handle them and what will get them to give the 'thumbs up' to your proposal.

These people don't care about your service (well not much). Perhaps one or two people are committed to fulfilling the need, in that the idea is their brainchild, but the rest are hearing your pitch to be informed, or more likely to judge why your solution won't work. I'm not a pessimist, but if you take this viewpoint, you're ready for that nasty question that can spike the presentation and rob you of all the good work you've done up till now. When you remember that they don't care about you or your solution, you ensure that you deal with reality, and not with what you hope they're thinking.

Addressing the concerns of individuals seems like a blindingly obvious tactic, but surprisingly most presentations and proposals *don't* account for answering the questions of the diverse audience. Therefore, ensure that you know who's attending so that you can map your presentation to their roles.

Roles are generic and people are unique. If the CEO you're about to meet was an operations person earlier in his career, bear that in mind. He's likely to be more now-based than future-based. People may change a little over their careers, but at their core they remain the same.

### Selling to committees

Often, prospects assemble a committee to manage big purchases or are involved as a steering group throughout the project.

In effect, selling to committees is a special case of 'selling to different roles'. Everything in the preceding section applies, plus:

- ✔ **Committees are weird.** They've a pecking order, they play internal politics and sometimes lack focus on the task at hand (that is, they've hidden agendas). Enjoy!

- ✔ **Some committee members may have little or no knowledge about your area of service.** This situation is common with the boards of commercial and public organizations. You have to keep things simple and clear. They're not idiots – they just need you to help them understand the need and value and why they should choose you.

- ✔ **When the committee can meet may control the timeframe.** This factor can slow down the sales process.

> ✒ **Committees can be risk averse and need lots of evidence that your offer is a safe bet.** Most of the committee don't want to be responsible for the ultimate decision. You need to convince the influencers (who want the solution) and whoever holds the money; the rest will probably follow.

The more you deal with groups, the more likely you are to be facing 'avoid risk' rather than *carpe diem* (seize the day!)

### Selling against risk

Talking about risk upfront with your primary contacts is a good idea. The chances are that they're advocates for the project, maybe even for you. They may even be slightly frustrated if a committee's involved: all they want to do is get on with it.

Understanding the primary contact's risk concerns helps you to counter them (see Table 14-4).

| Table 14-4 | Risk Factors that Impact Prospects |
|---|---|
| **Risk Factor** | **How to Counter** |
| Career | If your prospect's career would be threatened if you fail, educate the person on the process, benefits, case studies. Introduce him to the team he'll be working with. Invite him to your office or do a Google Hangout. Get to know the person and build trust that you can make the prospect a hero. |
| Resources and Timing/Timeline | Does the contact have the right people and the time for this? Meet the person, assess how knowledgeable he is and find out what else he has on his plate. Explain your approach and how you can support him throughout. Be realistic about what he'd have to do and when. Be straight about any 'drop-dead' date and whether that date is realistic. |
| Budget | Contacts are up against a tight budget with no wiggle room. Discuss the scope. Maybe you can delay some of the work until next year, making the project less risky overall. |
| Opposition | Prospects always have alternatives to you – such as doing it themselves or using the CEO's son, who's a kick-ass at something or other. Your contact may not be willing to fight for you. If so, go rogue. If you sense that your contact isn't supporting you, go over his head. Ask your CEO to call his CEO and say how pleased he is to be in business conversations with the prospect. If you're the CEO, maybe someone in your network knows someone in the prospect and can make a side call. Get creative. |

Rarely do you (or indeed does anyone) have services to offer that precisely fit the customer's situation, and so a slam dunk is unlikely. In contrast, sales are often lost to the 'do nothing' option. Not acting is much easier for prospects, and risk is a great excuse for choosing inaction. Make sure that your value proposition is crystal clear and that you spell out the benefits, preferably as ROI.

Contacts don't get fired for hiring IBM. In large companies, complexity is high and decision-makers go for the most trusted, dependable vendor. If your firm becomes the best at a specific service, you can be low risk too; maybe not quite IBM, but getting there.

During the sales process, talk about the risks and how you'll handle them during the work. Build mitigation for the risks into your plan for the job. Chapter 16 has more on this subject.

## *Limbering up to pitch*

I assume that after you complete qualification (see the earlier section 'Okay, You're In! Qualifying Leads into Prospects'), you typically create a quote or proposal and present it to the prospect. In a competitive situation, you need to show up as the best to win: best at selling, best in specialized knowledge, best at doing these kinds of projects.

Prospects buy from people. If the prospect refuses to meet with you ('just email me your quote'), walk away. Don't bend to everything that prospects want – if they expect free work upfront, explain why you don't do that. (You don't, do you? If so, stop it!)

Focus your efforts on the customers that you want to win. Proposing and pitching well takes a lot of effort so make sure that you:

- ✔ Focus on the prospect's need/pain, not on yourself.

- ✔ Customize your presentation/proposal to the customer, instead of making it generic and talking too much.

- ✔ Share the budget before the pitch, to avoid 'sticker shock'.

- ✔ Get ready for the tough questions the prospect is going to ask. Don't shy away from the problematic, simply hoping that everything goes okay.

- ✔ Prepare fully for the meeting and don't look disorganized.

- ✔ Manage the time on the day.

- ✔ Stick to your guns about how the project needs to be done, instead of letting the customer's opinions sway you from what you know is the right way.

The better you can follow these strong practices, the more in control you are. To do the preparation well:

✔ **Try to negotiate the agenda (see the earlier section 'Gathering the tools to help qualifying') with the prospect.** The more formal the process and the more competitive the bid, the more likely the contact is to tell you what he wants to see in the pitch. If you need flexibility to do the meeting differently, ask for it and say why.

✔ **Choose who's going with you.** Get that person's ideas for the proposal and pitch.

✔ **Profile who's going to be present from the prospect's side.** Check these people out on LinkedIn. Make sure that your whole team is in the know and allocate team members to take care of specific contacts within the prospect firm.

✔ **Create a pitch presentation that demonstrates how your service meets the prospect's needs (specifically).** It also needs to present the value from the point of view of each influencer/decision-maker. Don't forget that some people won't have met you or even know what you do.

✔ **List all the questions that you don't want the prospect to ask and get the answers prepared.** Decide who on your team is going to answer each one. Prepare some tough questions to ask the prospect as well.

✔ **Prepare your proposal.** See the sidebar 'Writing good proposals' and figure out how you're going to pitch it.

✔ **Rehearse your presentation.** Decide on a master of ceremonies and who talks about what. Allocate time to each section. The MC is in charge of moving things along and ensuring that action items get noted at the end.

✔ **Consider 'leave-behinds'.** What can you leave with the prospect: for example, copies of your proposal and presentation, examples of work?

You don't have to go in armed with PowerPoint presentations if that's not your style. Your presentation can be entirely verbal with the right props to keep the show going. Mostly, after listening to you for a short while, prospects want to talk about themselves, so plan sufficient time for discussion and questions, with some to spare.

## *Writing good proposals*

Proposals and quotes for services work come in all shapes and sizes. Some are gargantuan, hundreds of pages long. Some are two pages with a 'sign here' at the bottom. You have to determine what's right for you. But unless your service is simple and quickly delivered, or you work for an hourly fee and do whatever the customer asks, you usually write proposals that are separate from a legal contract and can be revised after an initial presentation.

### Following useful principles

Whatever the situation, follow best practice. At a minimum, your proposal needs to lay out the customer's need/problem clearly and what you're going to do to solve it, the deliverables, the assumptions you're making and the timeline and cost. If your proposal is long, create an executive summary (a one-page synopsis of the content of a proposal, including the pricing).

You may want to include other information with your proposal, but the best proposals keep it short and to the point and provide additional information (marketing materials, methodology, further explanation/education) separately, or as appendices.

Above all, you want to make it easy for the customer to say 'yes'. Consider giving options for level of service (where you want them to buy the middle one). Make the top one look like a Cadillac – expensive, lots of bells and whistles, and a bit of overkill for the customer's situation. Make the bottom one the down-and-dirty version – low cost, 'we guide you, you do the work', no wiggle room. The middle one is what the customer needs and what you want to sell.

As an alternative, give the company a core option and then a menu of all the extras it can add. Make sure that those options are distinct and not dependent on each other (or package them in groups).

### Being personal

Although you may have a boatload of boilerplate text lying around, make your proposals personal. Write as if you're in a conversation. For example, have a letter to the buyer as the first page, summarizing what the proposal is all about. Use the prospect's company name throughout. Talk specifically about its scope, feedback and timing. Avoid long pages with nothing about the prospect.

### Responding to requests for proposals (RFPs)

RFPs, whether public sector or commercial, are far more rigid in their requirements. This situation is where your boilerplate comes in handy. Read the RFP cover to cover and make an early decision as to whether you're going to respond. If you can ask questions, do so in minute detail (you normally submit them by email or online). You must follow the procedure and the proposal requirements meticulously, otherwise your bid can be eliminated. Often the response format is strict, so you have to adapt your boilerplate to their requirements.

You may not even get a chance to meet the selection team: if not, I recommend that you don't bid – remember that people buy from and sell to people and you may not like them! In the case of RFPs, don't offer options unless asked to. You have to propose and price exactly what the customer is asking for – even if you don't agree. Get yourself to the shortlist and then you start the discussion about better ways of solving the problem. If you provide options in the response, they can't evaluate apples to apples against others and you won't make the shortlist.

## 'Let's dance': Pitching on the day

Celebrate! You made it to the pitch, and so you have the possibility of a win. Now you need to manage what happens on the day. Obviously, ensure that you arrive a little early and have enough time to set up.

Make one person responsible for setting up the presentation if you're doing one (projector, hand-outs and so on), while other team members connect with your primary contact or other people who may come into the room early. The ten minutes before the meeting kicks off are precious – use them to get to know the people. If you did your research, you have something to say to each one. You need them to like you before they'll buy, so work on that first.

You're about to go into a delicate dance. You want to manage the situation *and* have the prospect delighted. You need to get your information across *and* answer all questions. You need to be respectful and polite *and* train the customer for what working with you will be like.

If you or your team get nervous in presentations, remember that you're looking to 'buy' the customer, and be on the lookout for whether the company's a good fit for you. Ask your folks to focus on evaluating the customer – it distracts them (while they're not speaking) into doing something useful and improves their listening. Otherwise, they're just in their own heads rehearsing what to say when their time comes.

Here are a selection of simple 'dos' for pitching well:

✔ **Start with introductions:** You want to put names and roles to faces. Ask people to state their biggest concern about the project – you may get 'Nothing really, I'm just here to listen' or you may hear some specific items you need to cover quickly. Don't introduce your team members – let them do it for themselves. It gets them talking. Keep introductions short.

✔ **Invite the prospect's representatives to interrupt you and ask questions:** The more they talk, the better. Just tell them if you want to address their question later.

✔ **Be clear:** Don't waffle and don't over-complicate. Customers want things to be easy, so make understanding how you can help them straightforward.

✔ **Repeat any questions you're asked by the customer, but in your own words:** Doing so ensures that you're answering what the person's really asking and gives you time to think about your answer.

✔ **Ask them questions:** Tough ones are really good – they give you breathing space and test the cohesion of the prospect's team. These questions often uncover whether they're in any disharmony. Be ready for how you're going to deal with their different viewpoints.

✔ **Listen carefully and take notes:** Ask about anything you're unclear on.

✔ **Talk about what working with you is like:** Explain how the project gets started, what happens along the way, how it wraps up and what happens afterwards. You're creating a future of working with you for them to step into. Make it personal, for example: 'Sunitha will help you organize the kick-off meeting. Jeff, she'd be working with you on that, right?'

✔ **Be ready to talk budget and make sure that your numbers hold water:** If they ask, say that you're willing to negotiate dependent on a deeper discussion about the scope. The presentation isn't the time for negotiation.

✔ **Capture action items for both parties and note next steps:** Be clear about the person or people to contact and when you can expect to hear from them.

Some people like to end a presentation meeting with a few 'trial closing' questions, namely, testing whether the prospect is leaning in your direction. Typical questions are: 'Does what we presented meet your immediate needs?'; 'Aside from the final details, are you ready to move forward with us?'; 'Are you speaking to any other vendors?'; 'If all were equal, would you go with us?' Use questions like these ones where you think appropriate.

The end of a pitch is as important as the beginning. Are the prospects staying behind, talking to you? If they're running out the door, try to discern whether they just have another meeting or are turned off. You need to look for your allies and spend time with them.

Don't forget to debrief with your team. Let them vent everything they have to say and then gather feedback about what worked and what didn't. After all, you'll be going through this process again and again.

## *The inquest: Assessing how the pitch went*

Follow up with the prospect to confirm action points and when you're going to hear from the company. Do so with a call and confirm in an email.

The time from the pitch to the decision is a dangerous one and lots of opportunities 'go dark' at this stage. Why is that? Unfortunately, most of the reasons why buyers go off the radar are related to issues that needed taking care of earlier in the sales process:

- **You didn't align with the prospect:** Perhaps the company's pain wasn't big enough or you were unable to sell it on the larger (negative) implications of choosing a 'do-it-ourselves' approach or doing nothing.

- **You didn't get to all the people who mattered:** You need to insist on interacting with all stakeholders so that you can answer individual questions and counter any objections.

- **You were too focused on yourself and not enough on the customer:** Remember that firms don't have to do business with you. They'll probably survive anyway.

Use your personas (descriptions of roles within the customer company) and the customer journey to take care of these issues next time.

You have to deal with the specter of 'do nothing', which is the most common reason why buyers never buy – at least not this year. Your responsibility is to push the case for urgency – the danger to the prospect of not buying needs to be bigger than that of buying.

# Chapter 15

# Closing the Sale to Your Satisfaction

***

### In This Chapter

▶ Concluding the deal

▶ Handing over to delivery

▶ Reviewing how everything went

***

*A*fter you've worked so hard qualifying a lead and pitching to a prospect (as I describe in Chapter 14), getting the call that a customer has selected your company is the high point of the relationship so far. Everyone likes to be wanted and this customer wants you. Well done! You're about to increase your revenue and contribute to your company's growth.

You're now in the final stages of closing this deal and getting ready to start the work. Typically 95 per cent or more of verbal acceptances close, but you still face a short journey before you get ink onto paper, a journey I lead you through in this chapter.

After the contract is signed, you then have to negotiate a delicate transition between the sales and delivery departments to set the project on the path to success and take onboard any lessons along the way. Therefore, I also help you answer questions such as: 'How can sales help the delivery team be successful with the customer?' and 'What steps are necessary to make sure that you learn everything you can from the sale cycle, win or lose?'

# 'Signed, Sealed, Delivered': Closing the Deal

A solid business requires solid contracts, because the success of your business depends on profitable work and a well-crafted and negotiated contract is a major contribution to doing work that pays.

Sometimes, you give prospects a contract and they sign meekly, like lambs. More often, though, they have questions or changes. This section helps you negotiate powerfully and get the contract signed.

## Picking your way through negotiation

When you get a verbal acceptance from the customer, you're entering a period of negotiation that ends when the contract is *executed,* namely signed by both parties.

But before you go into negotiation, you need to establish a few rules to abide by while the to-and-fro with the customer is going on. In the end, rules are made to be broken, but for every situation you need to bear in mind the deal-breakers that you must avoid.

Immediately after a verbal 'We want to work with you', the customer may start changing things around – or it may wait until a contract's on the table. Be ready in advance. What are your rules? What do you expect: for example, is payment to be online and are deadlines going to be adhered to?

Here are two common areas in which customers sometimes negotiate after a verbal agreement, plus my suggestions for how you can best respond:

- ✔ **Scope:** If *scope* (that is, the description of the work that you're going to do – see Chapter 14) is increasing, so must price. If scope is decreasing, make sure that it doesn't compromise the quality of the work or go so low that the deal is no longer worthwhile.

- ✔ **Price:** If customers want a lower price (for some reason they never seek higher ones!), you can negotiate by agreement with your team as long as you ask for a concession (say, better payments terms or direct deposit).

If customers want to talk about scope and price, try to have those conversations and come to an agreement *before* the contract is prepared.

You can still say 'no'. If customers really want to work with you, by which I mean that they don't have a second choice waiting in the wings, they often let you have your way if you stick to your guns.

## Getting to the real 'yes' without begging

If ever you need to be in control during the sales process, this is it. You're moving towards a contract and you have to bear in mind a few crucial things for this phase of the relationship. Think of this stage as a pre-nuptial agreement. Although you're both excited to be getting on with things, the legal stuff has to be processed before you can walk up the aisle.

Here are a number of tips for handling this period of the relationship:

✔ Tell the customer that this point is going to be the low one in the relationship, but that you'll both get through it and things will improve afterwards. It may seem direct, but straight talk gets you respected. Customers prefer it.

✔ Find out quickly whether the customer wants to give you its contract or is going to accept yours. Ideally, you want to use your contract format, but you may have to deal with the customer's. The larger your customers, the more likely they are to insist on their contract and you may not like what it contains. If they 'don't mind', go for yours – much easier. I explain more on contract details in the next section.

✔ Don't lose your nerve – you don't want to appear desperate. After all, the customer wants this deal as much as you do.

✔ Conduct the conversations in the same way as you did in earlier stages of the sales cycle (see Chapter 14). In other words, continue to 'train' the customer in how you want things to go. Schedule times to discuss key matters at hand, confirm action items at the end of the meeting and set deadlines for when those action items need to be accomplished.

✔ Don't hesitate to blame your legal advisors for how long everything is taking – they get paid lots and can take it.

A salesperson should be competent to handle most of the questions that come up during negotiation, but for certain items you need to consult or escalate, internally or with legal advisors. Both parties need to be comfortable with compromises, so don't be shy of asking for something in return if a customer wants to change the agreement.

Don't drop to your knees and beg for the work, no matter how much you need it. Also, don't use tactics such as 'if we don't start next week, we may not be able to fit you in until the month after next' (unless that's true, of course). The customer can see through any such white lies. They undermine the relationship, because now the customer can't trust what you say, and that impacts everything that happens while the work is being done.

Instead, be confident and authoritative – know your boundaries and what you're willing to accept. Be prepared to walk away with your head held high if you have to.

## Contracting for a win-win

Get a lawyer, unless your service is simple and you can capture a contractual agreement on two to three pages. You can obtain plenty of good templates for contracts at low cost (from sites such as www.legalcontracts.com and www.contractstore.com), but if you're not experienced with the legal implications, you can find yourself in dangerous territory.

In fairness, only rarely in services do parties have to go to court to resolve issues that occur during or after the work, but it does happen and it can take your business down. Services are usually a bit more flexible than products and this point is where a good lawyer, preferably one who's familiar with your type of work, helps you build a watertight contract, or to deal with one coming from the customer. Typically service contracts have a main agreement (Master or Services Agreement) and then a Statement of Work (what's actually going to be done). This format works especially well where you'll be doing more than one job for the client, or any follow-on work.

### Considering contract details

A standard contract has clear terms and conditions (Ts and Cs) that need to cover some of or all the following:

- ✔ A general description of the services you do (fully described in a Statement of Work)

- ✔ *Change orders* – a document added to the contract later to cover scope changes, and what the format for that document will be

- ✔ Payment terms

- ✔ Confidentiality agreements

- ✔ Ownership of the work – in certain circumstances you may want to retain ownership for reuse

- ✔ Warranties for the work

- ✔ Advertising and marketing – whether you can tell people about the customer and the work

- ✔ Non-solicitation of employees – the customer can't hire your people without a penalty

- ✔ Indemnification – setting boundaries that define what people can sue you for

- ✔ Under what circumstance each party can terminate the contract

- ✔ Arbitration – detailing the conditions for reaching agreement without going to court

- ✔ Other terms covering rare but important eventualities, such as mergers and takeovers, acts of God and the like

Now you know why you need a lawyer!

You need liability insurance. You can choose specific types of insurance for services companies, so make sure that you're well covered. I've had friends who found themselves in a litigation situation where insurance saved their bacon.

### Handling potential deal-breakers

When you have a good format for a Master Agreement and a Statement of Work, you should only need to consult your lawyer if the customer disagrees with a *material* item, namely something you can't just step over because doing so is too risky for you. I've only experienced a handful of such situations in my career.

Material items aren't the only potential deal-breakers. Sometimes the customer pushes you on areas that you really don't want to give way on. Table 15-1 covers some of the most common ones, whether they're deal-breakers and how to handle them.

| Table 15-1 | Negotiation Guidelines | |
|---|---|---|
| **Area of Negotiation** | **What to Do** | **Deal-breaker?** |
| Liability or guarantees | Beyond regular liability insurance, if the customer tries to make you responsible for loss of business, or anything you have no control over, push back. Get your lawyer involved. | Yes |
| Payment terms | If the customer wants terms longer than (say) 30 days, resist or request an upfront payment of some size to cushion the blow. | Maybe |
| Cancellation | Make sure that all terms for cancellation are fair — you should be able to cancel if the customer takes way too long to do its side of the work or is repeatedly late in paying. | Maybe |
| Pricing or scope | If these topics weren't agreed earlier, that's a mistake. You're late in the day to be sorting them out now. Clarifying deliverables in the Statement of Work is okay. | Yes, if the deal undermines your profitability |

Both sides need give and take in contract negotiation. Don't let it turn into the customer taking and you giving. That's a no-no.

Sometimes, contract negotiations start to go south. If it looks like you're ready to punch each other's lights out, have the CEOs talk, or anyone who can get you out of the impasse. Bringing in senior people who aren't emotional or angry is a great approach. Keep this tactic as your last and final measure, but I find that if the top people talk, they usually reach an agreement that everyone can live with. Never underestimate the power of escalation.

When the customer signs, celebrate! Somehow, I think you'll remember that tip.

Contracts are a difficult area to practice, but two aspects do allow you to try something with the help of others. First, you can get the opinion of your business mentor/advisor on contracting. Even if the person is in a different business, some principles are universal. Second, work with your sales team on the issues that you will and won't give way on during negotiation. The earlier Table 15-1 is a good starting point and you want everyone in your team on the same page, to avoid any rogue contract change slipping through and biting you in the rear-end later.

# 'This Much I Know': Managing the Transition from Sales to Delivery

After a contract is signed, you need to take care of important business called *handover to delivery*.

Often the people who're going to deliver the work aren't all that involved in the sales process, if at all. Therefore, you have a lot of valuable information in your head that you need to get over to the delivery folks. You're part of a team and you can't leave the playing field yet.

During the sales process, you've had a number of meetings with the customer. Beyond the obvious (scoping the work and creating a proposal – see Chapter 14 – and surviving contract negotiations as I describe earlier in 'Picking your way through negotiation'), you have a lot more to offer the delivery team in terms of useful information.

You can't just throw the contract over the wall to delivery and hope things go well. A lot of services projects falter right at the beginning if handover is skimped. Don't do it.

In this section I help you think about how long you should stay involved, when to pull out and when you may want to step back in again. Bear in mind that delivery wants to get started and you want to be helpful, but without cramping its style.

## Staying on the team

Be there to support the team during the transition. Your presence also gives the customer representatives comfort that the person they know best in your organization is still around while they get acquainted with new people.

Although you want to hang around for a while, you also don't want to outstay your welcome:

- ✔ You're not a delivery person (unless you're one of those unfortunate people who has to sell *and* deliver) and you don't want to interfere with delivery. Let delivery do its job. Don't be looking over its shoulder all the time.

- ✔ You have to get back to your other important work – closing the next deal, finding the next opportunity. Hanging out with new customers can be comfortable and sometimes that's valuable. But you're not in business to be comfortable.

You can be a great help at this time. Don't become a hindrance.

## Passing on all you know

Some of the knowledge that you need to communicate to the delivery team is contained in documents (such as proposals and contracts), some is in notes and some is in your head. Time to turf it all out, so prepare to share:

- ✔ Background to the customer's business: what it does, how long it's been around and whether it's in growth mode.

- ✔ How the customer found you.

- ✔ The customer's need and goals for the project.

- ✔ The proposal and Statement of Work with the list of the deliverables and perhaps a timeline for the work, or project plan, if that was part of the proposal.

- ✔ All the contacts you have in the customer, their contact details and how they've been involved up to now.

- ✔ Who on the customer side is going to be heading up the project and who else will be involved? See Figure 15-1 for a few proposed connections between your team and the customer's team.

- ✔ The customer's 'hot-buttons': what the customer is sensitive to.

- ✔ Anything unusual that you need the delivery team to be aware of.

- ✔ What you think is important to cover in the kick-off meeting with the customer.

When you've handed over all the information you have, think about this time being a good point at which to have the project manager step in and take over. Ideally, you should attend the kick-off meeting with the customer, not to lead it but in case queries come up. If you did your handover job well, the kick-off goes smoothly and the project is off to a good start.

One area that's often neglected is the matrix of relationships that needs to exist between your company and the customer. Modify this matrix for your own purposes, but make sure that the sort of diagram in Figure 15-1 exists so that everyone knows who's expected to take care of whom in the customer organization.

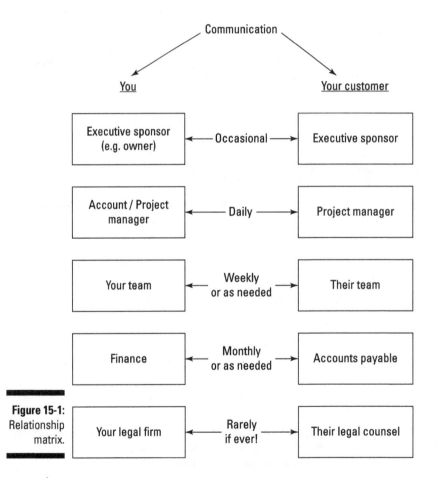

**Figure 15-1:**
Relationship
matrix.

Pay particular attention to all the relationships in Figure 15-1. Make especially sure that the finance people are connected and that details of invoicing are clear. Do they need accounting for hours and expenses? Do deliverables have to be signed off by the customer before payment can be made? All too often, the first month goes by, the time arrives to invoice the client, but nobody knows where to send the invoice or what needs to go with it. Payment is delayed because the relationship wasn't set up right. Make it someone's responsibility to thrash this stuff out.

## Backing out gracefully

Attend the kick-off meeting with the customer: make sure that you transitioned well to delivery and that nothing surprising comes up. If it does, you have to cycle round with the delivery team to clear up any outstanding questions or issues. If this process requires further conversations with the customer, you may well need to be part of them.

If the kick-off has gone smoothly, your account manager/project manager should be well in control after the kick-off meeting. Offer your support, but let that person know that individually you need to move on.

You may be asking, when should I jump in? Well, that has to be down to your judgment. As in any management situation, you want your staff to know that they have the authority and the responsibility for handling the customer, in good times and bad. Even so, sometimes they may need your help.

## Re-engaging with the customer

You may be the designated escalation point if issues arise with the work. If so, you have to respond to customers, and quickly, if they call.

If you're not the escalation point, you may still need to get involved again when:

- ✔ **Questions come up about the scope.** You're the only person who was at every meeting prior to the sale, so make sure that you have good notes, emails and other evidence of what was agreed.

  Refer to the contract – it supersedes all other documents. You may have to get involved in some straight-talking with the customer.

- ✔ **The customer doesn't like the team: that is, 'we want you back'.** The customer's representatives miss you and aren't overly impressed by the team now working with them. In this case, promise to look into it and check in with the team about how things are going. Ask your head of operations/delivery (if you have one) to dive in and see what's going on.

The best solution is for that person to support the team and handle the situation with the customer. If you have to be the one, ask incisive questions, because the team often don't want to admit that they're struggling (that is, the customer may be right). Only insert yourself when you absolutely have to and only in an oversight role.

✔ **The customer questions the billing and no one can seem to get the issue resolved.** Sort this problem out as soon as possible, otherwise you may be facing a loss and you don't want the problem to drag on. If the problem is just a misunderstanding, you can probably reset the expectations, but if you have real disagreement, use your negotiation skills to make a compromise – perhaps a discount or some other incentive to secure future billings. Often, the customer just wants someone to listen – or it wants to try it on! Be firm and fair.

When talking to prospects, writing proposals and negotiating contracts, try to under-promise and over-deliver. The opposite is a disaster, and typically results in something you don't want: a disappointed or even angry customer.

Fortunately, you can also be called in for positive reasons. The customer wants to praise the team and to thank you. Perhaps a representative wants to talk about a new opportunity or introduce you to a new prospect. Be gracious about giving your time and also gently guide the customer to the account manager if that's more appropriate.

# 'Say Hello, Wave Goodbye': Finishing Up the Sale

You're nearly done. You just have to complete your admin and paperwork, review the sale (for good or ill) and stay available for new opportunities down the line.

## Tidying up: Capture everything

As I describe in the preceding section, the information you have about the customer is highly important. Make sure to update your customer relationship management (CRM) tool with all your notes and documents and take care of some final items:

✔ Check that the data about the customer in your SFA/CRM system is up to date and accurate. Make sure that you've captured the lead source, size of company and anything about the sales cycle that was noteworthy (for example, what went well and what didn't).

✔ Ensure that the files in the CRM are the latest versions.

✔ Make sure that the contract was signed and that you have a copy in the CRM (even if the official copy is elsewhere). Too often, contracts can't be found a year or two later when you next need them.

✔ Ask the customer whether you can do a press release about the fact that you're working together. Say that you'll be back to see about a testimonial or case study.

## *Learning from experience: Win/loss reviews*

About two to three weeks after contract signature, ask the customer whether you can do an interview (called the *win/loss interview*). Although most salespeople do ask why they lost a deal, they rarely ask why they won – they're just too excited.

Conduct a formal interview (with losses too) to find out who else was in the running, what they liked about those competitors and what they didn't like. Find out why they chose you, if they did. Ask them to describe your company in three or four words and what would cause you to lose their business. Ask informally how things are going with the work.

What you discover from these conversations is great information for the team and also for marketing, so share it.

## *Recognizing the value of evaluation*

As the project nears its end, you need to get involved again. Attend internal team meetings that are wrapping up the project and any post-project review meetings. The agenda should include what happened in the sales process as well as on the project. In other words:

✔ Review the whole experience.

✔ Pick out what worked especially well and make sure to use those things again: that is, make them part of the best practices of your firm.

✔ Look at what didn't work and what to change for future engagements.

✔ Ask what may be next for this customer, such as any follow-on work or new opportunities. Capture those in your CRM and start working them.

Beyond internal review, you also need to do a post-project review with the customer, something I cover in Chapter 17.

# Part V

# Managing Your Customers for Business Success

| 1. Customer Overview | 2. Contacts | 3. Customer Needs/Pains |
|---|---|---|
| a) Background<br><br>b) Industry trends | a) Existing<br><br>b) Desired | a) Top of mind issues<br><br>b) Which can we solve? |
| 4. Current or most recent service | 5. Future services | 6. Benefits / ROI |
| a) Working on now<br><br>b) Previous services | a) What could we sell them?<br><br>b) On what timeline?<br><br>c) Which role or contact would buy? | a) What benefit would the customer get from this new service?<br><br>b) What would the ROI be? |
| 7. Goals for this quarter | 8. Actions to take | 9. Other Information |
| a) (Complete as needed)<br>b)<br>c)<br>d) | a) (Complete as needed)<br>b)<br>c)<br>d) | (Complete as needed) |

Repeatability, I say, repeatability is key to dealing successfully with your customers over time. Check out the great bonus article at www.dummies.com/extras/businessdevelopment.

## In this part . . .

- ✔ Understand the growth potential hidden in your customer base.
- ✔ Leverage customer relationships for greater success.
- ✔ Train your team to look out for new business.
- ✔ Implement a robust customer-review process.
- ✔ Expand your business within the same industry.

# Chapter 16

# Generating Success from the Customer Relationship

- - - - - - - - - - - - - - - - - - - - - - - - - - - - - - - - - - - - - - - - - -

## In This Chapter

▷ Sharing the customer within your company

▷ Producing useful information from the customer relationship

- - - - - - - - - - - - - - - - - - - - - - - - - - - - - - - - - - - - - - - - - -

*A*s I'm sure that you're aware, relationships of all sorts are fundamental to business success: relationships within even a small team in your company; relationships among the different departments within your firm; and, the subject of this chapter, the relationship of your firm with your customers.

When a prospect converts to a customer (as I describe in Chapter 15), the relationship between your company and the customer enters a period of transition. Unless your company is small, with a handful of people doing everything, the people who shepherd the sale through aren't usually the ones who deliver the work.

This transition is a delicate matter, as is customer management in general. Conflicts between different *functions* (departments), for example sales and delivery, can arise over perceived ownership of customers, which can threaten your business development intention for this customer and there-fore your revenue. So although I address this chapter primarily to account and/or project managers, marketing and salespeople are also likely to find it valuable.

I lead you through two important aspects of the customer relationship:

✔ **How to avoid hogging the customer:** Sharing the customer creates max-imum value for your business.

✔ **How to leverage the customer relationship for ever greater success:** Perhaps expanding your business with that customer and/or opening opportunities with new firms.

# *Back Off, He's Mine! Remembering that the Customer Belongs to Everyone*

A person whose specific role is to manage customer relationships (for example, someone with a title of account manager or project manager) often resents others buzzing around, disrupting the work or confusing the customer. Certainly, the idea of identifying one person as the primary point of contact for the customer has merit, but if that person feels as if he 'owns' the relationship, the result can be less productive for your company than it could be otherwise.

You don't want your staff squabbling over customers like teenagers in the schoolyard arguing over who's going out with whom. In this section I examine what a thriving customer relationship looks like, covering the necessity of sharing and collaboration, as well as describing the ideal result – long-term, continuing business with that customer and perhaps with its contacts. To get that result, you have to play nicely in the playground.

## *Sharing the customer relationship*

Take a quick look at the customer lifecycle diagram in Chapter 2, Figure 2-1. You can see that, depending on where the customer is in the lifecycle at any given moment, the function that 'owns' the customer changes. As a result, one person or team can't possibly handle the relationship throughout the entire process:

- ✔ Marketing supports the customer in the early stages, growing its understanding of the consequences of its business pain and how your company can solve it.

- ✔ Sales takes over later to convert a prospect into a closed deal.

- ✔ Your turn (as account and/or project manager) comes after the customer has signed the contract. Your role is to make sure that the work goes well and to identify new or extended work opportunities.

The problem is that marketing and sales want to stay in the picture and get in on the act. The salesperson wants to interview the customer during the first month for feedback on the sales process, marketing keeps pestering you to see whether it can do a press release and, in the meantime, the customer calls to say that one of your business's people isn't experienced enough for the work. Why can't marketing and sales butt out and let you get on with taking care of the customer?

To help clarify, bear in mind that the relationship has two sides:

- ✓ Delivering the work successfully
- ✓ Developing the business

In the heat of the project, business development typically gets neglected, or may not even be considered at all (ouch!).

Table 16-1 shows some key aspects of the customer relationship under the two headings.

| Table 16-1 | The Two Sides of the Customer Relationship |
|---|---|
| *Delivering the Work* | *Developing the Business* |
| **Primary goal:** Completing the work on time and on budget. Having a happy customer. This goal involves some of the following tasks: | **Primary goal:** Having a happy customer. Leveraging the customer for more business, referrals and marketing pieces. This goal involves some of the following tasks: |
| • Managing the project plan and budget. Resisting *scope creep* (extra work that creeps in but isn't part of the contract) and creating *change orders* (writing extensions to the contract for extra work). Making sure that invoices are accurate and payment comes in. | • Sniffing around for the next project for this customer. |
| • Ensuring that the team is on task. | • Expanding relationships with the customer organization (usually for more business). |
| • Reviewing deliverables to make sure that they're satisfactory. | • Gathering fodder for marketing activities (evidence of why customers hire your firm and love your work). |
| • Managing meetings with the customer. Responding to customer communications and concerns. | • Asking the customer for introductions to other prospects in its network. |
| • Wrapping up the project and getting sign-off. | • Asking for references and testimonials. |

You don't need to be a rocket scientist to figure out who's interested in the outcomes of all these tasks: the business owner, marketing, sales, finance and the rest of the team in general all have a stake in things going well.

But a conflict exists between trying to handle the relationship from a delivery standpoint, whether as an account manager who's probably more attuned to business development, or as a project manager who's focused on managing the work to deliver on time and on budget.

## Collaborating for customer success

Although the revenue target, the next project or leveraging the customer relationship may not be your specific responsibility as account and/or project manager, such things are undoubtedly important:

✔ The easiest way to get additional revenue is from existing customers. Typically, getting new work from an existing customer requires only a quarter as much effort as making a sale to a completely new customer.

✔ The best type of lead is a referral from a person that the new prospect trusts. Your customer has contacts that you want to get to know.

✔ Customer case studies/references are proof that your firm is competent.

All the business development tasks that I show in the right column of the earlier Table 16-1, and more, are perfectly legitimate at the appropriate stage in the project, so collaboration between account/project management and other functions is important.

Here I discuss how you can stop other internal parties from treading on your toes and yet still be open and collaborative.

### Understanding the psychology of the team and the customer

You're not in account/project management by coincidence – and neither is it coincidence that salespeople are into selling and that marketing is into doing its magic with early-stage customers. Job descriptions don't come into it – instead, certain people do certain jobs due to psychology. If you map the capabilities to do a job to people's underlying personality traits, you discover some interesting parallels. In fact, if you follow a career that aligns with your strengths, you're far more likely to be successful. (I talk more about personalities and the customer lifecycle in Chapter 4.)

If you feel like a round peg in a square hole, you haven't quite found the right place for your talents.

In the context of business development, the skills show up as follows:

- **Inventing:** The process of creating new services offerings, getting them out to the marketplace and measuring results – tends to suit entrepreneurs, business owners, visionaries and marketing.
- **Presenting:** The activity of positioning services with customers and getting their buy-in – suits sales.
- **Producing:** The effort of getting the work done and managing all the details of the customer project and relationship – suits account/project management.
- **Judging:** The business of handling the money and legal niceties – suits finance and legal.

Business thrives when all four skill sets are represented in your company and when they work together towards the ultimate goal – increasing revenue and profit while doing satisfying work.

The same logic applies to your customers, so start identifying the personality types there too and match them to roles. You'll be surprised how often they're a close fit.

### Knowing who does what

When you sort out what type of personality does what job, and connect this idea to the need to serve customers, you can see that sharing the relationships is going to be the most productive approach: it allows the team to spread out the load of customer management and get some varying and often useful perspectives. Table 16-2 contains some suggested pairings and the logic behind them. (Refer to Figure 15-1 for a useful relationship matrix.)

The model in Table 16-2 suits a larger customer; for smaller ones, trim down the team quite a bit. For example, the CEO can't necessarily pay attention to every customer.

When you, as a business owner or senior leader, align roles and/or concerns between team members and those at the customer organization, your firm has a robust and supportive vendor/customer relationship and gleans a lot of useful information along the way.

As account or project manager, ensure that you're copied in on all communications and invited to all meetings, even if you choose not to attend. Part of the role is to avoid disruption, so if anyone, such as the CEO or salesperson, wants to meet with the customer, they should gather intelligence from you first. Nothing's worse than someone from your company marching in to the customer and finding a big issue is going on that they knew nothing about and could've helped with if only someone had told them.

| Table 16-2 | Matching Who Does What in the Customer Relationship |
|---|---|
| **Your Company** | **The Customer** |
| CEO (inventing): Point of strategic contact. Should reach out to the customer periodically (beginning, mid and end of project, or every three months). | CEO: Interested in what's next, getting strategic advice, surrounding themselves with trusted advisors: wants return on investment (ROI). |
| Account manager (presenting/producing): Has oversight of all the work going on in the project. High-level advice and direction to guide the sponsor(s). Looking to expand relationships. | Project sponsor: Needs to see the project(s) be successful. Probably holds the budget. Concerned to see the project succeed and to get on to the next thing. Often juggling multiple responsibilities. |
| Project manager (producing): Managing the day-to-day matters of projects. | Project manager: Ditto. |
| Team members (producing): Doing the work. | Project contacts: Providing information so that the actual work can get done. |
| Controller/finance (judging): Wants efficient billing, quick payment, and speedy resolution of issues. | Accounts payable: Wants to delay payment as long as possible. Wants cost reduction (and so is interested in ROI). |
| Salesperson (presenting): Looking for the next opportunity/chance to pitch something. Wants to keep in touch with existing relationships and get new ones. Can relate to multiple levels in the customer organization. | Various: When vendor is trusted, has a problem they want fixing. Looking to see whether your firm can do that or refer them to someone else. |

### Managing the project to a successful conclusion

Unless your firm's on retainer, the project is eventually completed, hopefully successfully. From a business development perspective, this completion is a significant achievement:

- ✔ You can turn a satisfied customer into an advocate for your business.
- ✔ You can leverage customer testimonials, case studies and references for future work.
- ✔ You can look for additional business from the current project sponsor or from other people in the customer organization who need your services.
- ✔ You may get referrals to other prospects.

The foundation for creating these opportunities doesn't get put in place at the end of the project. It develops along the way through the interactions the team has with all the customer contacts.

Customer contacts talk to each other! Every team member has the responsibility to handle customer communications with care and to report issues quickly to the account manager/project manager.

What are the significant actions that ensure a solid customer relationship from which your firm can reap benefits later? Whatever your role, be well briefed before you meet the customer. Do your research on its business and people. Take responsibility for everything, even things that are not your responsibility.

For account/project managers, here are a few specific ideas:

- ✔ Have a really good kick-off meeting (see Chapter 15).
- ✔ Create a risk-assessment and mitigation plan.
- ✔ Share status regularly, so that the customer knows what's happening on the project.
- ✔ Be open about issues. Never sweep concerns under the carpet. Customers prefer to hear the bad news early, so communicate about any problems and your proposed solutions.

    Whether it's technically your problem, the customer's or another vendor's, it is always *your* problem.
- ✔ Wrap up the project effectively. In your haste to be done, don't neglect to get customer sign-offs and feedback (more on that in Chapter 17).

Check out *Project Management For Dummies* by Stanley E Portny (Wiley).

Some of the interactions that need to occur during a project can be pretty uncomfortable. Practice is necessary to become confident handling what is, after all, routine on projects – things not going according to plan.

Relationships with customers *improve* when your company deals with issues effectively, but they deteriorate when you hide things.

### Caring for your people

A saying goes that if you have happy people, you have happy customers. Keeping your people happy doesn't just mean a beer keg/wine on Friday afternoons. Folks who work in services businesses want to do well, learn things, advance their careers and pursue interesting work. Yes, they want to earn more money too, but that alone is never enough.

If you, as the account/project manager, have line management for project teams, or you're just managing their project participation and performance, your role includes leading, coaching and growing your team. Your business can gain huge benefits by addressing this aspect as follows:

✔ **Keep your staff from walking down the street and taking another job – keeping them provides continuity of the team and makes your customers feel secure.** Your firm incurs a big cost when it loses people.

✔ **Identify future leaders.** Some team members are fine where they are – others want to progress. You should know these preferences about your team and help people get the outcomes they want.

✔ **Encourage team members to discuss progress of the work and ask for help or advice if they get stuck or encounter a problem.** When you're open about project challenges with your staff, they reciprocate. Don't rule by fear.

✔ **Handle the occasional underperforming team members – your firm can't carry people who aren't productive.** Work with HR and management to see whether you can move the person to a more suitable position within the company. If you have to let someone go, do it quickly and kindly in accordance with company policy.

✔ **Include junior people in senior meetings whenever possible.** Create an opportunity for them to show their expertise. Give them feedback to encourage their communication skills.

✔ **Support staff development programs in your business.** Try to secure training, performance reviews and other means to expand your team's capabilities. Encourage your management to develop career paths for all job roles. People stay motivated when they know that they can progress career-wise.

## Yasmin comes up smelling sweetly

Yasmin has a software implementation business where the projects are extremely complex. Her staff-development strategy includes bringing new team members in and placing them on well-established teams for their first project. The team allocates a mentor for the 'newbie', preferably someone in a similar role, who spends around two hours per week sharing information about the project methodology, how to deal with issues or concerns, and who to talk to if something comes up that the new staff member doesn't know how to tackle.

The support they receive prepares them to contribute much more effectively on subsequent projects. Yasmin's people stay with her, she delivers successful projects and her firm is highly respected in her space.

A strong delivery team is priceless in supporting the growth of your company. No one can influence that on a day-to-day basis as much as an account or project manager. Make time for it.

## Creating a lifetime customer

Quite simply, the underpinning for a spectacular customer relationship is *trust*. Throughout the customer lifecycle, your firm needs to build trust with the customer in order, ultimately, to create a customer for life.

Even if your business's projects are short, your customer base is worth nurturing. Initially, though, the following items help you to be the best you can for your customer:

✔ **Create delight:** Delighted customers are a joy to work with. Give them your best and they tend to see your firm that way. They forgive small irritations quickly (but not too many!). To delight, you need to deliver flawlessly, take customer feedback and show that you've applied it, and then say thank you. Small things work – a gas gift card if they agree to do a case study, for example.

✔ **Be a trusted advisor:** When customers are interested in your opinion across every area of their business, you know that you've made it into the hallowed ranks. As an account/project manager, you want to be extra valuable to the customer. Don't forget that each contact in the company is worth time and effort. Know your stuff – their business, trends around your offer, other people they could work with who you trust. Be objective in conversations, not self-serving.

✔ **Connect socially:** If you share leisure interests with your customers, even better. You get more quality time on the golf course than in the office. Don't fake it, but when a customer invites you for holiday drinks at his home, that's where you find yourself mixing with other trusted advisors.

The higher up your contacts are in the customer organization, the more able they are to take straight-talk. Leaders don't like 'yes-men' – they want your honest opinion. Lower down the organization, by contrast, straight-talk can be threatening, because junior people don't have the power to pursue an outcome that you may be recommending. These people want to keep their heads down and out of trouble. The exceptions are people who see themselves as future leaders.

# Tell Me What I Mean To You: Securing Value from Your Customers

Over and above delivering a project to your customer's satisfaction, your firm can obtain plenty of value out of your customers – if you bother to ask for it. Therefore, I talk you through carrying out a formal customer review and keeping in touch with customers in the future. This post-project work is the most neglected area of business development and yet it has huge potential for more business – if you just ask. This section gives you a formal process for asking for what you want – a good ongoing relationship with your customer, feedback on how to do better, and, of course, new business. It also forms the foundation for deeper client development work that I cover in Chapters 17 and 18.

## Understanding your value through the customer's eyes

Whatever value you think you bring to your customers, their view is sure to be quite different: it definitely pays to ask.

You want to understand your value (or, heaven forbid, lack of it) in a number of areas, and the best way to do so is with a formal customer review process. Although you can sometimes gather useful bits of information informally along the way, they tend to get lost in the day-to-day rushing around. Using a properly constructed review, usually in the form of a questionnaire, is the way to go. You can also compare how different customers view you qualitatively (through their comments) and quantitatively (through their scores).

### Itemizing what customer reviews cover

The aim of a formal customer review is to get an impression of the relationship with your firm's customer overall and across all stages of the project. To do this, you need questions relating to the following:

- ✔ **Project:** Quality of deliverables, the time it took and the outcomes.
- ✔ **Staffing:** How does the customer rate your firm's staff on the project?
- ✔ **Communications:** Are they sufficient and of the right type?
- ✔ **Others aspects:** How the sales process went and the transition from sales to delivery and invoicing.

One of the best practices for customer review processes is to have the customer compare you to its ideal vendor. The customer can then score your performance by comparing to a somewhat objective, unemotional standard. You also want to gather specific comments, especially if a score is in the lower range.

### Conducting the customer review process

Although automating the process with an online questionnaire is tempting, pause for a moment and think about how you personally tend to fill in questionnaires. Are you slow and thoughtful, or do you get through it as fast as you can? Most people do the latter.

Instead, the preferred approach is to get with the customer in person and ask the questions face-to-face: you need 30–45 minutes. I suggest having two people present – one to ask the questions and one to do the scribing, or filling in the form on a tablet: listening while you're writing is difficult.

If necessary, you can do the interview on the phone, but doing so is much less valuable. The fact that you take the trouble to go to the customer's office to get the feedback is impressive. Plus, you get to see the person's body language, which can tell you a lot!

Ideally, the person interviewing the customer shouldn't be someone who worked on the project, including the account/project manager: better that the interviewer is the owner or another account manager, because then the customer is more likely to 'spill the beans'.

Don't interrupt or get into a debate about what the customer is saying. The trick is to make sure that the person is fully heard, without someone starting to argue or justify. The customer's point of view is valid, even if you don't agree with it. Your role is to listen, record and ask for clarification if need be. Don't push back: you're not a hard-bitten cop trying to catch out a low-life criminal in *Law & Order*!

You may have to interview several people at the customer organization – you want as much feedback as you can get.

To see what a typical customer review form may look like, check out the snippet in Figure 16-1, which shows one section of a customer review. You need to create one appropriate to your own business.

Figure 16-1's form uses a concept called *conformance*: shorthand for whether you measure up to that perfect vendor to which the customer is comparing you. Using a scoring system allows you to see areas of excellence and under-performance at a glance.

| (VENDOR)'S COMPETENCE AND PARTNERSHIP | | (1) Does not conform | (2) Conforms rarely | (3) Conforms somewhat | (4) Conforms mostly | (5) Conforms always | N/A | Comments (important for ar |
|---|---|---|---|---|---|---|---|---|
| | Frequency | O | O | O | O | O | O | |
| Communication | Usefulness | O | O | O | O | O | O | |
| | Accessibility | O | O | O | O | O | O | |
| Flexibility (e.g. can work around my team's schedule) | | O | O | O | O | O | O | |
| Risk/change management (e.g. brings issues to the table quickly, creates solutions) | | O | O | O | O | O | O | |
| Proactivity (e.g. suggesting alternative approaches, adding value) | | O | O | O | O | | | |
| Competence in the area of my project | | O | O | O | O | | | |

**Figure 16-1:** Sample from a customer review form: The customer enters a rating of 1 (low) to 5 (high) in the appropriate spaces or N/A if not applicable.

Additional comments: ................................................................................
..............................................................................................................

## Feeding back to the team

Whether you think that some of your customers are a pain in the neck or not, it's a good day when you get all fives. But the comments often give you the highest value feedback, because they tell you specifically what the customer thinks, what you may be able to use to build testimonials and collateral or, if the comment was negative, what you need to work on internally to improve.

Ideally, share your customer review metrics with your executives, together with the comments, and aggregate them with results from other customers to give you an overall score. You can set good goals around those scores to see how far you can raise them.

You also want to share the individual review results with the team that did the work. As well as making the team feel good (generally) about what the members have achieved, doing so prompts discussion about improvements, which is always beneficial.

Be circumspect about how you divulge comments about individuals, especially if negative. Even particularly positive comments about one person on the team can make the others feel that, even though they were working their socks off, they weren't appreciated.

Start putting together your own customer review form. Write down the areas you'd like to ask questions about and then start brainstorming questions with your management and sales and marketing folks. My own version includes sections for the overall relationship, the project, the team, our competence and partnership (as in Figure 16-1) and how we compare to other vendors. It also has a section where I ask whether the customer would be a reference or is willing for us to write a case study. I ask about future work and referrals to other departments (see the next section 'Asking for more').

## *Asking for more*

One of the great things about a customer review process is that by the end of the main part of the review, the customer is lulled into a state of appreciation (assuming that you've done an okay job, of course). This point is where you stop asking for information and ask for what you want.

Here are a few ideas of the sorts of things you can request at this stage in your relationship:

- ✔ **Testimonials and/or case studies:** Sometimes, the contract excludes these things, but if not ask for them. Don't expect the customer to do any work. Write up a summary of the customer, the challenge it faced, the solution you provided and the results you produced. A direct quote from a customer can be a perfect testimonial. Sometimes the results from the project don't show up for a few months, so you may have to come back later for data for a case study.

    Give this information to marketing and let them draft the testimonial/ case study for the customer's approval. (Check out the template for a case study in Figure 16-2.) If you have any good emails from the customer commenting on the excellence of your work, be sure to give those to marketing too.

    Creating case studies for customers can be a tricky business. You have to follow their rules regarding usage of their logo or other brand elements. They may have style guidelines that help marketing. Find out who needs to approve a case study and how long the process is. Bigger companies tend to move more slowly and be more formal; it can take weeks.

- ✔ **References:** If your customers regularly take up references before they do business with you, you need a fresh supply of new customers willing to provide one so that you don't exhaust your favorite customers. Most give you a glowing reference, even if some minor issues occurred during the project. Customers like to help.

- ✔ **Future work:** If you've been communicating effectively with the customer throughout the project, you may have some sense of what's coming next for its department. At the end of the project, you can definitely ask.

✔ **Additional contacts:** You can also ask if you'd benefit from any introductions to others in the organization. If you do good account planning (see Chapter 17), you already know who you want to get close to. Upselling to an existing customer is much easier than acquiring a new one.

✔ **External contacts:** The customer may be willing to introduce you to other relationships within other companies. After all, they're not locked up in their offices for eight hours a day – they're out and about at networking events, conferences and social functions discussing business.

---

Gather the following information and give it to marketing to create the case study.

| |
|---|
| Customer name: |
| URL: |
| Company description (what they do) (<10 words): |
| Headquarters location: |
| Summary statement of what client now has that it didn't before and the major benefits (<50 words): |
| Statement of client requirement (what it needed), what you did and the tangible deliverables (<100 words): |
| Customer quote: ' _____ ' |
| Name and title of the person giving the quote: |
| The challenge (detail on what the client needed) (<66 words): |
| The solution (specifics of how the solution was envisioned, developed and delivered. Use bullets as much as possible) (<220 words): |
| Results (benefits statements and tangible results, including ROI, e.g., quantitative measures of performance improvement if possible) (<250 words): |

**Also provide:**

* Client logo
* Client contact for case study approval

**Figure 16-2:** Case study template.

As the final section on the customer review, include questions that cover the above items. You have their attention – so use it!

If you have any information you can give informally to salespeople about the customer and your results, share it. Salespeople can use this material verbally with prospects, even if a formal case study isn't available yet.

The later stages of the project, during project review, as I discuss in Chapter 15, are the ideal times to bring the salesperson back into the account, especially for developing and exploring possible new projects with other departments in your customer organization or with wholly new companies. This approach saves a lot of time, because you may well have another customer you need to be working on. Yup, salespeople have their uses.

## Turning the customer into an active advocate

After the work is done, you can easily forget your faithful customer: after all, you have to move on. However, if you can keep in touch with your prior customers, they keep you in mind when a new opportunity arises.

See whether you can:

- **Join the groups that your customers belong to, offline and online.** It helps you understand who and what they're interacting with. Don't be shy to ask them whether you can join them at a specific event. They'll probably introduce you to anyone they know or just enjoy spending time with you.

- **Ask for introductions to people they know.** LinkedIn is a great source: you can do your research and be specific about who you're trying to connect with.

- **Help customers if they ask you for advice.** It may be a referral to another firm that can help them with a problem or some information that they don't know where to find. Make yourself useful.

- **Follow up on introductions and contacts.** When you sign a contract with a new customer referred to you by an existing one, send a little gift to the customer contact who introduced you.

- **But make sure that doing so is acceptable:** in some companies and almost universally across the public sector, you won't be allowed.

Don't try to be all things to all customers: select the ones you believe can provide value to you and then make some effort in their direction. The more value you provide to your customers, the more they'll want to reciprocate: it's simply good for business.

# Chapter 17

# Joining Together to Maximize Business and Customer Value

. . . . . . . . . . . . . . . . . . . . . . . . . . . . . . . . . . . . . . . . . . . . . . . . . .

## In This Chapter

▶ Making business development everyone's business

▶ Considering the role of account planning for customer growth

▶ Turning the delivery team into great business developers

. . . . . . . . . . . . . . . . . . . . . . . . . . . . . . . . . . . . . . . . . . . . . . . . . .

*T*he key to good customer management is to have great account managers, so in this chapter I focus on your account/customer/project managers (and their boss) who lead the teams working on the customers' projects. These people can have various titles, but they're usually part of delivery (sometimes called operations) and they lead and can encourage the whole of the delivery team to get involved in business development in one way or another.

Although business development looks as if it belongs to the marketing and salespeople and is nothing to do with anyone else in the organization, when you accept and communicate that everyone in the business is responsible for it, you increase your chance of thriving. The account managers are the lynchpin.

In this chapter, I look at how account managers need to be effective in business development, and how to motivate the whole of your company to push the business-development bandwagon and support your plans for growth. I describe the roles of account planning and account managers in this task and show how delivery can be vital by obtaining invaluable feedback for you.

# You Know It Makes Sense: Seeing How Business Development Benefits All

If people in your organization think 'business development isn't *my* job', you're coming out of the gate at a distinct disadvantage. I'm not exaggerating when I say that everyone in your company contributes to the health of the business in one way or another: remember that a healthy organism grows and prospers.

In this section I look at how every function in your business contributes to business health, including making everyone a 'business developer' (in a general sense) and encouraging effective motivation and communication.

## Creating an organization in which everyone sells

Your aim is to create a 'selling' organization, one in which everyone is pulling in the same direction for new customers, happy customers and high profit.

This goal may not be as far away as you think. Table 17-1 shows how your people may be contributing to business development already, without even knowing it. All these roles are working on behalf of the company to grow your business and make it successful and every one of them has a part to play in the development of your firm.

| Table 17-1 | How Your People Contribute to Business Development |
| --- | --- |
| **Role** | **How the Function Contributes to Business Development** |
| CEO/owners | Provide leadership, customer confidence and expertise and are often the best 'salespeople' in the company. Can smooth over difficult customer situations. |
| Finance | Handles customer invoicing and payments with accuracy and efficiency. Looks after collections, minimizes bad debt, keeps costs low and maximizes profit. Supports investment and growth. |

| *Role* | *How the Function Contributes to Business Development* |
|---|---|
| Human resources | Finds the best people who perform well. Takes care of employee concerns and takes the lead on ensuring employee satisfaction, resulting in good work and delighted customers. |
| Marketing | Positions the company and brand in the marketplace and is ultimately responsible for generating leads. Makes sure that the company's reputation is taken care of and enhanced. |
| Sales | Converts leads into deals. Leverages relationships and partnerships to deliver more opportunities. Cross-sells (develops and sells to new contacts) and upsells (to existing customers). Represents the company in the marketplace in a wide variety of ways. |
| Customer/account/project management (usually part of delivery) | Acts as the day-to-day face of your company to the customer, offering business advice, communication, issue resolution and smoothing over less critical customer situations (and critical ones sometimes). Looks for new opportunities, gets case studies and testimonials, and asks for referrals. |
| Delivery team | Does the work with integrity and efficiency. Provides the ultimate value to customers by solving their business problems, hence creating customer advocates. Provides the proof to new prospects that your firm can do what you say it can. |
| Customer service | Handles customer questions and concerns on a day-to-day basis, often when the main work is over. Used where customers need ongoing services (as in support or maintenance agreements). Creates happy customers. |
| Legal | Avoids risk by making sure that contracts are robust and that no one sells the company down the river. |

Beyond their day-to-day work, which is already a significant contribution, people like nothing more than being able to find or refer a prospective new customer. Not everyone has the knack for doing so, but you can encourage the whole organization to think of itself as a selling organization, looking for new opportunities and new customers, working on higher profits or more efficient ways to do the work, or being extra attentive to the customer and impeccable in communication.

One way to achieve this goal is to motivate the behaviors that you want, for example:

- ✔ Offer an incentive when an employee relationship results in a new deal.
- ✔ Give a bonus to anyone who refers a new employee, with a second payment if that person stays for more than six months.
- ✔ Create a competition for the most profitable project/customer team.
- ✔ Set up an annual bonus pool to share the profits with your employees.

The reward doesn't always have to be money, of course: company acknowledgements, gift cards or even a party work well too. Mix it up a bit, so that people don't always expect cold hard cash.

Doesn't that all sound peachy – the whole organization pulling together to get the results that everyone wants? Oh, if only things were always like that!

When you move your business towards a model of unified purpose, you're doing 'business development' on your own business.

## Being a motivating business

In many firms, unfortunately, some people, in whatever role, prefer to point the finger and lay the culpability for sub-par results at someone else's door. When you think about this behavior, it can seem like cutting off your nose to spite your face, especially if you're a business leader. You want to motivate, not accuse.

### Ensuring that your firm doesn't demotivate

Picture the following scenes:

- ✔ Marketing is unable to generate solid leads – should they be pilloried by all and sundry?
- ✔ Sales wins a new contract, but the scope turns out to be bigger than you anticipate and the project looks as if it will lose money – is the department incompetent?
- ✔ Sales is going through a dry spell and can't seem to win a deal – is that the salespeople's fault?

To a certain extent, when things don't go well, people do have to step up and get into action, which means admitting the problem and asking for help. But when a culture of blame exists in your organization, asking for support can be very difficult.

Imagine a customer calling you and yelling down the phone about a poor deliverable. Do you look to convict someone of the crime? Are you a motivating or demotivating force?

Picture instead a context in which a new project manager identifies that a project is turning out to be more complex than anyone expected and goes to talk to the salesperson to share the situation and find out about the history of the sale. The discussion uncovers what happened and they go to your CEO to explain the state of affairs and propose next steps. They set up a meeting with the customer and negotiate a modification to the scope so that the project can proceed. That would be a great outcome.

You can no doubt see that communication pays a vitally important role here (check out the later section 'Talking about team communication').

### Motivating everyone to do their bit

Here are some ways in which everyone in the business can do their job while pulling together as a team and acting in the company's best interests:

✔ Inspire people about the role they play in the company. If you ask one stonemason what she's doing she may say, 'I'm carving this block to this pattern.' If you ask another he may say, 'I'm building a skyscraper.' Awareness of the wider context (the big picture) provides the inspiration. Take a look at Chapters 7 and 13 for rolling out your business development strategy.

✔ Incentivize people for the right behavior (see the earlier section 'Creating an organization in which everyone sells' for some ideas).

✔ Create structures, processes and opportunities for collaboration across functions. In other words, you want all the people from Table 17-1 to feel part of a selling organization, to harness the potential that inherently exists if they'd only work together.

You can achieve all the above only with good plans and consistently great communication.

## Talking about team communication

At the root of issues with business growth is a weakness in team communication. Here are a few of the sorts of things that arise as common problems:

✔ The functions of marketing, sales, customer management and delivery become separate from each other, each doing their 'own thing'.

✔ Important information about prospects and customers doesn't get shared across the functional boundaries.

- ✔ People are heads-down, working on their own tasks and ignoring the contribution that they could make to others on the team.

- ✔ Feedback from customers or between departments is often weak or non-existent. The company is busy doing work, but not using the customer or internal resources systematically to improve and elevate the offer.

Of course, everyone relates to the mindset of 'this is my job and that's someone else's'. Wanting to draw boundaries that help define and limit responsibility is natural. The risk of this conventional 'job description' mentality, though, is that it fails to maximize the potential and value of every employee.

Look at the customer lifecycle diagram in Figure 2-1 and use it for this exercise with your team. Ask each of them to look at the diagram and to note down the following:

- ✔ The part of the customer lifecycle they think they own

- ✔ Where they see their function overlapping into other parts of the life-cycle, owned by someone else

- ✔ How they think they can contribute to other parts of the lifecycle

The results of this exercise are often illuminating. Most functions feel that they can provide useful information to help develop and enhance services, hone marketing messages to help them have a more positive impact, support the sales process to make it faster and less risky, and support customers and partner relationships for maximum mutual benefit.

Use the feedback from this exercise to develop good communication practices for your company.

Table 17-2 shows types of communication that are worth your time and attention and make a difference to the growth of your business. Almost every company benefits from addressing these aspects.

| Table 17-2 | Communication that Contributes to Company Growth |
| --- | --- |
| *Communication* | *How it helps* |
| Marketing emails and other outbound communications | Staff members often don't know what's being communicated to your target market. Keeping the team informed as to what's going out, what new collateral has been created and where your company is advertising offline or online, is helpful for everyone in conversations they have with prospects, customers and partners. |

| *Communication* | *How it helps* |
|---|---|
| Scope of a prospect's project | Salespeople often try to figure out how to meet prospect requirements so that they can create a proposal quickly. Sharing the scope of a prospect's project allows the delivery team to help – maybe they've dealt with a similar situation before. |
| Informal information coming from a customer | From good news to bad, customer feedback in any form is valuable to the team. Fold positive feedback into marketing messaging that can be used by sales and leveraged to boost team self-esteem. You can share and jointly tackle negatives and consider new ideas for future enhancements to almost every aspect of the business. |
| Significant communications or updates | Throughout the customer lifecycle, the whole team should know about certain key events – a customer signed a contract or Statement of Work, a project won an award, a case study just got created, the website had a facelift. Try to avoid anyone saying 'I didn't know that!' |
| Organizing the work in easily accessible project folders | To avoid being bombardment with TMI (too much information), organize documents in a repository and make sure that everyone knows where to find them. Some solutions even allow you to set alerts when specific types of documents get updated. |
| Joint account brainstorming/ planning | A customer is a valuable commodity – do some account planning for your most significant and valuable customers (see the tip in this section on scheduling marketing and sales reviews and also the later section 'Making the Most of Account Planning'). |
| 'I have an idea' suggestions | Create a simple mechanism for gathering and sharing good ideas. Take them seriously and see whether they're worth implementing. |
| Any intelligence coming from market research, competitor activity, customer and partner feedback | Share formal information – great blogs or whitepapers, activities that competitors are doing, formal feedback from customers and partners. |

For your periodic meetings, do the marketing and sales review in the morning (check out Chapter 13) and a customer review and any training in the afternoon (see the next section). Get these meetings scheduled at the beginning of the year and don't allow people to duck out. If customer needs come up, your team has to say that they're not available on those days. Mondays and Fridays are good days for these meetings, because customers tend to be a little less active. Also, don't schedule status meetings and the like for those days (or move them if they are already there).

Good communication pays off big time in increased revenue.

# Making the Most of Account Planning

Before everyone starts running around looking for new customers, a good idea is to create a focus for business development activity. One area that most companies neglect is their existing customers. Sure, they're happy to take the call when a customer gets on the phone to talk about new work, but they're not usually proactive in their customer management. That starts with account planning and gives the team goals and tasks to get their teeth into.

As part of your business development plan (see Chapter 6), you set some pretty ambitious goals. You break your revenue plan down into three categories:

- ✔ Revenue that you can rely on (already covered by a signed contract, that is, booked business)
- ✔ New revenue that could come from your existing customers
- ✔ Revenue that needs to come from completely new customers

Part of your strategy is to make sure that you maximize revenue from your current customers.

This section details the essential role of account planning as the foundation of good customer management and I concentrate on new revenue from existing customers. I cover understanding where your revenue will come from, how to achieve your goals and creating your firm's account plan.

If you're a project-based company (one job and you're done), this section's material on the potential to *upsell* (increase or add new business with your existing contacts) or *cross-sell* (develop new contacts and sell to them) may be less relevant. Even so, these practices turn your account managers into superstars, so use what's going to benefit you.

## *Analyzing where your revenue will come from*

Maybe you have existing contracts that roll right into next year, January and beyond. Maybe you have ideas on where you're going to find new business within the customer base. The thing is, you don't achieve your goals by accident. You need to plan to get there and that starts with account planning.

Your revenue is going to come from new clients too. I cover this aspect in Chapter 6, where I also talk about your current customers. Use Chapter 6 for preliminary planning (including Figures 6-1 through 6-4).

I'm assuming that you have a spreadsheet with your goals broken down to revenue coming from customers (and who they all are and where the money is expected to come from). If you don't deliver on that part of the plan, you put a lot of pressure on your sales team to sell more than they originally anticipated – or you just won't reach your goal.

## *Turning goals into reality*

Account planning turns those desired numbers into a real possibility. If your account/project managers are naturals at customer/account management, they already have ideas about how to expand the business with your customers. Capitalize on their insights.

If your account management function is weak, however, you may have to use salespeople (perhaps that's you) to drive new business in existing customers. Therefore, add to your strategic initiatives for the year the goal to strengthen your account management team and practices. Use Chapters 16 and 18 to help you. The later section 'Growing, Growing, Gone! Account Managers' Role in Your Growth Plans' also includes ideas on how to get account managers comfortable with upselling.

What you need to include in your account planning depends quite a bit on the size and nature of your customers and your service:

- ✔ If you work with mainly mid-sized businesses, say $100–500 million (£63–347 million), the account planning can be fairly straightforward, because the power to buy tends to lie in a few hands.

- ✔ If you deal with mega-businesses, the situation is quite different and more like handling several smaller businesses that just happen to come under the same umbrella. Done well, you can have a meal-ticket for life from Fortune 1000 companies, but you need to invest in excellent account managers who probably can split their time between getting new opportunities as well as billing some hours to cover their costs.

If you can apply your service across different departments or divisions in a customer, you have a lot of potential for expanding the work you do. But when your service is more focused on a single department or function, it may lend itself to a long-term contract situation.

Either way, start account planning modestly and work up from there. I've seen account planning documents that are 20 pages long. Personally, I prefer something like a sales battlecard (see Chapter 14): 1–2 pages only and revised every three months with updated goals and actions.

## Deciding what to include in your account plan

Here are a few things that you may want to include in your account planning:

- ✔ **Information about the customer, the current relationships and work being done.** This information serves two purposes:

   – It reminds the account manager of the status quo.

   – It informs anyone else who's going to be involved in the account of the current situation.

- ✔ **Key metrics about the current work.** Examples are profitability and Days Sales Outstanding (DSO), namely how long customers take to pay you.

- ✔ **Date of last customer review and the scores and key areas being worked on.** See Chapter 16 for all about this process.

- ✔ **Additional relationships you want to develop in the customer organization.** These relationships may be people to whom your current contacts can introduce you, or people you can just go after on your own. Again, the customer review process from Chapter 16 is helpful in asking for internal referrals.

- ✔ **Potential new opportunities identified.** Perhaps through conversations with the customer, or ideas on what you can offer that the existing contacts or new ones may be interested in.

Pin the account plan over account managers' desks: nothing works as well as keeping it front-of-mind. Figure 17-1 shows an example account-planning template. Fill the boxes in the order as numbered – it helps you develop your thinking around how to impact results with each customer.

| 1. Customer Overview | 2. Contacts | 3. Customer Needs/Pains |
|---|---|---|
| a) Background <br> b) Industry trends | a) Existing <br> b) Desired | a) Top of mind issues <br> b) Which can we solve? |
| 4. Current or most recent service | 5. Future services | 6. Benefits / ROI |
| a) Working on now <br> b) Previous services | a) What could we sell them? <br> b) On what timeline? <br> c) Which role or contact would buy? | a) What benefit would the customer get from this new service? <br> b) What would the ROI be? |
| 7. Goals for this quarter | 8. Actions to take | 9. Other Information |
| a) (Complete as needed) <br> b) <br> c) <br> d) | a) (Complete as needed) <br> b) <br> c) <br> d) | (Complete as needed) |

**Figure 17-1:**
Account-
planning
template.

Part of the annual cycle is to prepare an initial account plan for each major account. Don't get too ambitious – set a few simple goals for the first quarter and then revisit and update at the quarterly meetings (check out Chapter 13). Use account managers and delivery team members in account planning – they all have insights into how to develop a customer more fully.

By all means skip customers without potential, but don't neglect the customer review process. New opportunities show up in surprising places – you never know who your contacts know until you ask.

# Growing, Growing, Gone! Account Managers' Role in Your Growth Plans

Before you send your account managers out into the hostile world of upselling and cross-selling (see the preceding section), consider doing some staff development. Selling doesn't come naturally to some account managers, who often just grow into a role or do it by default, instead of being born to it. Time spent in regular training sessions is a gift that keeps on giving.

This section delves into what account managers need to get comfortable with.

## Showing account managers how to do business development

To be successful in upselling and cross-selling, your account managers need to start looking at the bigger picture – not just to see how much money you can beat out of your long-suffering customer contacts, but how you increase your value to them and create potential value for others in their company. This bigger picture requires more than suggesting that they use your x, y or z service, now that they're done with a, b and c.

Your account managers need to do the same sorts of things that business development leaders do to add value and sell new services, except that they're doing it in the narrower context of a single customer (or maybe two or three). So if you're an account manager, what does that look like? Here is a selection of things to work on:

- ✔ **Know your customer inside out.** What are the company's goals, what business moves or changes may be coming, where is it showing up in the news and what are its competitors doing? Much of this information is freely available on the Internet, or various information services can deliver it straight to your inbox (something your salespeople are likely to be using already).

- ✔ **Understand the organization structure and where your current contacts sit within that structure.** Some information tools give you that too, or you can build your organization map in a customer relationship management (CRM) tool such as Salesforce or as part of your account planning documents (jump to Chapter 15 for more on CRM). The key point is that to increase business within upper mid-market or large customers, you need to develop new relationships, preferably by introduction.

- ✔ **Know what the trends are in your customer's market space, or in yours, that may provide opportunity for new business.** If everyone in the customer's industry is getting into, say, enterprise-wide collaboration tools, or dealing with new legislation or end-of-life product, maybe that gives you an opportunity. If your other customers are starting to engage your company to help with some new, innovative initiative, you should be aware of that and share it with your customer.

- ✔ **Know the right questions to ask each customer.** Good knowledge of the customer's business is the starting point for figuring out what may be next on its mind. If you can pose questions that get the customer thinking, or that lead to a discussion of new opportunities, that's awesome.

- ✔ **Be willing to share information that's useful to your customer, even if the information is of no direct benefit to your firm.** The perfect account manager is a trusted advisor and trusted advisors do what's good for the customer, not for themselves. In the end it pays off.

No one is better at these tasks than top salespeople. If you have folks like that, good on you. Use them to share their best practices with you to hone your account management skills. If your salespeople need to up their game, joint training sessions are really beneficial.

Table 17-3 shows what these training sessions can consist of, giving topics to cover and approaches that work. Make these sessions active and collaborative, not just boring sessions on what people should be doing.

| Table 17-3 | Account Management Training |
|---|---|
| **What to Do** | **How to Do It** |
| Account planning | Share the format of the account planning template (Figure 17-1) and your revenue goal for the year/quarter. Fill in what you know today and share it with another account manager or salesperson, who should ask questions. More details and ideas come out of a paired discussion (two heads are better than one). Fill out the rest as homework. |
| Customer review process | The key to developing and growing a customer is the customer review process (at the most formal level) and all the weekly or monthly opportunities to talk informally with the customer about how things are going. Many account managers have difficulty asking for anything, so carry out paired role play around the customer review process (Figure 16-1): make sure to include questions that ask for a case study, a testimonial, a reference, a referral or even just what the contact is going to focus on when this project is done. One person plays the customer, the other the account manager. Then switch. |
| Share best practices in customer profiling | Have team members share their favorite sources of information about customers, industries, staff changes and so on. Agree how to capture and share such information as the customer moves through the lifecycle. Decide also where to keep this information. |
| Win/loss and status/deliverable meetings | Sales and account managers should share how they capture information to improve performance at different stages in the lifecycle. For example, for salespeople, the win/loss interview tells them what they did well and where they can improve. For account managers, they often find out at status meetings, or when a deliverable is in review by the customer, or during that customer review process. |
| Best practices | Get examples of best practices from team members, such as an action they took or information they used to get a result with a customer. |

## Playing around with roles

When working with a group of account managers in a software training organization, the discussion quickly moved from the customer experience to some role play on asking customer contacts who else in their organization may benefit from the training.

After two or three role-play attempts with a co-worker, account managers started to say that they felt more comfortable about asking for introductions. The next week, an account manager called me to say that he'd been introduced to a contact much higher up in the customer's organization and they were discussing making the training a corporate standard for all departments.

Sales and account management should get in a room together once a month if possible. Account managers benefit from seeing how salespeople are comfortable talking about opportunities, budgets and asking for the business.

In case you're wondering, salespeople do account planning too, except that the 'customer' is still a 'prospect' and no actual work is being done yet. Even so, salespeople know that profiling the customer in some depth is one of their keys to success. They may use the CRM to gather the information, but if they're not researching the customer fully – well, they should be!

## Thinking about monthly, quarterly and annual reviews

When you have an account plan (or a number of them), it needs first to get put into action and second to periodically get reviewed and refreshed. Set up a regular meeting schedule to provide a forum for account plan reviews:

- ✔ **Monthly meeting:** To look at achievements from the prior month and plan for the next month.
- ✔ **Quarterly meeting:** To review the past quarter and plan for the next one, making any necessary adjustments to the existing plan.
- ✔ **Annual meeting:** Does account planning for the next year.

Owners and management, marketing, sales and delivery team members may want to attend and contribute (or learn). Account managers should take turns to discuss their accounts.

*TRUE STORY*

## Raj goes large!

Raj runs a software development company and believed that his team had previously underperformed. Growth seemed to be just a matter of luck rather than planning.

I worked with Raj and his team to facilitate their annual planning cycle. During the planning process, we uncovered a whole new business opportunity, which his firm could easily position with its customers and potentially double revenue from each client. With a plan in hand, team members became alert to what they needed to find out, what they should act on and how to expand their customer's value using this new idea.

At the end of the first quarter, one account manager had three contract extensions and was starting to see new revenue coming in, above her original account plan. The next quarter's plan included getting every customer to sign-up for the extended service and to have sales discuss the opportunity with new prospects during the sales process. Major win for Raj's company!

As an account manager, you use these meetings to see whether you're:

- ✔ Delivering on the revenue goals.
- ✔ Expanding your relationships in the customer.
- ✔ Expanding the people or departments in the customer with whom you're doing business.
- ✔ Getting good customer reviews and acting on the feedback.
- ✔ Feeding back information to people in your company: marketing, sales and delivery (see the next section).

# Bringing Delivery to the Feedback Party

Account managers aren't an island – they're surrounded by a delivery team, some of whom may be future account managers. Think of your team as feet on the street and use them to the advantage of your company. What's the significance of having a capable account management and delivery team? In the end, the work on the ground with the customer is at the heart of your business, so in this section I look at leveraging your whole team to deliver on business growth.

## *Spreading delivery's tentacles into the market*

When the delivery team is doing its job, staff members are looking to be the best they can at delivering the customer work flawlessly, quickly and efficiently.

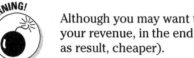

Although you may want to bill customers every hour in the week to maximize your revenue, in the end you're caught out if a competitor does it faster (and as result, cheaper).

Where delivery really has the advantage in business development is that it works right at the coal face. The team hears what the customer is saying, sees what issues come up and gets to know the hopes and dreams of your customers. It gathers intelligence at a whole different level, like an octopus, reaching out into different aspects of your customer's business and feeling for what's there.

## *Gathering new ideas and best practices*

Each delivery team has its own perspective on its customer(s) and from the work it has done with prior ones. Somehow, you have to aggregate that knowledge into a collection of valuable experiences and information that you can use for your business.

The following is what's of highest value to you:

- ✔ **Information about your direct impact on the customer's business.** This information tells you whether your services are relevant, whether you're delivering them the right way and whether they're providing the right value that the customer is more than happy to pay for. This information allows you to improve constantly how you serve your customers to maximize your value to them.

- ✔ **Information about whether customers love working with you.** If so, maybe they want you to extend your services to encompass a little more – to go a little further. Think carefully about whether you can do as good a job with extended services, and if you can, go for it. If the plan is a decent one, you should be able to cross-sell this extension to many of your other customers as well.

- ✔ **Information about when you see a whole new trend in the marketplace.** It may be a threat (such as the fact that your service is being replaced by newer approaches) or a whole new opportunity for your company. Your customers may be seeing the same trend and they'll share with you what they're thinking. Take their views seriously – they're the ones with the check book.

Figure out how to collect customer intelligence and how to use it and combine it with your own ideas. If it doesn't get captured, it typically gets lost and forgotten.

## Ensuring that sales learns from delivery

When account management is a robust discipline in your company, sales has a lot to learn from delivery. Delivery is all about making things happen in reality – having customers achieve their goals, delivering the work as perfectly as possible, managing the ups and downs of a services engagement, and keeping things on track and on budget are significant skills.

Now, I'm the last to suggest that salespeople are universally sloppy, but some of them really are! They want to be performing in front of a prospect, sharing how great your company is and the excellent results the customers will get if they just sign on the dotted line. What salespeople often don't do so well is meticulous record-keeping. The evidence is that top-performing salespeople (and account managers) do pay careful attention to note-keeping.

I discuss the downside of inadequate record-keeping in Chapter 16, which covers handover from sales to delivery and how to make that go smoothly. When sales gets a chance to collaborate with delivery, it can benefit hugely, especially by examining areas that don't work as well as they should, such as a weak kick-off or a messy completion.

Sales also needs first-hand understanding of the real value of your services to the customer, even if they're specific to that customer. If that value gets captured (shared across the team, written up as a testimonial or case study, quantified and qualified), account managers can use that information in their selling.

A great case study coming to you in an email isn't the same as a verbal communication by the account manager and other team members about the difference they made to that customer.

## Making delivery feel valued

Sometimes, the delivery folks feel like the workhorses of the company. They're heads-down every day, sometimes working long hours to get the job done on time.

When you enrol your delivery team in the idea that *they* are your frontline intelligence army and that what they uncover is priceless, you can elevate their perceived importance (and perhaps find a way to compensate them for what they may see as an off-hours effort). Plus, when the whole team (marketing, salespeople and account managers) places high value on using what delivery says, the pivotal role of delivery becomes evident to everyone.

No one talks to the customers as often or as deeply about the real issues as the delivery team. Make the most of their input.

# Chapter 18

# Standing Tall To Get More Customers: Vertical Industries

. . . . . . . . . . . . . . . . . . . . . . . . . . . . . . . . . . . . . . . . . . . . . . . . . . . . .

*In This Chapter*

▶ Benefitting by going vertical

▶ Applying your knowledge to a vertical

▶ Implementing vertical-specific campaigns

. . . . . . . . . . . . . . . . . . . . . . . . . . . . . . . . . . . . . . . . . . . . . . . . . . . . .

*F*or most businesses, expansion is the name of the game. Whether your focus is a little more revenue every year, a path to a great exit by selling your company or you're into world domination, growth matters. When a business grows, employees experience a thriving, dynamic and exciting environment; if a business is static or in decline, things feel turgid, because in essence business is a game and you play games to win.

I write a great deal in this book about how to attract, acquire, retain and leverage your customers, but business development involves much more than just the next customer, and then the next, and then the next. . . . For example, Chapter 17 describes approaches for a *first, next, next* strategy, where each successive customer you acquire builds on the last and things get easier.

In contrast, this chapter looks at growth from the point of view of *verticals:* the specific industries your customers are in and your value to their specific situations, given that industry context. I discuss the importance of verticals and whether going vertical is suitable for you. Also, I show how to leverage your customer-management success with one customer throughout the vertical.

I use a variety of target verticals as examples, but my thoughts apply to any vertical, so you can translate the ideas to your own business.

# 'The Only Way Is Up!' Understanding Why Verticals Matter

In this section, I explain what verticals are, why they have such potential for some firms, whether you should join the fun and what customers within a vertical want from you. You can use this section to start your assessment of whether verticals would be good for you to pursue.

Here are a couple of definitions:

- **Verticals:** Companies that are in the same line of business, for example Retail, which can be subdivided into sub-verticals like Apparel, Footwear, Grocery and so on.

- **Horizontals:** Similar to verticals, horizontals represent a line of business, but one that cuts across verticals. For example, Manufacturing is a particularly broad category and apparel manufacturing is hugely different from electronics or convenience food manufacturing.

Two connected dimensions significantly impact the value of your company in the market:

- **Specialization:** Although you may be tempted to try to be everything to everyone, that approach opens you up to extensive competition and to being mediocre in some areas of delivery. Staying narrow and going deep is much more valuable – like drilling for oil.

- **Verticalization:** As a special case of specialization, serving one or just a few verticals makes your offer much more valuable than a general offer from your competitors.

To discover more about verticals, see the sidebar "River deep, mountain high': Verticals and horizontals'.

Figure 18-1 shows an extract from a SIC code table that indicates categories of specific industries. Each major vertical and all the subdivisions are shown as two, three or four-digit codes, dependent on how granular you're getting (see also siccode.com/en/pages/industry-codes). A NAICS (North American Industry Classification System) code table is also available and similarly used to categorize companies (see www.census.gov/eos/www/naics).

When you're collecting company data for business-development purposes, make sure that you get the SIC code for each company. Doing so allows you to segment your database by industry and therefore tailor specific marketing campaigns with information that's relevant to the vertical. Check out Chapter 11 for more on building your prospect database.

---

## 'River deep, mountain high': Verticals and horizontals

A vertical conjures up an image of something that goes from top to bottom, like a column on a building, as opposed to side to side, or horizontal, like the sidewalk outside your home.

If you think of the marketplace as a rectangle, you can divide it into columns where each

represents a slice of the marketplace – a specific industry, such as agriculture, healthcare or education (see the following minitable, which is, of course, far from complete):

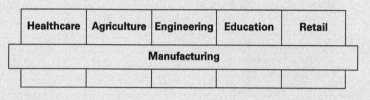

| Healthcare | Agriculture | Engineering | Education | Retail |
|---|---|---|---|---|
| | | Manufacturing | | |
| | | | | |

As a wrinkle, some categories that look like verticals, such as manufacturing, are really more like horizontals. Manufacturing companies do some of the same things whatever product they're manufacturing. They also inherit certain constraints and opportunities from the vertical for which they're manufacturing (for example, a pharmaceutical company has to be concerned about the FDA, HIIPA and the Affordable Care Act), so manufacturing 'cuts across' verticals as shown above. You get the picture.

To look at the wide variety of verticals, download a standard industrial classification (SIC) code table and check out the diversity (Figure 18-1 shows an extract from such a list).

The SIC categories are broad slices – for example, a healthcare insurer (such as Aetna, Cigna or United Health) may have different concerns from a healthcare provider (such as a hospital). How detailed you get in thinking about verticals depends on how specific your service is.

---

## *Working with verticals makes sense*

Customers believe that they're different, even if you know that they're not. Therefore, they think that vendors that have worked in their space are more valuable than ones that haven't – and they're right about that.

If you've gleaned specialized knowledge from working with a company in a specific vertical, you're more valuable to other companies in that vertical. When you position your service in their language (words specific to their vertical) and you have case studies to show that you know what you're doing, you're automatically going to rise to the top of their consideration list.

In addition, any work you do for a similar company is essentially 'repeatable'. You have so-called domain knowledge about how the firm's business operates that you don't have to relearn, so the customer spends less time teaching you. Plus, any distinctive services, know-how or other components of your solutions are highly valuable. You may have insights, solution tips and tricks to pass on, which make the delivery of your service much more cost effective for the customer (and more profitable for you).

| CATEGORY DESCRIPTION | SPECIFIC SIC CODE |
|---|---|
| **Medical instruments and supplies** | D384 |
| Surgical & medical instruments | D3841 |
| Surgical & medical instrument mfg (pt) | D3841 |
| Surgical appliances & supplies | D3842 |
| Paper (except newsprint) mills (pt) | D3842 |
| Sanitary paper product mfg (pt) | D3842 |
| Electromedical & electrotherapeutic apparatus mfg (pt) | D3842 |
| Surgical appliance & supplies mfg (pt) | D3842 |
| Dental equipment & supplies | D3843 |
| Dental equipment & supplies mfg (pt) | D3843 |
| X-ray apparatus & tubes | D3844 |
| Irradiation apparatus mfg | D3844 |
| Electromedical equipment | D3845 |
| Electromedical & electrotherapeutic apparatus mfg (pt) | D3845 |
| **Ophthalmic goods** | D385 |
| Ophthalmic goods | D3851 |
| Ophthalmic goods mfg | D3851 |
| **Photographic equipment and supplies** | D386 |
| Photographic equipment & supplies | D3861 |
| Photographic film, paper, plate, & chemical mfg | D3861 |
| Photographic & photocopying equipment mfg (pt) | D3861 |
| **Watches, clocks, watchcases, and parts** | D387 |
| Watches, clocks, & watchcases | D3873 |
| Watch, clock, & part mfg (pt) | D3873 |

**Figure 18-1:** Extract of a standard industrial classification (SIC) code table.

You can also take on board new customers much more quickly, guide them more effectively and streamline your services from your prior learning. Over time, you can become the go-to vendor for your service in that vertical. Just think how much you'd like to hear the following statement about your firm: 'Do you need a product development plan for your new wearable heart-monitoring device? If so, go to Jim at PQR Inc. His company specializes in product design for new biomedical devices.' Gives you a nice warm feeling inside, doesn't it?

## Identifying your verticals: Is going vertical right for you?

To start deciding whether to pursue a vertical strategy for your firm, examine your current client list and look for any natural candidates:

✔ Do you have more than one customer in any given vertical? Do you have compelling customer case studies, testimonials and references?

✔ Have you done any work for customers that had vertical-specific deliverables, namely where your work directly impacted your customers' results, cost reduction, avoidance of risk or the like?

✔ Have you needed to acquire a deep understanding of your clients' specific business functions compared to other verticals?

If the answer to any of or all these questions is yes, you may have a case for going vertical.

When you've identified two or three candidate verticals, you can start to dig deeper into what may make your offer particularly compelling in those verticals.

As with any other business-development ideas, look and think before you jump. Carrying out research along the lines I give in Chapter 5 is a great idea, *before* you invest in marketing and selling into a vertical.

Before you finally fix on your verticals, see Table 18-1, which presents ideas for characteristics of verticals that would make them good candidates.

| Table 18-1      Characteristics of Compelling Verticals |
|---|
| *If the Vertical . . .* |
| Has a wide enough customer base to support, say, 20 percent of your business, or more. |
| Has other associated verticals that are similar in nature that you can also embrace without too much of a stretch. |
| Is well represented in your geography and/or in other regions, such that you can gain some traction in specific markets. |
| Is thriving – preferably advancing in terms of growth, new technologies. |
| Has challenges that your service can resolve. |
| Requires specialized knowledge to enter into as an employee (for example, requires specialist degrees or prior experience, or you commonly see people moving from one firm to another within the vertical). |
| Is likely to be current for a considerable time and/or you can continue to develop your offer to keep pace with the needs of the vertical. |

The bottom line is that you want the vertical to have promise of future growth for your company, and not to be in a state of decline.

While you're about it, check what the competition looks like. If a vertical has a promising opening for services, someone's probably already dominating that market. Make sure that you can compete with more advanced thinking, better technologies or by producing better results.

I'm sure that you can name certain verticals where their sphere of work simply evaporated, went into serious decline and/or is threatened by some upstart idea. Newspapers, film photography, on-premises server farms, hard-copy printing, books and CDs, the list is endless. Alongside those are new and upcoming categories of online services, geo-specific services and data (that rely on knowing where something is on the map), big data analytics (crunching the huge amounts of data available today for business insights), hybrid vehicles, video telecommunications and live media streaming.

If a vertical is having to update itself, or is trading in the latest, progressive trend, make sure that you can guide your customer to the next important thing it needs to be considering in your area of expertise to help it stay current and leapfrog the competition. You need to be up-to-date too.

## Listening to what customers say about their vertical

If you look at the career of a friend whose firm has stayed within a given vertical, you may wonder why it did so, instead of veering off in some other direction.

Some people who work in verticals bring highly specialized skills and knowledge to their jobs. Your firm also has specialized knowledge that's vertically based – after all, every customer you have is in a vertical and some of their knowledge rubs off on your team. This section helps you think about the specialized knowledge you may need to be even more valuable to specific verticals.

Here's an example to illustrate. Imagine a procurement officer who's working for a hospital group. When a new hospital is looking to fill such a role with a new employee, here are some of the sorts of things that person would need to know:

- ✔ Who the suppliers are, where to source from and how to negotiate.
- ✔ Knowledge of products and technical goods, such as X-ray equipment, pediatric equipment, specialist supplies and so on.
- ✔ The nature of supplier systems and procurement systems.

✔ Knowledge of procurement procedures, authorization workflows, budget approvals, quality controls, returns and refunds.

✔ How to project manage the fitting out of a new hospital so that all the procurement is done in time.

The first requirement for such a job is often 'specific hospital or solid health-care procurement experience'. Someone working in vehicle parts procurement for a chain of motor vehicle dealerships wouldn't have the specialized knowledge for how to fit a hospital.

Imagine that you're a professional services firm that helps organizations design, set up and operationalize their procurement processes. Consider how easy or difficult breaking into the hospital arena would be if you'd never worked with a hospital before.

Clearly, it wouldn't be easy. Like a prospective employee, you need prior experience. You may even need a specialist team member from that industry (usually at high cost).

Often, firms break into a vertical by luck. I had a huge break into the automotive arena many years ago, when a vendor let a major motor manufacturer down and I just happened to get introduced by a business contact of mine. I did tens of millions of business in that industry over the next decade. Selling services into that vertical became easier and easier because I discovered how it worked.

Customers in a specific vertical have good reason for wanting your firm to bring some specialized knowledge with you – knowledge about *their* sphere of work and about *your own* and how the two are *related*. They also may be looking for:

✔ Specialized certifications

✔ Specialized quality control

✔ Legal knowledge

✔ Familiarity with complex processes

✔ Knowledge of the supply chain (how products and services are brought to market)

When you can demonstrate that you have the knowledge and expertise in the vertical, you're highly valued, you beat out the competition more easily and you can often charge more. Nice!

# Leveraging Your Knowledge for Vertical Success

After you pick a vertical to focus on and have completed your background research (see the preceding section), you need to redefine your offer to fit your chosen vertical. People working in any vertical think that they're 'different' – a fair point of view, because clearly differences exist between, say, car dealerships and colleges. In this section, I describe isolating the differences between firms in different verticals, adapting your experience to appeal to a vertical, digging deep or stretching wide and assessing your readiness to go vertical.

Where firms pull off 'going vertical' they often close deals faster and at a higher rate, get better referrals, become ever more expert and valuable. It can be the making of a services business.

## Understanding similarities and differences between verticals

Despite different business contexts from vertical to vertical, much about how you deliver your service is independent of the customer's vertical. Make sure that you fully define your offer using Chapter 5.

Compare a recent customer from outside your chosen vertical with one inside it. How much of your service was delivered exactly the same and what aspects had to be done differently?

I expect that this little bit of research shows that you have to rethink your delivery approach to encompass the vertical knowledge you have or need to acquire. Preferably do that *before* you start trying to get new customers. You don't want to be doing that sort of thing on the way to a customer meeting!

Assume that you're an industrial architect. Compare designing a hospital with designing an automotive parts production line. Table 18-2 takes a look at what's the same and what's different about customer interactions, the knowledge required and how you deliver your service. By the way, I'm no architect, so the table is by no means intended to be a definitive answer for architects!

**Table 18-2    Verticals: What's the Same/Different About Customer Interactions, the Knowledge Required and How You Deliver Your Service**

| The Same | Different |
|---|---|
| Your overall methodology for gathering requirements | The detailed questions you'd ask about requirements |
| The tools, techniques and architectural knowledge you bring to the design process | The best practices for building layout, access, services, space planning, fitting out and so on |
| Methods for optimizing work environments and work flow | Specific knowledge about staff types, activities, movements and needs |
| Presenting deliverables and various stages | Different influencers and decision-makers within the customer's organization structure |
| How to price construction, pricing tools | Knowledge of materials, equipment, fitments and furnishings specific to the vertical's requirements |
| How to go through planning permission, budget approvals, financing options, hire contractors, supervise construction | Specific local and regional construction restrictions, laws, union/workforce constraints and so on |

# Breaking down your services experience from a vertical perspective

Everything you know about how to be successful with customers is still valid; you just need to think about how to layer the vertical knowledge onto your best practices.

For example, if your typical process includes a kick-off meeting and then a series of discovery meetings, you're probably using questionnaires to make sure that you're gathering all the right information. Are those questionnaires okay in a generic form, or do you need to adapt to include vertical-specific questions? In most cases, the answer is yes, you do need to add a vertical flavor to your questionnaires.

Use your knowledge of working in the vertical previously and incorporate your experiences into a modified delivery methodology or process so that you can expand your team and do the work really well as your new customers sign up.

If possible, test your ideas with someone from the industry: perhaps a prior customer or someone who works in that vertical can validate your process. At the very least, that person can give you cultural insights into how businesses in that vertical work.

## Finding gold in them there vertical hills

The narrower and more specialized the vertical, the more valuable your specialized services become. You have to choose whether your service lends itself to going wide with a vertical or whether going narrow and deep is better. Say that you have an appointment-setting solution that you've customized for doctor's offices by adding a whole bunch of practice management features. Do you stick with doctor's offices (stay narrow) or can you easily repurpose your solution to dentists, chiropractors or psychiatrists (go wide)? How about hospitals or veterinary practices (go wider still)?

As another example, e-commerce emerged in the late 1990s and has exploded. Lots of opportunities exist to offer services to companies that want to go online, but lots of competition too. Like manufacturing, e-commerce is more like a horizontal than a vertical: e-tailers have to provide lots of common things.

But some areas of e-commerce, such as selling alcohol online, are highly specialized. If you choose to be an expert in the complex business of selling wine online, with all the local restrictions, tax implications and authoritative sources of information, you'll probably find more gold than if you offer general e-commerce websites (which are becoming highly commoditized, in other words, it's a price-driven market). People have already come out with solutions for wine-specific sites. That doesn't mean you can't do well – you just have to find the prestigious customers who want to stand out from the crowd and need your expert advice.

Whether new technology is rampant in your space or not, you have to keep on top of the latest thinking.

Look carefully at the market potential of your vertical offer. If you can add a few customers by positioning a vertical offer, go for it. Sometimes it pays to be opportunistic. If, however, you're looking to increase your valuation for a potential acquisition, you want to make sure that your offer has a long lifespan and is going to be worth the investment in time, staff and geographic reach.

## *Checking whether you're ready to go vertical*

When you have an outline of how you're going to deliver your service to vertical customers, what the value is to them and what your project is going to look like, you're nearly ready to turn to the marketing and sales effort (in the next section).

Before you do that though, assess your readiness by taking a look at Chapters 6 and 7. Like any other area of your business, you want to be clear about your goals and how to achieve them. Get feedback from your professional advisors as follows:

- ✔ **Legal:** You may need a slightly different contract format.

- ✔ **Accounting:** What are its perceptions of this market segment?

- ✔ **Friends and family/trusted advisors:** Get their take on your ideas for verticals. They work in different industries and can give you a perspective beyond your own. They can also advise you if you're going too far: spreading yourself too thin with a wide vertical or going too narrow and becoming so niche focused, you can't branch out.

Beware of contracts that may preclude you from working with another company in the same vertical. If exclusions are necessary, make sure that the customer defines a specific list of companies that it doesn't want you to work with, namely their direct competitors, and then only if your service gives the customer a competitive advantage. If your service is general, such as legal advice on healthcare law, don't accept exclusions. But if a custom marketing strategy is the one that helps your customer sell more, you may have to accept some exclusions.

# *Designing and Executing Vertical Campaigns*

I cover much of what you need to go to market in general in Chapters 10 and 11. You just need to repeat the planning process for your marketing with the specific vertical in mind.

## *Writing vertically based promotional materials*

As with any good marketing materials, map out the buyer's journey. Understand the roles you'll be interacting with and how they relate to each other:

- ✔ Who's the typical budget holder/decision-maker?
- ✔ What areas of pain is the organization experiencing?
- ✔ How do you tackle those pain points?
- ✔ What results do you produce?

Try to get one or two vertical case studies done: they're convincing to buyers. Don't forget to ensure that you have materials for sales to use too. Plus, make sure that the language you use in your materials is accurate for the industry: create a glossary of industry abbreviations for internal use. Perhaps consider a training session for your employees to 'launch' a new vertical initiative.

## *Getting your vertical message out there*

Beyond the direct buyers, make sure that you understand the organization structure of your targets, what the pecking order is and who you need to influence.

Vendors often get pulled in because the CEO saw an article about a risk that his company needs to take care of or an opportunity it mustn't miss. Ask yourself the following questions and add these channels into your marketing activities:

- ✔ Where are these influencers spending their time?
- ✔ What are they reading?
- ✔ Where are they networking?

Beyond your usual channels, try to get your message in front of industry experts – bloggers, journalists and other influencers who report on industry trends, problems and solutions. Consider vertical-specific trade shows – you may be the only vendor of your type attending them and so could make a killing.

# Part VI
# Making Influential Friends: Partnerships

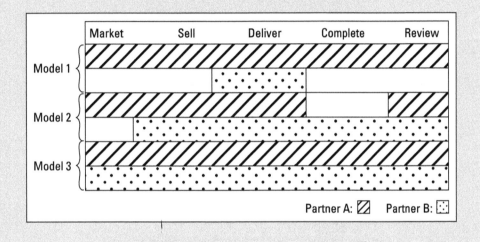

# In this part . . .

✔ Discover what types of partnerships you can seek.

✔ Stay focused on what your firm does best.

✔ Weigh up whether partnering is right for your company.

✔ Get what you really want from a partnership.

✔ Implement a partnership that's a success for both parties.

# Chapter 19

# Seeking Partners for Mutual Benefit

*Y*oung or small companies that are struggling to survive often try to hog all the work, keep their costs down and stop others from encroaching on (what they perceive to be) their business. Although superficially understandable, this strategy is shortsighted for all sorts of reasons. After all, you're willing to use your network to spread the word about your company and recommend people and companies in your network to others (you scratch my back . . . ). So why not consider doing the same thing where you spot a real, mutual benefit. That's what partnerships make available to you.

This chapter discusses partnerships as a route to significant business growth. I detail the main types, explain the importance of sticking to your core strengths at all times and supply some high-level considerations to bear in mind when you're weighing up whether partnering is going to be good for your company – or not.

Partnerships can bring you leads, credibility, access to a wider customer list or additional product or services capabilities that you don't have. Whatever the benefit, your business development practices (and results) shift when you partner well.

Just to be clear, I'm not talking about businesses that are *founded* as partnerships, as is typical of law, accounting and consulting firms, among others. In such businesses, a group of equals owns a part of the business and shares in the profits.

My definition of the kinds of partnerships I cover in this chapter (and in Chapter 20 on making partnerships successful after you take the plunge) is as follows:

*A partnership is a relationship between two business entities sharing a common goal.*

# Considering the Types of Partnership Available

You may think that a partnership is a partnership is a partnership. If so, all I can say is, does only one type of human partnership exist? Not at all, which is why in this section I describe some of the more common forms of partnership into which services firms enter.

Table 19-1 gives broad definitions of the different types of partnerships that may be appropriate for your company, as well as an example of each type.

| Table 19-1 | Partnership Types, Descriptions and Examples | |
|---|---|---|
| **Partnership Type** | **Description** | **Example** |
| **Channel partner** | Where the two companies enter into a formal agreement. One has a product or service that it wants to provide to customers and it needs other companies to help make that happen. In other words, one company is treating the other as a 'channel sales' partner and both benefit from the relationship. | Eric's business installs monitoring equipment at oil-extraction locations. His channel partner provides the equipment and software and sends him leads. Eric introduces his clients to the opportunity of onsite monitoring as a cost-reduction/quality-control advantage. |
| **Referral partner** | A step above your business contacts and informal support. A referral partner is a company to whom you can send leads and who can send leads to you. It may be entirely informal, or have a referral contract where either party gets a fee or commission on the referred work. | Chris's company does process-improvement consulting for manufacturing, including sales and customer-service optimization. Her friend, Mandy, uses Salesforce (a sales team tool) and has an implementation company that customizes Salesforce for clients. The two firms have a referral agreement that pays each a percentage on referrals to each other's clients. It works well because they're tackling different aspects of the same problem. |

| Partnership Type | Description | Example |
|---|---|---|
| **Working partner** | Implies that the two companies work together within the same customer organization, symbiotically or even under a common contract to deliver a single project or set of services. Working partners often act as *sub-contractors* (that is, your partner does work on contracts that you have with your customers, but you're the 'prime' – you own the contact and the partner is 'under' you); who's the sub-contractor on any given project can vary. | Raquel's marketing company specializes in organizing large-scale events for major brands and their customers. The focus is on the complexities of booking and managing events for 50,000 people or more. Its design partner, Bridget's company, does all the offline and online design for the events. When one of Bridget's clients wants to do a trade show, she asks Raquel to help. |
| **Alliance** | A form of partnership where two companies agree that a major business benefit exists in defining a deep working arrangement for a specific purpose, such as launching a new product or penetrating a new market. This type is most common between larger companies of roughly equal size. I don't spend time on alliances – suffice to say that they're complex legal relationships and if someone wants one with you, you'll know. Get help from your lawyer. | John created a unique and highly promising e-commerce add-on for dealing with abandoned carts. A prior colleague, Steven, has software that can form part of the solution. They create a joint venture, which is equally owned and funded by their two companies, to develop and bring the software to market. |

# Sticking to What You Do Best

As you work through the stages of business development (and through this book), you build up a vision of your company as a well-focused business that provides good value to its customers and has a clear story to tell the marketplace. Knowing your firm well is central to whether you should keep yourself to yourself or reach out to others.

You know that focus is important. You focus on being the best at what you do, on the right kinds of customers that are a good fit for you, on your geography, specific verticals (see Chapter 18) or size of customer.

In this section I cover deciding whether to stick to your plan – and nothing's wrong with that at all – or whether to widen your business offer.

## *Keeping to your set path*

Imagine that you get tempted to expand your services. Perhaps a customer you've worked with for a while and who really trusts you asks whether you can help with 'another matter'. Or an employee has read about the latest thing and thinks you should 'get into it'. Or a potential investor wants to 'do its own thing' inside your company.

None of these ideas are necessarily bad, but assume for the moment that they don't align with your business strategy, so you decide not to pursue them. You refer your customer to someone else that you know can help. You tell your employee that her idea is really interesting, but that the company is focused on a different direction. You decline the investment.

What you're doing when you make these decisions is keeping to your chosen path – maintaining focus. Provided you're really confident about those decisions and doing well in business terms, good on you.

## *Going deep not wide*

Sometimes certain business situations arise where an opportunity to expand your reach through formal partner relationships is a good idea. Indeed, I'd go so far as to say that most successful and larger services firms used partnerships as a strategy to secure their growth. Without them, they wouldn't have been so successful.

Any small business is well advised to find ways of *deepening* its services (that is, become more and more expert in a narrow area) rather than *widening* them (that is, adding completely new services, hoping to do better in the market). The marketplace has a distinct preference for firms that have a concentration – deep expertise that solves knotty customer problems. When you're small, going wide tends to dilute your market reputation, because you become defocused. For more on this dilemma, check out Chapter 18.

So what are business owners to do if real opportunities come up that are somewhat outside their expertise? Should you dive in and try to take advantage or would a partnership be better?

Think of situations you've been in recently where you were tempted to launch into something new and compare them with the first column in Table 19-2. Then consider the choices you had before you – to go it alone or to partner. You don't have to agree with me, but expanding services and/or partnering are strategic decisions, so you want to consider carefully what each might mean for your firm.

| Table 19-2 | To Go It Alone or to Partner? | |
|---|---|---|
| *If the Customer Says . . .* | *Go it Alone* | *Partner* |
| Now that you've finished the work, can I call you if I just have a question or two? | Yes. Create a support contract structure so you can charge fairly and allocate the right people to cover the work. | Maybe if you don't want the bother of 'small' projects or ongoing maintenance work. |
| That XYZ system or process you implemented is great. Do you do ABC systems as well? | No, most likely you'd mess it up. | Find a good referral partner, or even a working partner if overlap exists between the two systems/processes. See Table 19-1 for details of these partnerships. |
| Thanks for that great contract template. Can you help me with a new business idea I have? | Depends. If you work with start-ups that's fine. If not, don't go there. | You may want some working partners with other specialties. |
| Our company in Dubai needs the same work you just did for us. Can you take that on? | Maybe, if you're confident about working at a distance, or your team is willing to travel. | May be worth finding a local liaison partner who can front the work and/or give you some cultural guidance. |
| The strategy you developed for us was perfect. Can you implement it for us? | No, unless that's what you already do. Keep to the strategic work. | Partner for the implementation services. |

Sometimes, partnering is the answer and sometimes it's not. Bear in mind, though, that partnering takes real effort. Spending some time thinking it through can save you a whole load of time and wasted effort later.

# *Traveling Alone or Partnering Up*

The question is, are you going to stay single or get married? The difference between marriage and partnering is that you don't have to be monogamous. You can have a number of partners at once, including a mix of different types. What marriage and partnerships do have in common is that you want to look before you leap, and after you're in you have to work at it.

In this section I cover what you need to consider when making this decision: including when not to partner and, if you decide you want to try it, projecting what a partnership would look like for your firm.

## *'We belong together': Finding reasons to partner – or not*

Why should you partner? What advantages can you expect from doing something that's going to take attention, energy and investment?

Think of partnering as a way of increasing your capacity for success. When you partner with another company of whatever size (and the partnership is well founded), think of it as if you just grew your firm and its capacity to reach out to and serve the market. In fact, in the best partnerships, the sum of the parts is greater that the whole. Together, you're stronger and more powerful than you are on your own.

Here are a few key questions to ask about a potential partnership:

- ✔ **Why are you considering partnering?** What's the context for the partnership and what sort of business case would be necessary so that the partnership makes sense for both parties?

- ✔ **Is it just opportunistic?** Is it to meet one customer's need, or is it aligned with defined growth strategy? Either way is fine, but you need to be clear, which in turn helps you structure the right partner agreement.

- ✔ **Would this partnership align around common goals?** Can you find a partner alike enough in philosophies, values, services, methods and pricing?

- ✔ **Do both firms broadly serve the same markets?** Or can you find a partner who operates in markets that you want to get into?

- ✔ **What type of partnership would make sense: referral, channel, working or alliance?** Check out the types in the earlier Table 19-1.

You have to consider whether the effort and investment is worth the results you get from the partnership.

To bring about financial advantage, both parties need to be willing to invest in the partnership and undertake some mutual or joint activities that drive a result. The situation is exactly the same as for your own business: you can't just set up your nameplate, sit behind your desk and wait for business to show up. In fact, you can use a lot of the material in this book to consider how to strategize for and implement an effective partnership. Chapter 20, for example, gives a quick guide to creating a successful partnership.

So why would you choose not to partner? The bottom line is everything. If partnering activities don't lead to new business, directly or indirectly, partnering not worthwhile.

If you've ever been involved in an unsuccessful partnership, try to estimate how much time or other resources you spent on the effort. Where else could you have spent that money? Unfortunately, a lot of partnerships go this way because both parties lack a commitment to make something happen. If the opportunity is a reality and not just pie in the sky, two good businesses working on something together produce a result.

If you can't even take a stab at the value you'll get out of the partnership, don't go into it until you can, which may take a few joint conversations to clarify the goals, plan and investment.

Beyond that, don't get into a new partnership if:

- ✔ **You're desperate for business, unless by some miracle your partner is bringing you an immediate deal.** Desperation doesn't make for objectivity and you need to be objective.

- ✔ **Your resources are already really stretched.** In other words, you, or someone relatively senior in your organization, have/has no time or energy to work on this relationship.

- ✔ **You're financially stretched right now (that is, cash flow is tight).** Relationships take investment and your focus should probably be on getting the cash in and building a financial cushion.

- ✔ **You have one or more new strategic initiatives on the go that are important to you.** Again, unless the opportunity's immediate, wait a quarter or two and reopen discussion at that point. You don't look any the worse from being clear about your priorities – quite the contrary.

One thing's for sure – when you start working with partners, it impacts how your business operates. That's why you need to be cautious and thorough before you proceed.

In the end, nothing focuses the mind like putting a deal on the table. If you have an opportunity that you want to offer to or share with someone, you'll be amazed how quickly the partnership can come to life. By contrast, a lot of partnership discussions can be hot air: polite, even enthusiastic, but still hot air. Unless and until a financial advantage exists for both parties, it signifies nothing. Even if an immediate opportunity does show up, you're better to be prepared instead of being carried away by enthusiasm.

## 'Picture this': Considering your business with partners

Like any relationship, partnerships have their upsides and downsides. Enjoy the upsides and make sure that you're willing to put up with the downsides.

Acquiring new partners is like having one or two additional demanding customers to please. New partners bring new contracts to manage (between the partners), new things to do in sales and marketing, new administrative tasks and even new ways of delivering your services. You may also expand your geographic reach and be traveling more. You may have to invest in training for your staff, so that they can team more effectively with your new partner.

Imagine what having a significant new partner would look like. Check out the sidebar 'The ups and downs of partnerships' and consider whether a partnership can look like that for you or whether it would be something more modest. Is a great opportunity sitting right in front of you that would take more than you can do alone? That's what you're looking for when thinking about partnering up.

---

### The ups and downs of partnerships

Sally had a great career in software development, eventually owning her own company and building business solutions for the telecom industry. She was fortunate to form a partnership with a major telecommunications company and offer her software to its channel partners as a preferred vendor. Her feet hardly touched the ground. She was dealing with a huge organization with the marketing, sales and partner management resources that she had only dreamed of.

After just a couple of months, however, the partner commented that her marketing was sub-standard. Sally had to make a big investment to tackle that problem – and quickly. Life got pretty stressful for a while, but the result was a great outcome. The effort she and her team made generated four new clients a month and led to astronomical growth. Without this partnership, she would still have been a small company, struggling for every deal.

# 'Service Firm WLTM Companion for Business Growth': Finding Good Partners

Assuming that you're considering going the partnership route, you need to do a bit of preparatory work before you can go out looking for 'the one' – at least you won't have to trawl dating websites, post adverts saying 'Would Like To Meet', or haunt dimly lit bars. You do, however, need to profile your 'possibles' and decide on your business goals (which is a bit more complicated than desiring 'long romantic walks on the beach').

Of course, a lot of partnerships do arise in an ad-hoc way. You meet someone and get talking, find that you share common interests and think that a partnership may be a good idea. But no matter how random the conversations seem, you probably wouldn't be open to the idea unless you'd already thought that this kind of partnership would be beneficial for your company. Think of it as being like deciding to buy a particular make and model of car – suddenly you see them everywhere, where you'd never noticed them before.

I had a big influx of business a short while ago and started to consider outsourcing some of the work and what kind of a partner I'd want. Within 24 hours, I received a LinkedIn request, which I normally accept if the company looks interesting, but this one was exactly what I was looking for. Within a month, we'd set up a partnership. Would I have paid any attention to this particular CEO and his company otherwise? Undoubtedly not. He would just have been one of my thousands of LinkedIn connections.

Do your thinking in advance, because it opens you up to connections that may lead you to the partners you want.

## Creating partnership goals

Some partnership types are likely to be more appealing to you than others. Some partnerships may be essential to your business and you definitely want to prioritize getting those into place. Others may be more like experiments or nice-to-haves.

Based on the different types of partnerships that I describe in Table 19-1, what sorts of goals can you set up? Table 19-3 gives you a breakdown of what to look for and expect from different partnerships and what you may need to be ready for.

**Table 19-3**      **Partnership Types, Goals and Commitments**

| Partnership Type | Possible Goals | Commitment |
| --- | --- | --- |
| **Channel partner:**<br><br>(a) You implement what the partner offers.<br><br>(b) Your services dovetail with the partner's. No referral fee is involved. | One party brings leads/opportunities to the other (or it goes both ways). Set a percentage of your business for next year that you'd like the partnership to produce for you (e.g., 10 percent of net new business). | (a): Requires a commitment. Often fees from you to the partner, training for your people, marketing effort, partnership management, detailed reporting.<br><br>(b): Requires a marketing effort to position the partner's services, that is, become familiar with what it offers, use some light collateral from it to share with your customers, follow up diligently on opportunities. |
| **Referral partner** | A one-way or bi-directional referral agreement. The benefit is a percentage of the sale (typically 5 percent or less), so this isn't a big money spinner. Consider the minimum deal size and how many referrals you're likely to generate. | Each party 'looks' for opportunities for the other. This requires proactive discussions with target customers, who typically are in the same market segment as your firm. Anything else has you acting as a sales rep for the partner, which isn't typically worth your time. |
| **Working partner** | In this partnership, the companies work on projects together (typically one leads the engagement and the other is a sub-contractor). One-off projects are draining, but if you can see three or four customers a year or more, the collaboration becomes much easier. | This partnership is similar to expanding your company. The partner's people become part of your delivery mechanism, so you have to get close to make it work. You also often have to adapt your marketing, sales, delivery and administrative processes. |

When you've defined your goals for a potential partnership, make sure that they represent a win-win situation, in other words – that both parties benefit. Put your goals into your revenue plan and estimate the costs of running the partnership and making it successful (more on this topic in Chapter 20).

Typically, a partnership takes quite a long time to produce results. Unless both parties are ready to go to market with the partnership concept, it takes a while for alignment around common goals and how to work together. Given a typical sales cycle of three months in services, anticipate a year or more before you see revenue. Make sure that you're willing to wait.

## Getting your criteria together: Profiling ideal partners

To profile your ideal partners, you need first to get clear what you want and second what you're looking for in the partner.

### Things that you want

When you think about your services, what's lacking in your business or what would expand your opportunities?

Don't be tempted to try to meet every sales opportunity, whether it fits your services or not, by hiring to fill your capability gaps. Although not out of the question, you have to remember that doing so changes the nature and dynamic of your business.

Picture an architect firm that spends time understanding its clients' needs and creating great solutions through its design. The firm doesn't build anything – it usually hands over to a contractor and provides supervision to make sure that the dream gets realized. If the architect chooses to hire construction managers as employees, suddenly the firm is running a whole different sort of business.

Consider the big consulting firms whose sweet spot is to offer strategic advice and direction to their clients. In some cases, they've the capability to implement their strategy, but often they partner with smaller firms who have the detailed knowledge to implement a new manufacturing quality control process, for example. For the range of consulting that they do, trying to be expert in every type of implementation would bog the whole company down.

So consider partnering before you opt to start a whole new design department, or add an auction department to your real estate business, or build a lawnmower repair shop next to your vehicle service center.

Here's a checklist of things that may be important to you when profiling partners. Add to it as necessary for your particular situation:

- ✔ **Ensure that you have a strong value proposition for the partnership.** For example, if you have to turn away a lot of business because you don't have an auction department, estimate how much business you'd get for your company if you partner with a local real estate auction firm.

- ✔ **You need sufficient knowledge of the specialist area of a potential partner to be able to talk about it with confidence.** Or you need to learn pretty quickly. Often people believe that what the other partner does is easy, but their work is no easier than what you do and you need to get your head around it.

- ✔ **Remember that your future may have a merger or acquisition in it.** You may choose to focus on partnerships that have that potential.

- ✔ **The partnership has to support your overall strategic goals.** Partnerships are a multi-year relationship, so although you may be slavering over the potential of quick wins, the real money comes from a long-term effort. Don't distort your whole business purpose for the sake of some ready money.

When you start looking for partners, or evaluating ones that just show up, this checklist gives you a strong foundation for assessing whether they're going to pay off for you.

Your own network, especially your friends, family and advisors, are your best advocates and counsel. Share your thoughts with them and run prospective partners by them to see what they think. They can be more objective about your business than you can ever be.

### Things that you need in a partner

What a good partner looks like and what you need to check for all depends on your goals for the partnership.

Consider the following ideas:

- ✔ **Both firms have complementary skills:** Close enough to be useful, but with minimal overlaps.

- ✔ **The partner is really good at what it does (just like you):** Go for strong partners, not so-so performers. If they're good at what they do, they're usually more organized and effective at partnering too.

- ✔ **Find someone with a common customer base with you:** For example, same types of companies, same size, same geography or same industries.

✔ **The partner has resources in the geography you're interested in:** These may be local, or you may be trying to break into a new market.

✔ **The partner is trusted in the marketplace it operates in:** No bad reports about it, no bad press or complaints to the Better Business Bureau. The track record looks good and the website is respectable.

✔ **The partner is big enough to invest time and money:** In marketing, training, business changes, extra administration.

✔ **Both firms are a similar size:** Or at least you feel confident that the partner won't swamp you or be too small.

✔ **You're creating a win-win situation:** The benefits don't have to be 50/50, but it can't all go one way. Even if you pick up commission for a referral, that's not going to be enough for a solid partnership.

# Chapter 20

# Pursuing Your Plans for a Successful Partnership

. . . . . . . . . . . . . . . . . . . . . . . . . . . . . . . . . . . . . . . . . . . . . . . .

### In This Chapter

▶ Fitting partnerships into the business development lifecycle

▶ Initiating a powerful partnership

▶ Building success together

. . . . . . . . . . . . . . . . . . . . . . . . . . . . . . . . . . . . . . . . . . . . . . . .

*I*n Chapter 19 I describe what you need to consider when deciding whether a partnership is right for your company (in the analogy I make, whether you want to marry or stay single). Here I assume that you're following the marriage route and need to look around for a suitable spouse. Therefore, this chapter lays out the characteristics of a successful partnership and how you can create one.

Instead of reiterating all the good business practices I cover throughout this book, I highlight some of the unique management communication and team-work challenges and opportunities that partnerships offer.

If you follow even half of the advice in Chapters 19 and 20, your partnership has a much higher chance of success than the average one. Good luck and much prosperity.

# Locating Partnerships within Business Development

As you launch into setting up a partnership and using it to drive maximum revenue, you start to experience some of the same parts of the business development lifecycle that I cover elsewhere in this book, when I talk about the customer experience and business development lifecycle (see Chapters 2 and 3).

Think about your partners as customers, because doing so makes you concentrate on setting goals, bringing value to the relationship and getting results. What you're selling is quite different, of course: your ability to create and run an effective partnership. If the partner 'buys' it, some sort of partnership agreement gets signed and you're off into the delivery stage.

Other aspects of the customer lifecycle are also useful, for example, creating defined projects (for example, joint marketing activities), avoiding *scope creep* (that is, getting side-tracked), *completing powerfully* (signing off that a task is done) and carrying out a periodic partner review process.

# Partnering Up Effectively

Partnerships are all about creating a win-win situation. You achieve your objectives, the partner achieves its own and everyone's happy.

Unfortunately a lot of partnerships die on the vine pretty quickly, by and large because people want things easy. Building and growing a business takes effort (in other words, doing all the 'business development' stuff), but with partnerships they imagine that the fruit is going to drop off the tree of a beneficent partner, right into their laps. Don't fall for this dangerous delusion: partnerships take real work.

In this section I examine what it takes to get from a twinkle in the eye to the great partnership benefits and accomplishments: new and exciting customers, working alongside other professionals that you respect, increased revenue and fulfilled goals. Specifically, I cover becoming familiar with – and finding out about – your potential partner, staying realistic and establishing shared targets. I also take a quick look at what may be creating problems in a partnership that seems to be floundering.

I use a *working partnership* as the fullest example of a partnership. Other models (*referral* or *channel partnerships*) are a subset of working partnerships (you can find definitions in Chapter 19).

In a working partnership, you may be going to go to market together: aligning your offers, doing some co-marketing and co-selling, delivering the project as a single team and sharing the spoils. I follow that model, but you can adapt it easily to any other variant.

## Dating: Getting to know each other

In essence, a partnership is *created.* It doesn't have a life of its own, at least not initially: it is what you say it is.

The best partnerships are created at the executive level, or at a minimum are sponsored by the executives of the company with full support and enthusiasm. Forming a partnership starts with getting round a table and talking – CEO to CEO, or a broader group if needed.

You need to go into the discussion with what's important to you clear in your mind:

- Is the potential partner competent at what it does? Does any evidence show that it's at least as good as you are? (If so, great!) In other words, you have to pitch each other and buy into a relationship.

- Be open and honest about what you want from the partnership and the potential for producing that result. Is it aligned with your goals?

- Be equally interested in what the partner wants and the potential it sees. Are its goals a good fit for yours? Can you feasibly support its goals?

- Check in with yourself – are you committed to what the potential partner wants as well as to what you want?

- Are you seeing commitment from the potential partner to go to market, together with all that entails?

- Do you both have the resources and time to make things happen? I assume you do, otherwise you shouldn't be having the conversation, but does the potential partner have the same stomach for investment?

- Can you see real market potential in the partnership?

- Do you like the potential partner? Do you want to work together?

If the answer to any of these questions is 'no', walk away before you waste time and energy pretending the partnership will work. It won't.

The final point about whether you like the people you're eyeing across the table is pretty important. If they show up as a bunch of arrogant jerks, they may not be a fit with your organization. Any common passions, interests, lifestyles or causes are a great foundation for a partnership. If you have nothing in common, leave the partnership paperwork in the drawer.

Mostly, partners simply want more business. Well, so do you, so that's honest. The problem is that, in the heat of early discussions, you may fail to dig deep enough to find out whether the partner knows what getting that result requires. What it often *really* wants is for you to introduce it to your customers or to provide leads. In other words the partner is going after the low-hanging fruit. Don't buy it, or at least, don't commit yet. It's too early.

## Testing the cultural fit: What do you have in common?

When you know a bit about each other, you want to go through a few more steps before sealing the deal. To begin, involve a wider group from your company and from the potential partner. Even if just for educational purposes, you benefit when people from the partner understand your company and how you operate and vice versa.

You also want to look for the same degree of liking, commitment and alignment of goals that you felt in the early discussions, except that now you can get feedback from other team members.

If you didn't initiate the discussion, here's your chance to check out the potential partner and provide your own feedback. Be candid internally, and then, if a partnership gets created with which you're not wholly on-board, set your reservations aside and *act* as if you're committed.

Table 20-1 provides a few topics for the second discussion and things you need to watch for. You have to provide the same information about yourself too, so the table is also a good checklist for preparing for such a meeting.

| **Table 20-1** | **A Deeper Partnership Discussion – What to Talk About** |
|---|---|
| *Important Topics* | *Aspects to Find Out and Share* |
| What the potential partner does and how it does it | The breadth and depth of services and how projects are conducted. How close are the two approaches? Can you make the approaches fit each other? |
| The customers it serves | Who are the companies that the partner works with today? Who has it worked with in the past? Are the partner's customers anything like yours? Will it be able easily to help your customers and prospects, and vice versa? |
| The customers it *wants* to serve | What are the partner's plans? Do both businesses want to get into new areas or work, new *verticals* (industries), geographies? |
| How it measures success | Are you both tracking the same things? Is reporting back to each other on progress going to be easy? Can you align case studies and testimonials? |

| Important Topics | Aspects to Find Out and Share |
|---|---|
| How the partnership will be set up | Who'll be the primary points of contact? Where will the parties need to work together? What structures do both firms envision for managing the partnership? |
| How customers will be handled | Who'll handle the customer management and customer communications? Will this situation vary, or is one partner likely to predominate? Who'll handle issues and fixing things? Are the partner's customers happy (like yours) and how does it achieve that? |
| What preparation the partner sees is needed to kick off the partnership | Are joint marketing materials needed? Do people need any training in each other's capabilities? Do the salespeople need to be aligned? |
| The likely biggest obstacles to success | What causes issues in the businesses today? What are the weaknesses? Will these things impede the partnership? |
| Whether the partnership looks balanced | Given all the above, is the partnership looking like a fair arrangement for both parties? |
| How both parties feel at the end of the discussion | Check your gut. How do you feel? Trust your instincts. |

No doubt you can see from the table that you need to like each other, respect each other's work and not be greedy but be willing to share costs, effort and the benefits.

You may feel as if opening your kimono in this way is risky. But don't forget that people respond to authenticity and are more likely to trust you when you temper your strengths with an open admission of areas you're working on. No one's perfect, so be suspicious of any firm that tries to look faultless. It can't possibly be, so to put it plainly, such a firm is obfuscating or downright lying – neither of which has any place in a partnership.

After this critical meeting, get your team together to discuss the partnership. If you're feeling especially organized, prepare a checklist where team members can rate the partner and write down feedback. I provide an example in Figure 20-1.

Take team feedback seriously. In the end, many of your people are going to interact with the partner *on the ground,* selling and delivering work for customers, which is hard enough already without adding problems. On a positive note, the team may see huge advantages in working with a new partner – and that would be a real bonus.

| | Score 1–5 (5 is high) | Notes |
|---|---|---|
| **Credibility** | | |
| Size | | |
| Customers | | |
| Website | | |
| Marketing | | |
| Certifications | | |
| Testimonials/Case Studies | | |
| | | |
| **Fit** | | |
| Fit of service with ours | | |
| Target customers and markets | | |
| Potential value to our customers | | |
| Potential value of partnership to us | | |
| | | |
| **Value/Pricing** | | |
| Does their value proposition mesh with ours? | | |
| Is their pricing structure compatible with ours? | | |
| What project revenue do they expect? | | |
| | | |
| **Compatibility** | | |
| Are the organization charts compatible? | | |
| Do the roles within their organization match ours? | | |
| Do the methodologies look similar? | | |
| Do their deliverables match ours for depth and quality? | | |
| | | |
| **Trust** | | |
| Do I like them? | | |
| Do I believe what they say? | | |
| Can they do what they say they can? | | |

**Figure 20-1:**
Team checklist for partnership potential.

Internally, you're probably at a go/no-go decision point. You have three options:

- ✔ **Proceed:** Your team is aligned and enthusiastic. They see the potential and they're willing to commit to the work. Proceed to the next section.

- ✔ **Decline:** You don't think a fit exists, or you have other objections or concerns. Give the potential partner your decision, and, without being offensive or deceptive, explain why. Unless you're really convinced by what its representatives say in response, don't be swayed by promises to do things differently or attempt to 'fix' things.

- ✔ **Defer:** Maybe the opportunity has potential but the timing isn't right. This situation may be for all sorts of reasons, so share your thoughts and recommend revisiting the partnership in 3, 6 or 12 months. Put a note in your calendar to have a further conversation at a later date to see whether the time has come.

## *Setting boundaries to stay realistic*

When you've decided to go ahead, what the partnership *isn't* going to be about is almost as important as what it *is* about. A bit like when you're working on your offer (see Chapter 5), this stage is all about maintaining focus, not running all over the place chasing rainbows.

Partnerships can be heady, so get real. If your new partner is excited about this relationship, it's probably looking at you through rose-tinted spectacles (even if you did try to be honest about your shortcomings). Take a long, hard look at yourself. What benefit do you really think you can bring to the partner, with everything that you have going on today? Maybe it really is a slam-dunk, but I guess that nine out of ten partnerships underestimate the level of effort involved (pretty much in the same way that they underestimate effort in any area of business that they're not yet expert in).

With a specific partner in mind, here are a few questions to ask yourself:

1. **Can you meet the partner's goals that you know about (see the next section)?**

2. **Is your existing team enough to take on this new effort and if necessary can you reduce its work in other areas?**

3. **Are you willing to appoint or even hire a partner manager and invest in some other services, such as developing marketing materials (collateral creation) or getting new leads?**

4. **What else would you have to do to make this work and are you up for it?**

If the answer to any of the above is 'no' or 'I don't know', consider stepping back or, if you really want to proceed, starting small. What can you realistically suggest to your partner as your initial commitment? When will you evaluate how things are going? Can you enrol it in a more modest endeavor? Unless the opportunity is *time-critical* (jump on it now or it's gone), you may be better setting clear limits on the expectations and efforts.

Now, consider what you're expecting from your partner. Are you being realistic, or are you wearing rose-tinted glasses? Based on your observations, from both sides, set boundaries for the partnership. Define realistic goals, determine a reasonable investment and maybe even consider doing a one-year pilot with limited expectations. In some cases, you can't be half-married and a pilot is unfeasible, but at least consider this possibility.

By the way, larger companies are no better at partnerships than smaller ones. In fact the bigger they get, the more money they pour into partnership structures, tools and resources, so the harder they find spotting what's not working.

## *Agreeing shared goals*

You have your own agenda in creating this partnership – things that you want to achieve for your business that are specific to your growth and your future. Those objectives are for your eyes only, and, believe me, your partner has some of its own.

Therefore, you also want to create some *common* goals with your partner – things that you can both commit to that will drive the partnership forward.

Create a two-by-two grid on a sheet of paper or your word-processing program and label the four boxes with the following headings. Then create bullet points that provide a framework for your partnership and why it matters to you:

- ✔ **Strategic goals:** These goals support your primary goals and provide a pathway to a bigger future – maybe even as a united company, or as a partnership that has its own wings (that is, a partnership that becomes a force in the marketplace). As an example, you may be creating a new, unified service offering.

- ✔ **Tactical goals:** These goals meet a need, such as keeping your revenue levels healthy or improving your profitability. An example would be increasing your pipeline and portfolio of customers.

- ✔ **Long-term goals:** A clear market need exists for what you can do together and it has longevity (probably for the next 3–5 years or more).

- ✔ **Short-term goals:** An immediate market opportunity exists that's probably of short duration, one you can go after together or with each other's help. Maybe you both want to be in the other's geography. After a year or two of supporting each other's effort to break in to a new geographic area, you may not need each other anymore.

Lofty or humble, get clear about the shared goals and don't puff them up into something bigger than they are. Tell it how it is, at least for the near term. If things go well, you can go big later. Set some near-term objectives, get them achieved and then create some new ones.

As you finalize your ideas, make sure to build them into your revenue plan, figure out your costs and present them to your 'friends and family' before inking the deal. You're about to make a commitment and you want objective feedback beforehand.

If you create an informal partnership, with no goals and no contractual basis, it withers within months, as the poet TS Eliot wrote in 'The Hollow Men', 'Not with a bang but a whimper'. Mostly, after initial enthusiasm, activity declines, no results are produced and people stop communicating. The thing is left hanging out there like an empty promise.

## From tiny seeds . . .

Some friends of mine wrote a great book on selling and they asked me to review it. I knew their plan was to create an online course from the material and I saw a lot of potential in that. So I read the work and made comments. They then asked me to find a partner to build the online version, so I did. Then we signed a referral agreement for me to get them some customers.

At that point, I planted the seed that, if we managed to increase their customer base through my efforts, perhaps we should consider a deeper partnership. Can't tell you more – you'd have to sign a non-disclosure agreement (NDA)! I'm sure you get it. Start small, build from there.

You need to do two more things to bring the partnership to life:

- ✔ **Sign that contractual document:** Be clear about what the partners will and won't do, what's allowed from a marketing perspective, how you'll operate together, especially around a customer, and who gets what piece of the financial pie (for example, if one partner brings a deal to the table, does it get a cut of the deal?). Find a decent partner contract online and run it by your lawyer. It needs to contain a lot of the terms and conditions that you write into your master services agreement.

- ✔ **Share the news:** Let your whole staff know about the new partnership and get them excited about its real potential: such a partnership is going to impact them, for sure. Decide whether to issue a press release or tell your customers or business network. The more you commit publicly, the more likely you are to do what's necessary to achieve the desired result. No one wants to make a noise about something and then fail.

## Understanding why partnerships don't work

If your partnership isn't working out at any stage, the reason is probably down to one or more of the following:

- ✔ Its benefits aren't worth the effort.
- ✔ It has an under-investment of time and money.
- ✔ It contains some cultural conflict.
- ✔ It features inadequate communication and collaboration.

To mitigate these issues, make sure that you establish the partnership properly and put the necessary work into execution (see the earlier section 'Setting Up a Good Partnership'). It still may not work, but at least you gave it your best shot.

# Going to Market Together

I assume that you've selected a partner who's said 'yes', signed on the dotted line and watched the eager bridesmaids trample over each other in a vain attempt to grab the thrown bouquet. But as all newlyweds know, or discover quickly, the wedding is only the start of the work.

In this section you discover all about establishing a primary contact, deciding how to work with your partner, settling responsibilities and considering customer ownership, as well as optionally proceeding with white labeling or co-branding. If the last two points don't apply to your firm, I also discuss something of interest to everyone involved: dividing the spoils!

## Appointing a partner manager

Make sure that your partnership has a defined primary contact on both sides to organize collaboration, handle communication and deal with the road-blocks. If no one's at the helm, misunderstandings and challenges arise, and things tend to fall through the cracks, with everyone thinking that 'someone else was going to do that'.

Initially, that person can have many other responsibilities, but later you may need a dedicated partner manager, especially if you have more than one part-nership to run. This person needs to be a great communicator, motivator and decision-maker and be able to deal with issues promptly and effectively.

Does that remind you of anyone? Take a look at your customer managers and see whether you can perhaps promote one. If your partner manager can also be the customer manager for the first project, so much the better, because the person gets to see the partnership at work first-hand.

## Creating a unified go-to-market strategy

You need to define how you're going to work together with your partner, both to get customers and to serve them. You can work on these things as you go along, but being clear about *what* will need attention is a good idea.

At the core of the relationship is your ability to deliver the services to the same level of quality and customer satisfaction with your partner as without it. Problem is, you've devised all sorts of ways of doing that, and so has your partner, and those ways aren't going to be the same.

Chances are that, if you're in the same broad area of services, you find more alignment than difference. But even what you *call* something, say the stages in your methodology, can cause extreme confusion if you don't align the terms. In fact, getting a new customer is relatively easy compared to delivering for the first time with a new partner.

Use the checklist in Table 20-2 and see which items are relevant to your situation. Put those items on your to-do list of things to discuss and hammer out with your partner.

| Table 20-2 | Checklist of Things to Do when Setting Up Your Partnership | | |
|---|---|---|---|
| *Important Areas* | ✓/✗ | *Important Areas* | ✓/✗ |
| Mission and vision | | Feed structures and payment styles | |
| Positioning | | Methodology: stages and tasks | |
| Services and how they align/dovetail | | Methodology: deliverables and their formats and depth | |
| Market segments you serve | | Account management philosophy | |
| Go-to-market approach | | Team constitution and experience | |
| Marketing materials (websites, collateral) | | Project-management methodology, reporting, risk management, change-order process | |
| Campaigns/lead generation | | Communications process (internally and with the customer) | |
| Sales approach and tools | | Customer sign-off process | |
| Pipeline management and reporting | | Customer review processes, cross-sell and upsell strategies | |
| Proposals, letters of agreement, contracts | | Service review process, change management for services delivery | |

You may take so much for granted in your own business that you forget that you're going to have to go through a re-invention when you acquire a new partner. Luckily, you both have great experience and a great track record of success to draw on.

Truthfully, you can't tackle everything up front. Just have your checklist completed and use it to allocate time, when the time is right, to have a working session to crash through the details. For example, when a customer gives you a verbal 'yes' (in others words, you have a win, but are still in contract negotiation), bring the team together and work on the team composition for the project (who's going to be on the team from which partner), the methodology (how you'll organize the work) and deliverables (the actual, tangible things you have to deliver to the customer).

## Defining roles and responsibilities

One of the biggest areas of confusion in partnerships is deciding who does what. The allocation of roles and responsibilities depends a great deal on each partner's strengths and weaknesses and what's obvious from the go-to-market strategy. At the core of the issue is: who owns the customer (see the next section for more) and who owns the contract? In most cases, the customer wants 'one throat to choke' – in other words, wants to be clear about the prime contractor and its primary point of contact for the work, which doesn't have to be the same partner, by the way.

Partner A and Partner B joined together to deliver a highly complex international website. Partner A does the user experience and design, Partner B does the implementation (builds the content management and commerce solutions). Typically, Partner B holds the contract because it has to support the customer long after Partner A's work is done. But in the early stages of the work, Partner A takes the lead, manages the project and acts as customer liaison.

As you get to know your partner, who does what becomes clearer. Figure 20-2 shows three of the many potential models for how partners work together.

In Model 1, Partner A is involved throughout and Partner B comes in only for the delivery. In Model 2, Partners A and B co-sell and co-deliver, but Partner B takes over the completion and probably the long-term customer relationship. In Model 3, both partners are fully involved throughout.

Interestingly, partnerships with obvious divisions make for great eventual mergers. If you're much better at marketing and selling than your partner, but your partner's strong at developing long-lasting customer relationships, this situation can be an even better proposition than where both firms are equally good at everything.

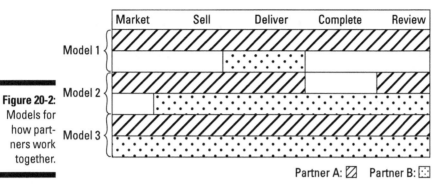

**Figure 20-2:**
Models for
how part-
ners work
together.

Here are a few more questions to ask yourself concerning roles:

✔ Will a prime/sub-contractor relationship exist that determines who's accountable for status reports, invoicing and customer management?

✔ Who'll be the project manager?

✔ Who'll manage communications?

Share your thoughts with your partner early on and determine who's on the hook for every aspect of the customer lifecycle.

## *Tackling the question of who owns the customer*

The area of who owns the customer can be a bone of contention, because the people who communicate with the customer most frequently gain more influence. Naturally, the choice has to make sense to the customer.

Take a look at Chapter 16 on customer management to review the pivotal role of a customer manager (often also called an account or project manager). What applies in your company also applies to a partnership. You need a customer manager who's willing to be a great liaison between the two organizations and the customer; but both parties must also be willing to keep the customer manager informed about day-to-day progress.

Trust is imperative in this relationship. Monitor your initial project with your partner carefully to make sure that the customer manager, whether yours or the partner's, is working out. Challenging people's performance when they work in another organization can be a touchy subject. Get it wrong and it can be the death knell of your partnership. That's why forming strong relationships across the partnership at every level is so important – so that you can tackle issues as they arise.

## *Wondering whether to white label or not*

Some firms base their whole business on acting as a sub-contractor for other companies. Often, such firms don't have a strong brand or a marketing/sales organization, but they do have a minimal website more directed at potential partners. When they work with partners, they take on the identity of the prime contractor (getting business cards and email addresses and acting as part of the prime's organization). They sometimes get involved in the sales process to help scope and price the project, but the owner or one of the delivery team often supports the partner in the sale.

This approach is a form of *white labeling*: wrapping someone else's product or service in your 'branding' and presenting it as your own. Originally from the music record industry, this term is now used in product manufacture and even in services.

The question is, however, will customers know that they're working with partners? Some firms hide the fact (whatever the contract requires). In truth, most savvy customers become aware during the project that some of 'your' people are sub-contractors. They may not care, because the work is getting done, they're happy and that's all they care about, or they may take exception.

The choice is yours, but I prefer to be open from day one. If you think doing so is a competitive disadvantage, you can hold off telling customers that you're using sub-contractors, but I suggest mentioning it while contracts are in process at the latest. The customer usually approves it with little resistance.

Your competitors are probably doing the same anyway, so it may not be the disadvantage you think it is. Indeed, white labeling is becoming the norm in so many services industries that it's probably much more common than anyone can detect on the surface.

## *Coping with co-branding*

Whether you're going public with a big story about your partnership, or just trying to get some deals together, consider whether and how to co-brand. You have your story and the partner has its story – and you may want to bring those narratives together in a way that makes sense.

*Co-branding* is when two or more brands are associated with a single service (or product). As always, the customer is what matters.

When you think about co-branding, consider the following:

- Are you combining the strengths of your companies into a more valuable service?
- Are you going to go to market together (market and sell in collaboration)?
- Is the customer going to work with a joint team, each party performing part of the service?

If the answer to all these questions is 'yes', you need to co-brand. In most contractual situations, you have to declare whether you're sub-contracting, so being overt about the nature of the partnership is necessary.

Discuss jointly the mission and vision of the partnership: who you are together that you aren't separately and what the brand guidelines should be. Mostly, partnerships choose to keep their brand 'as is' and create some modified marketing materials that tell the story. That's the simplest and least expensive approach. While doing that, you also need to agree a positioning statement (what you do and who you do it for), align how you present, create proposals and construct case studies.

Although you probably need to be open about your partnership, you also don't want customers to be confused. Ensure that you make understanding your partnership and who does what easy, and also create materials with a unified look and feel (for example, write your staff bios in the same style and ensure that your case studies are consistent in format).

## Sharing the wealth

How the money gets divided up depends on what model of roles and responsibilities you're using (see earlier Figure 20-2). If you're in Model 1, you're carrying the cost of marketing, sales and customer management, so you expect your partner to give you preferential pricing on the work. In other models, the balance is different.

Above all, don't avoid the conversation. Make sure that you:

- Have clear partnership terms in the partnership contract.
- Have agreed commission and pricing arrangements in advance for every type of case.
- Are clear about who's doing the invoicing and when the other partner will get paid.
- Have a solid sub-contractor contract in hand to use when your first project shows up. You can find plenty online, but make sure that you cover matters of insurance, pricing, invoicing and payment and what happens if a customer terminates the contract with the prime contractor.

# Part VII
# The Part of Tens

For ten useful questions to ask about a prospective customer, head to
www.dummies.com/extras/businessdevelopment.

## In this part . . .

- Make business development part of your daily activities.
- Stay on track towards your goals.
- Measure your business's performance.
- Use powerful resources to help with your business development.

# Chapter 21

# Ten Regular Actions that Benefit Your Business

. . . . . . . . . . . . . . . . . . . . . . . . . . . . . . . . . . . . . . . . . . . . . . . . . . . . .

*In This Chapter*

▶ Identifying regular tasks that make a real difference

▶ Taking small actions each and every day

. . . . . . . . . . . . . . . . . . . . . . . . . . . . . . . . . . . . . . . . . . . . . . . . . . . . .

*I*n your day-to-day life, you know that you gain beneficial results by repeating small actions every day: for example, walking a short distance to help get fit or memorizing a few additional words of a new language (*bien sûr!*). Well, business development is no different.

Schedule some time today for this chapter's ten actions and keep a log. You never know – the wonderfully unexpected may well show up.

## Making Five Business Phone Calls

Tackle the calls you don't want to (yes, those darned cold calls). Doing so brings your firm four benefits:

- ✔ You conquer your dislike.

- ✔ You maintain your company's presence in the market.

- ✔ You come to appreciate people who do this task all day.

- ✔ You're sure to uncover a lead at some point (on average, after about 100 calls – around four weeks from today).

Go to it!

# Calling Customers and Partners

Call every customer and every partner each month. Find out how things are going, what's on these people's minds and whether you can discover anything to which your team needs to pay attention.

Every three months, take these people out to lunch, or at least drop by. You get feedback, more work and referrals. Feed any actions to the marketing, sales or customer-management folks.

# Talking to Employees

Talk one-on-one with employees for 15 minutes every month. Find out what they're working on, what they enjoy and what's causing them grief.

You need to keep employee turnover down, so look for opportunities to motivate people to stay: provide new challenges and opportunities for career development.

# Reading Some Blogs

From all the noise on the Internet, select three or four bloggers who provide value to your firm or to your customers and read their posts fully every day. They make good fodder for your own tweets or newsletter (see the next section).

# Sending Out Three Value-Added Emails

You need to work hard at keeping relationships alive. Store interesting articles, blogs, events, white papers and the like, and send an item each to one new prospect, one new customer and one historical customer.

# Updating Your CRM/SFA

Salespeople and customer managers need to keep daily notes in your customer relationship management (CRM) and sales force automation (SFA) systems and share them with the team (flip to Chapter 11 for details). Make sure that you capture emails you send, too. Keeping the history saves time searching through emails and trying to figure out where your time is vanishing.

# Making Five New Connections on LinkedIn

LinkedIn is great for establishing new business connections: 80 per cent accept your invitation and 50 per cent respond to a message you send them, as long as this message is well crafted (check out Chapters 8 and 11 for more). Plus, you get access to their networks.

# Tweeting Something

Leave tweets from the company account to marketing, but you can certainly tweet or retweet something on your own account – and it doesn't all have to be business. Show your human side by tweeting about baseball, opera, mountain-climbing or mending old clocks. After all, people do business with people they like. Check out Chapter 8 for more on Twitter – and get comfy with it.

# Reviewing How Your Day Went

Ask yourself how each day has gone. Did you feel a sense of accomplishment? Could you have delegated any busy work? Did something not get done (in which case, reschedule it)?

Also, clean up your email inbox and your desk at the end of the day – doing so is a huge timesaver for tomorrow.

# Planning Tomorrow

Schedule everything you need to get done tomorrow (including working by yourself): for example, those five calls, the whitepaper you're writing, that customer you're calling. Don't let people sabotage what you think is important by interrupting what you're doing. Give them an open time to come back.

# Chapter 22

# Ten Key Metrics to Watch

*In This Chapter*

▶ Using metrics for revenue growth

▶ Putting metrics to work for business efficiency

*I*f someone asks 'How's business going?', can you answer accurately and with certainty? Part of business development is making sure that you can. Use the *metrics* (measurements) that I provide in this chapter to monitor the health of your firm. Doing so takes only a few minutes each week.

I discuss metrics of all sorts in much more detail in Chapters 6 and 7.

## Knowing How Big Your Sales Pipeline Needs to Be

Is your sales pipeline the right size? When you know the typical sales cycle and closure rate, you can set a target number for the value of your pipeline and increase it as your company grows. If it dips, you know you have to act. For more on pipelines, pop to Chapters 6 and 7.

## Maintaining the Right Number of Opportunities

You need to know how many opportunities you have at each stage in the sales cycle. You want a few in negotiation, a few more at proposal stage and more still at earlier stages. If the pipeline doesn't have that shape, carry out some rebalancing by focusing effort on specific stages (see Chapters 6 and 13).

# Shortening Your Sales Cycle

Here are two crucial questions that you need to be able to answer: how long is it from a new lead to a closed deal on average; how long until you see revenue?

Work on shortening the sales cycle. Use what you find out to be ever more accurate with forecasting your revenue (see the next section).

# Planning Projected Revenue

Get your backlog/projected revenue report going (see Chapters 6 and 7) so that you can plan for the customers that may be coming. If your sales cycle is long and projects are extended, creating that backlog is easy. But if both are short, use historical data and growth rates to take a stab at it. Use your backlog to plan staff numbers, new equipment and training.

# Producing the Right Number of New Leads

How many new leads do you see each week? Where are they coming from – the phone ringing, your website, replying to emails or adverts? Consult with marketing and sales and figure out whether the throughput is adequate, and whether the leads are the *right* leads: in other words, ensure that time spent on them is worthwhile. Check out Chapter 8 for more info on leads.

# Assessing Planned versus Actual Revenue

Check the actual revenue numbers for the month that are just in and how they match up to your forecast. Are you ahead of the game or behind? What actions do you need to take if you're behind? Make sure that you know how your company is really doing. Check out Chapters 7 and 13 for loads more revenue-based discussion.

# Checking Profitability by Customer

You need to know which of your customers are making money for you and whether some are much more valuable than others. Gathering together all the costs and calculating profitability can take a good deal of work, but if you can do it you have more evidence of the sort of customers you really want.

# Monitoring Cash Flow: Days Sales Outstanding

Cash flow is vital to every company – many an otherwise efficient firm has bitten the dust due to short-term cash flow problems. Look into: how fast your customers pay; whether they're on time or late; and what proportion of your revenue gets held up.

Watch this metric like a hawk and act promptly to collect.

# Keeping the Customer Happy with Satisfaction Scores

Happy customers make a happy you! Are your customers happy? Use a mix of satisfaction scores and qualitative comments to help find any weaknesses and fix them. Do so formally at specific points in the customer lifecycle – it does wonders for the customer relationship (see Chapters 4 and 16 for the lowdown).

# Minimizing Staff Attrition

Good people leaving can kill your business: remember that the best can get another job easily. Keep an eye on your turnover in staff and try to hire well and keep attrition down. You don't want a reputation as a revolving door.

# Chapter 23

# Ten Great Resources for Business Development

*In This Chapter*

▶ Visiting places for inspiring ideas

▶ Obtaining tools for growing your business

*E*veryone can do with a little assistance from time to time. Here are ten great resources available to help you with business development.

## Discovering Online For Dummies Resources for Business Development

You can find a whole host of tools that support the concepts in this book at www.dummies.com/go/businessdevelopment, www.dummies.com/extras/businessdevelopment and www.dummies.com/cheatsheet/businessdevelopment.

## Signing up for Business Insider

Business Insider publishes the latest news on a wide variety of business matters. To be simultaneously in the swim of and up to speed with what everyone's talking about, sign up for the categories you're interested in at www.businessinsider.com.

# Using the Business Training Institute

The Business Training Institute runs online training on a wide range of topics. Find seminars, webinars and videos from experienced business experts at www.thebusinesstraininginstitute.com.

# Improving with Influence Ecology

Although not specifically focused on business development, Influence Ecology (www.influenceecology.com) offers powerful courses that help ambitious people discover how to operate effectively in the current marketplace. These courses can transform your view of the marketplace. But be warned, it's a strenuous course – not for wimps!

# Casting a Wider Net with the American Marketing Association

American Marketing Association (www.ama.org) is the trusted go-to resource for marketers and academics, providing ways for marketers and academics to connect with the people and resources they need to be successful.

# Getting Better with the Sales Management Association

The Sales Management Association (www.salesmanagement.org) promotes professional development, peer networking, best practice research and thought leadership among professionals who support, manage, coach and lead sales organizations.

# Blogging for Success: Sales Benchmark Index

The Sales Benchmark Index at www.salesbenchmarkindex.com is my favorite blog for marketing and sales tools and concepts, both strategic and tactical. If you're wondering how to improve things or what to tackle next, this blog will swamp you with ideas.

# Being In with the In-Crowd: LinkedIn Groups

Join a few relevant groups on LinkedIn (www.linkedin.com/directory/groups), follow what people are talking about and contribute your own ideas or answer people's questions. It's a great way to study what matters right now.

# Leading with Confidence: Vistage

Get into one of Vistage's many leadership coaching groups (www.vistage.com). For business owners and CEOs, Vistage is an opportunity to be part of a group that keeps you accountable for your goals and results.

# Contacting the Author: RainMakers US

I'd be delighted to hear from you if you want to talk about your business and taking it to the next level. Get in touch at anna.kennedy@rainmakersus.com.

# Index

## • *N* •

## • *O* •

# About the Author

Anna Kennedy is Founder and CEO of RainMakers (US), Inc. The company offers business development consulting and professional services to small and medium-sized services companies who are ambitious for growth, but somehow stuck in the journey towards higher results. She is the inventor of a proprietary methodology, the 'RainMakers' Cookbook' for business development assessment and strategy development that helps clients examine their current state and plan for the achievement of their ultimate business goals.

As a student and practitioner of business development for twenty years, Anna understands the challenges of business development for business owners, executives and senior managers who were not 'born into' the disciplines that constitute business development.

After a distinguished thirteen-year career in the UK as a mathematics, computer science and business educator and author, Anna relocated to the US to take up an opportunity in professional services leadership. As Managing Partner at US Web and later at MarchFirst, Anna was involved in taking some leading US brands online in the early and heady days of the .com boom and ran the most profitable operation in the MarchFirst family. Those experiences provided direction for her thinking on how to create, operationalize, survive and successfully grow a services business. In 2003, she developed a model for customer lifecycle management that is an inspiration for many services firms today.

Today, Anna is a consultant, trainer and advisor to small and medium-sized services and product firms. She especially enjoys leading dynamic speaking engagements for small business owners and other with ambitions to be the best at business development.

Anna is married with four children and five grandchildren. Living in Pasadena, CA, she loves theatre, music and raising money for the Leukaemia and Lymphoma Society. You'll find her any weekday between 5pm and 6pm, walking round the Rose Bowl.

# Dedication

This book is dedicated to my husband, Liam Kennedy, who has given me unstinting support in anything I ever wanted to do throughout thirty five years of our relationship and marriage. His encouragement as I wrote *Business Development For Dummies* has been the rock I leant on when things got tough.

I also want to thank all the inspiring bosses I had before I founded my own business: Roger Howe (now Executive Chairman of Stemedica) for his guidance and development of me as a US business leader, through Jim Howard (now CEO of CrownPeak Technology), Andrew (Flip) Filipowski (the greatest entrepreneur I have ever known), Brian Diver (now President and COO at SD.I), to Jason Meugniot and Jon Provisor (owners of Guidance, Inc.). Thank you, all. Finally, a special thanks to Kirkland Tibbels and John Patterson, founders of Influence Ecology, who grounded my ambitions and helped them become a reality.

# Author's Acknowledgments

I want to acknowledge the people who started me on the Dummies journey – Dr. D. P. Lyle, author of *Forensics For Dummies* and Mark Layton (Mr Agile), Author of *Agile Project Management For Dummies*. As friends and business associates, they showed me the way.

I want to thank the team at Wiley for giving me this opportunity and for working with me throughout the process with total professionalism and unvarying support. To Claire Ruston and Annie Knight, Acquisitions Editors; Steve Edwards, Project Editor; Andy Finch, Development Editor; James Harrison, Copy Editor; Polly Thomas, Wiley Marketing, and many other Wiley people who make birthing a book about as easy as it can be.

Special thanks also go to Christopher Faust, CMO of Qvidian and the technical reviewer for the book, for his expertise, patience and priceless feedback as the work was in development.

**Publisher's Acknowledgments**

We're proud of this book; please send us your comments at `http://dummies.custhelp.com`. For other comments, please contact our Customer Care Department within the U.S. at 877-762-2974, outside the U.S. at (001) 317-572-3993, or fax 317-572-4002.

Some of the people who helped bring this book to market include the following:

**Project Editor:** Steve Edwards

**Commissioning Editor:** Claire Ruston, Annie Knight

**Assistant Editor:** Ben Kemble

**Development Editor:** Andy Finch

**Copy Editor:** James Harrison

**Technical Reviewer:** Christopher Faust

**Proofreader:** Kim Vernon

**Publisher:** Miles Kendall

**Project Coordinator:** Sheree Montgomery

**Cover Image:** ©iStock.com/antishock